Alternative Worlds in Hollywood Cinema
Resonance Between Realms

Alternative Worlds in Hollywood Cinema
Resonance Between Realms

James Walters

intellect Bristol, UK / Chicago, USA

First Published in the UK in 2008 by
Intellect Books, The Mill, Parnall Road, Fishponds, Bristol, BS16 3JG, UK

First published in the USA in 2008 by
Intellect Books, The University of Chicago Press, 1427 E. 60th Street, Chicago,
IL 60637, USA

A catalogue record for this book is available from the British Library.

Cover Design: Gabriel Solomons
Copy Editor: Holly Spradling
Typesetting: Mac Style, Nafferton, E. Yorkshire

ISBN 978-1-84150-202-1

Printed and bound by Gutenberg Press, Malta.

CONTENTS

Acknowledgements

This study has benefited from the guidance and support of many individuals and institutions. I would like to thank the staff of the Department of Film Studies at the University of Kent for three crucial years of undergraduate education, and especially Andrew Klevan whose energy, rigour and vitality as both a teacher and a scholar continues to be a source of inspiration. I would also like to thank the staff and students of the Institute of Film Studies at the University of Nottingham, where this book began life, for their helpful comments and suggestions in the early stages, especially Mark Jancovich for his careful assessment of the work. Nottingham and then the Arts and Humanities Research Council have supported me financially in my research and I thank them for the faith they have shown. Danny Rubin kindly agreed to be interviewed for this book and I am deeply grateful for the insights he gave into the writing and filming of *Groundhog Day*. I am also immensley grateful to Sam King at Intellect Books, who has guided the book through its publication with care, enthusiasm and dedication.

The Department of Film and Television at the University of Warwick provided a perfect environment for the growth and development of the thoughts and ideas contained in these pages. I am indebted to a host of fellow researchers who shared suggestions and sympathies throughout, and I would especially like to thank James Bennett and Tom Brown for their enduring friendship and good judgement. Many of the staff in the department offered insights into the work, both formally and informally, and I thank them for their generous investment. V.F. Perkins, particularly, has had a prominent influence on my work both as a teacher, colleague, and through a body of scholarship that is indispensable for anyone engaged in the study of film. I reserve greatest thanks for Ed Gallafent, whose generosity, vigour and understanding has driven the project and profoundly shaped its outcomes. I cannot adequately articulate his contribution so I simply thank him for the depth of his commitment.

Finally, I would like to thank my wife, Amy, who understands so much about films and whose humour, intelligence and support has constantly inspired me to work. This book is dedicated to her.

INTRODUCTION

Hollywood films have always exhibited a general tendency to contrast 'worlds' of particular kinds and orders. We might consider, for example, the ways in which the worlds of domesticity and criminality are brought together in Max Ophüls' *The Reckless Moment* (1949) and how, in that film, Ophüls succeeds in exposing the shortcomings of Lucia Harper's (Joan Bennett) conventionally safe domestic world precisely by having the criminal underworld invade its apparent sanctity. The integral detail in the film's elucidation of these shortcomings lies in the way that a supposedly unscrupulous blackmailer from the criminal world, Martin Donnelly (James Mason) is shown to offer the loyalty, sympathy and tenderness unavailable to her in her own world. Potential threat becomes temporary salvation, therefore, as a character from one world provides unexpected relief for a character who belongs to another.[1]

Similarly, we may think of Alfred Hitchcock's *North by Northwest* (1959) in which Roger Thornhill (Cary Grant) is forced to exchange his world of work with the world of international espionage. As with *The Reckless Moment*, this can, on the surface, be read as a move from safety to danger, from order to disruption. However, as with Ophüls before, it might also be said that Hitchcock makes his character's life precarious precisely to illustrate existing deficiencies and, particularly, to exemplify Thornhill's own shortcomings in one world by throwing him unceremoniously into another. This view is taken up in Robin Wood's landmark study as he remarks that, at the beginning, Thornhill is:

> a man who lives purely on the surface, refusing all commitment or responsibility (appropriately, he is in advertising), immature for all his cocksureness, his life all the more a chaos for the fact he doesn't recognize it as such; a man who relies above all upon the trappings of modern civilization – business, offices, cocktail bars, machines – for protection, who substitutes bustle and speed for a sense of direction or purpose; a modern city Everyman, whose charm and self-confidence and smartness make him especially easy for the spectator to identify with, so that at the start we are scarcely conscious of his limitations as a human being.[2]

Thus, as Thornhill is made to interact in a world completely foreign to him, he is forced to develop a set of resourceful survival instincts that contrast with his former 'irresponsible' complacency, as outlined by Wood. Indeed, Wood sees Thornhill's climactic effort of clinging to Mount Rushmore as 'the final test of stamina, with everything staked upon his powers of endurance and determination' – qualities emphatically lacking when we first encountered the character.[3] Just as the world of crime in The Reckless Moment could be described as an underworld, so the world of international espionage in North By Northwest acts as a kind of behind-the-scenes world, hidden from the everyday world Thornhill was previously part of. As with Lucia Harper, this other world provides surprising benefits to the character that contrast with the world he has left behind.

A discussion of worlds in these two films relies upon terminology inherited from everyday language, whereby we talk of contrasting social spheres as 'worlds' so that reference is made to a person's world of work as opposed to their domestic world, for example. In this sense, the term 'world' is used figuratively, rather than literally denoting another realm. This is the case in the two films mentioned as, in straightforward terms, the spaces that Lucia Harper and Roger Thornhill travel between are geographically located within the same homogenous world. However, in the following study I am concerned with a type of film that represents a more extreme version of this general tendency to contrast worlds, observable across Hollywood cinema. The films offered for scrutiny literally contrast more than one world within their narratives, presenting two (or more) divergent spaces that are dimensionally separate from each other.

This investigation connects with a tradition identified by the American philosopher Stanley Cavell when he suggests that 'Hollywood has always had a taste for contrasting worlds of the everyday with worlds of the imaginary (playing on the two primordial possibilities of film, realism and fantasy)'.[4] The potency of Cavell's succinct observation can be recognized in at least two ways: firstly in that a great multitude can be cited as conforming to the criteria offered (Cavell, for example, offers an initial list that spans over sixty years of Hollywood cinema[5]), and secondly in that it invites us to consider further how such an apparently inexhaustible array of films could be organized so that we might better understand what the films are telling us about the worlds they present and contrast. In that sense, the terms 'imaginary' and 'everyday' can be usefully expanded upon. It is my contention that, for example, the worlds of Oz (The Wizard of Oz), Pottersville (It's a Wonderful Life) and Brigadoon (Brigadoon) share a thematic correspondence as elsewhere worlds in which characters enjoy (or endure) an existence away from their everyday lives, yet none of those worlds are the same, as each film presents a different version of an alternative world, thus making that alternative important to the characters, and to us, for different reasons. A central aim of this book, therefore, is to attempt a more precise categorization of alternative worlds in Hollywood films that leaves us better placed to understand the contrasts and correlations that the films discussed wish to establish.

The three categories that I suggest alternative world films fall into are (i) Imagined Worlds, where a character dreams or hallucinates a world away from the world they inhabit, (ii) Potential Worlds, where a character visits an alternative version – or – alternative versions – of the world they inhabit, and (iii) Other Worlds, where a character travels to a different world entirely from the world they inhabit. These categories are explored correspondingly within the three parts of this study. Each part contains a chapter discussing the category of world in broad terms followed by two chapters presenting case studies of key films belonging to that category. I maintain that this kind of categorization is critically advantageous inasmuch as it allows for a more exact appreciation of the particular importance of the alternative world characters experience. In relation to the films, visiting a potential version of the world is fundamentally different to imagining a world or, indeed, travelling to a world that is different entirely. Each of the films discussed make this distinction imperative and rely upon our understanding of the alternative world presented in order to create meaning and significance within their stories. Dividing alternative worlds into three distinct categories also carries the advantage of providing a clear framework for discussion, making the terms of the debate coherent in each case. It is in accordance with this aim that each part of this study dealing with a category of alternative world begins with a foundational chapter that lays out some examples of films belonging to that category, addressing them in general terms and outlining some of the issues at stake in a critical examination of imagined worlds, potential worlds and other worlds respectively.

A concurrent aim of this study is to scrutinize in detail the ways in which seven key films make dramatic use of their alternative world, addressing how that alternative is given weight and significance within the narrative. This approach necessarily places constraints upon the range of films made available for consideration in the book, as I am committed to articulating the precise aesthetic handling of the alternative world (or worlds) in each of the seven case studies. However, I do not intend to suggest that these are the only examples of alternative world films that merit further scrutiny and, indeed, readers may recognize a series of correlations between the films I focus on and others not included in this study. The book is intended to stimulate exactly that kind of further contemplation and conversation among its readers, and so the fact that comparisons and equivalents can be found beyond the films I choose for extended consideration is by no means detrimental to its aims. Indeed, I would suggest that a number of the films covered in the opening chapter of each part of this study deserve further consideration, and I would hope that the nature of my brief analyses of each raises themes and issues that might be profitably expanded elsewhere, and by others.

With this in mind, having suggested that alternative worlds in films can be divided into the categories of Imagined, Potential and Other, I proceed to outline how those categories function within the seven specific films, proposing ways in which alternative worlds are handled and made crucial within those particular cases. This approach also marks a departure from a broader, narratological position that might be adopted to provide a more remote assessment of the films, identifying shared and divergent formal characteristics without necessarily debating the complex arrangement of those characteristics in each case. This critical stance certainly has its place within film studies and might logically be applied to a discussion of alternative worlds which potentially incorporates a wide corpus of films. However, such an approach might also risk failing to address the films with the kind of precision and rigour that I hope to attain here, suspending a detailed consideration of how each alternative world is composed, utilized and made important within particular films.

By adopting a method of closer scrutiny my work follows the practices of a critical tradition existent in film studies and sometimes referred to as interpretative criticism or textual analysis.[6] In essence, my adherence to this approach is a response to the complexity of the films I choose for discussion. In the seven films offered for extended consideration, the intricate arrangement of elements such as lighting, set, costume, décor, camera movement, editing, music and performance demands a level of detailed analysis that remains sensitive to such a complex form and structure. Like Deborah Thomas, I am acutely aware that:

> Not all films are up to close scrutiny...with some much more bountiful in the opportunities for thought which they offer than others. While some may be thin and merely formulaic, others appear almost inexhaustible as objects of reflection and discovery, sustaining readings and re-readings from many perspectives and along many lines.[7]

I would maintain that the films I select for sustained analysis merit such extended scrutiny, a fact that can only emerge through the analysis itself. More specifically, I contend that the films handle and utilize the convention of the alternative world in a manner that is neither 'thin' nor 'merely formulaic,' achieving instead a depth and resonance that justifies the attention paid to them over the following pages. This 'handling' and 'utilizing' of the convention is bound up in the films' representational strategies so that *what* is shown on the screen is inextricably connected to the *way* that it is shown to us: the compositional relationship of those elements listed above. In this sense, my approach corresponds with a guiding thesis provided by V.F. Perkins as he describes his concept of synthesis between 'how' and 'what' in films:

> Synthesis here, where there is no distinction between how and what, content and form, is what interests us if we are interested in film as film. It is that unity to which we respond when film as fiction makes us sensitive to film as film.[8]

Perkins' statement implies a subtle balance between content and form that, in practice, not all film-makers are able to strike. Perkins emphasizes this fact in a preceding statement concerning a director who is able to maintain a sophisticated synthesis between content and form in his films: Alfred Hitchcock. Perkins says of Hitchcock, 'He does not let us know whether he is finding the style to suit his subject or has found the subject to suit his style. He builds towards situations in which the most eloquent use of his medium cannot emerge as bombast'.[9] Synthesis, then, is a concept also associated with *excellence* in film-making, exemplified in the achievements that Perkins identifies in Hitchcock's work.

A study of alternative worlds in film is necessarily concerned with content but, according to Perkins' argument, such a study will unavoidably be concerned with form, as the two are inseparable in any film. *Synthesis* between content and form, however, may not be achieved to the degree of subtle cohesion that Perkins identifies in Hitchcock's work. Once again, close analysis reveals the extent to which that level of synthesis has been accomplished in a particular film, evaluating the balance of the relationship achieved between content and form. It would be inadequate, therefore, to describe the events of a film without also attending to the way in which they are presented to us, as how a thing appears becomes inextricably linked to what we understand it to be. Furthermore, synthesis between 'how' and 'what' in film becomes a measure of value and accomplishment.

The study is centred predominantly upon Hollywood cinema, but it is not my wish to imply that the convention of the alternative world is limited only to a particular national cinema. Indeed, throughout the study, periodic reference is also made to examples found outside of Hollywood cinema and it is quite possible that a counterpart study could be made of films existing beyond Hollywood entirely. Nevertheless, as is evident from the extent of my work, Hollywood provides a rich source of the kind of films this book seeks to engage with, affirming its appropriateness as a main focus. Furthermore, limiting key examples to Hollywood cinema provides a firm critical basis for the study, ensuring that the films discussed share a contextual background additional to their common trait of featuring alternative worlds in their narratives.

I also deal with films from different periods of Hollywood cinema, although the study is not intended as an historical investigation and, certainly, I make no case for the evolution of the narrative convention throughout the chronological advancement of Hollywood cinema. Rather, the selecting of films from different periods is intended to emphasize the endurance of alternative world narratives throughout the history of Hollywood cinema, illustrating the fact that stories continue to emerge which incorporate similar patterns and structures in diverse, inventive ways. With this in mind, each part of the study includes detailed examinations of films from both classical and contemporary Hollywood.

Ultimately, this book is concerned with the relationships that certain films establish between the two or more worlds contained within their narratives. Consequently, the term 'resonance between realms' becomes a guiding concept as I explore the ways in which those worlds are made significant in relation to each other within the films, and how those films make strong dramatic use of the worlds contrasted in the stories they tell. In each case, I am concerned with the ways in which alternative worlds impact upon characters that experience them, engaging with an investment in questions of individual self-awareness and fluctuating self-identity that all the films share. At its most basic level, therefore, this is a study of films that explore what happens to people when they move between worlds.

Notes

1. Tragically, in Ophüls' film, this union is torn apart when Donnelly is killed as he attempts to save Lucia and her family from recrimination. The bond between the two characters is made so profound in the film that, when Lucia returns to her domestic world once more with the status quo restored, a sense of loss and deep grief overwhelms the scene, compromising any sensations of relief or resolution. As a *Framework* editorial rightly concludes, 'The final image of the film – family integrity preserved, nasty truths once more hidden away – is one of the bleakest in the cinema'. *Framework* editorial 'The Reckless Moment' Framework 4, Autumn 1976, p. 20.
2. Robin Wood *Hitchcock's Film Revisited* London: Faber & Faber Ltd., 1989, p. 134.
3. Ibid. p. 141.
4. Stanley Cavell 'The Good of Film' in William Rothman (ed.) *Cavell on Film* New York: State University of New York Press, 2005, p. 345.

5. The films Cavell 'randomly' suggests are *The Wizard of Oz, Lost Horizon, It's a Wonderful Life, The Matrix, Being John Malkovich, Fight Club, Dogma, Waking the Dead, Groundhog Day, American Beauty, The Sixth Sense, The Cider House Rules*, the last three chosen for their pertinence as nominees for Best Picture in 1999 at the 2000 Academy Awards.

6. More specifically, I am influenced by the depth and precision found in the expressive criticism of writers such as Robin Wood, Andrew Britton, Ed Gallafent, Deborah Thomas, John Gibbs, Andrew Klevan and, particularly, V.F. Perkins. The work of these authors (to which I refer periodically throughout this study) might be linked directly or circuitously to the British journal *Movie*, which expounded a type of detailed interpretative criticism that has provided a crucial foundation for the practice of textual analysis within film studies. Similarly, the writings of Stanley Cavell, Gilberto Perez, George Wilson and William Rothman feature a sustained attention to intricate matters of style and meaning in film, providing a key influence for the shape and direction of this study.

7. Deborah Thomas *Reading Hollywood: Spaces and Meanings in American Film* London: Wallflower Press, 2001, p. 2.

8. V.F. Perkins *Film as Film: Understanding and Judging Movies* New York: Da Capo Press, 1993, p. 133.

9. Ibid.

1

ESTABLISHING CONTEXTS

There are certain critical debates already in motion within film studies that inform and augment a study of alternative worlds in film. However, such arguments rarely deal with the convention of the alternative world as a sustained point of interest or investigation. Indeed, most of the critics and theorists to whom I will be referring in this chapter are engaged in a much wider consideration of the nature of film and film narrative. Nevertheless, an awareness of these wider critical positions is pertinent to my study as films whose stories incorporate alternative worlds do not – cannot – exist in isolation from the countless other films that do not. There would be little profit in insisting that any category of film we might choose is entirely discrete, as such a rigidly confined attitude can only invite legitimate challenge and contradiction, thus undermining the stringency of the argument. Perhaps this would be especially true of the categories I am concerned with, which are observable across genres, styles, tones and periods of film-making. Self-evidently, by including an alternative world or worlds within their stories, the films I refer to do not reinvent the principles of cinematic storytelling. They do not cease to resemble other movies and remain as comprehensible (or potentially incomprehensible) as any other film. Indeed, the very fact that these films avoid stretching the boundaries of credibility and coherence to breaking point – that we do not reject them out of hand despite their narrative departures from established realities – should be a matter of some importance. This leads to the suggestion that there are traits discernible within narrative cinema generally that allow for, or provide opportunity for, the creation of alternative worlds within a film's broader fictional world. It is intended that an engagement with those more general traits, expressed through the critical attitudes covered in this chapter, will lead to a better understanding of alternative worlds as they occur in the films discussed.

Working from this perspective, and integrating the study of alternative worlds into wider discourses surrounding narrative cinema, necessarily draws attention to existing debates that detail and analyse some of the more general attributes that worlds in films possess. This area of enquiry has itself hardly benefited from sustained analysis, a fact acknowledged by those who attempt such an enterprise. Yet, an awareness of the rules, conditions and characteristics of created worlds in film can serve to position the device of the alternative world in a wider context, making it continuous with certain patterns and tendencies in narrative cinema that have been observed and debated.

Even before investigating debates surrounding the nature of created worlds in film, however, it is worthwhile to revisit the work of certain critical theorists who concern themselves with cinema's ability to create worlds at all. In order to evaluate descriptions of the fictional worlds as created and formed, we might first attend to the event of their creation and, thus, their form as they appear to us. This line of inquiry brings forth debates surrounding the event of the world film, and thus forms a stage before a consideration of the nature of worlds as created in film, which in turn represents a stage before a consideration of alternative worlds, as created in film, takes place. With this progression in mind, I will address each stage accordingly in this chapter, beginning with the broadest and wide-ranging.

The Event of the World in Film

Edward Branigan has endeavoured to explain some of the processes that are at work when we watch films and, indeed, this is a main purpose of his book *Narrative Comprehension and Film*.[1] At a point in this work, Branigan turns his attention to an area he determines as 'Story World and Screen'.[2] Adopting an approach founded in part upon some of the guiding principles of cognitive science, he states that: 'Narrative in film rests on our ability to create a three-dimensional world out of a two-dimensional wash of light and dark'.[3] At once, Branigan concerns himself with the form of the cinema screen, its two-dimensionality, but goes on to highlight the viewer's role in interpreting that apparent flatness as essentially three-dimensional, creating a textured world. His emphasis on the spectator's interpretative processes is consistent with his position, influenced by the field of cognitive science, well established in the study of film by the time Branigan's work appeared in 1992. The audience's interpretative process as he describes it is self-evident, perhaps indisputable, and film-makers would appear to have sought to exploit this almost from the beginning of cinema. For example, whilst various writers have challenged the authenticity of accounts that describe audiences' terrified reactions at seeing the Lumière Brothers' 1895 film, *Arrivée d'un train en gare à La Ciotat* (*Arrival of a Train*), for the first time,[4] there is no denying that this film makes early reference to the cinema audience's inclination to create three-dimensional worlds from two-dimensional images, so that a train moving towards the camera apparently connects with the audience's world-making cognitive process as outlined by Branigan: it looks like a train travelling towards the audience. The fun for some audience members may or may not have rested upon the make-believe notion that the three-dimensional world of the film could penetrate our real, three-dimensional world, regardless of the two-dimensional screen that separates them, rather than any serious belief in the possibility.[5] This is different, I think, from the effect elicited in us when we watch a film made from the placement of a camera in a moving roller coaster carriage. It would seem that our potential reactions here – apprehension, excitement, disorientation and others personal to the viewer – derive from the *involuntary* sensation of actually being on the ride, of being *within* the film world. At the very least, the passage of a train across a diagonal axis from background to foreground highlights the extent to which we have assumed the existence of a world in three-dimensions. In this way, the mere fact that we can speak intelligibly about the foreground and background of a shot is perhaps the most arresting proof that we understand the world to extend beyond the screen, three-dimensionally.

Branigan further distinguishes that 'Light and sound in narrative film are thus experienced in two ways: virtually unshaped *on* a screen as well as apparently *moving within*, reflecting and issuing from, a world which contains solid objects making sounds'.[6] Here, Branigan makes clear the duality, as he sees it, of the cinematic image: the fact of its two-dimensionality allied with its simultaneous illusion of a real three-dimensional world 'moving within'. Duality is a useful term here, as we are surely always aware that we are watching a projected, two-dimensional image and yet instinctively accept the cinema's convention of three-dimensionality. The images have been captured in the real world, and that realness remains intact as they are projected for us in the darkness. Branigan's observations here are perhaps familiar to the point of becoming unremarkable, yet the interpretive principles of cinema spectatorship he describes are fundamental to the advent of worlds created in film, and central to our accepting them as worlds.[7]

Branigan's assertions mark a contribution to existing debates surrounding the existence of 'worlds' in films. Stanley Cavell, writing twenty years earlier, had already concerned himself with the nature of the filmed world and, particularly, the viewers' relationship to that world as they experience it, as it appears on (or within, or beyond) the screen. As he moves towards defining precisely what is at stake for the viewer when images are projected onto a cinema screen, Cavell lays out some of the contrasting features of painting and photography.[8] Cavell moves away from Bazin's celebration of photography as having 'freed the plastic arts from their obsession with likeness' as he considers this perspective to be suggestive of an implicit competition between painting and photography, as though 'painting had wanted something that photography broke in and satisfied'.[9] He takes this position to be somewhat fanciful and, instead, details the differences between the worlds that painting and photography depict. Of particular interest to Cavell is the fact that the world extends beyond the area captured by the camera's lens in photography, whereas that same principle cannot be applied to a painting: 'You can always ask, of an area photographed, what lies adjacent to that area, beyond the frame. This generally makes no sense asked of a painting...A painting *is* a world; a photograph is *of* the world'.[10] Here we find a thematic correlation between Cavell's account of the photograph and Branigan's account of cinema. Both writers concern themselves with matters of space and distance, but while Branigan is interested in the three-dimensional *depth* of the cinematic world, Cavell articulates the existence of an 'implied world' that extends *in every direction* beyond the scope of the camera's lens that has 'captured' a section of that world. It becomes clear, therefore, that Cavell's theory of the 'implied world' in photography enriches an understanding of cinematic worlds, that the camera which produces a photographic 'snapshot' of its world is implicitly related to the camera which produces a filmed section of its world. As with photography, we are invited to attend to the existence of a world around the camera, outside of the section framed and recorded onto film.

For Cavell, however, a key distinction exists between the photographic image and the cinematic. This definition occurs when Cavell turns his attention specifically to the screen in cinema: he finds that it has no border or frame around it, as pictures and paintings do, but is itself a frame. The frame in cinema is more versatile than that of a photograph or painting as the camera moves or adopts different positions and distances; in this way it is 'indefinitely extendible and contractible'.[11] But Cavell finds the screen to be important in other ways relating to the film's world and the viewer's relationship to that world. He chooses to view the screen not as a surface which supports an image (he rejects this notion by contrasting it with the canvas in painting that literally does support its image) but instead as a barrier. He asks: 'What does the silver screen screen? It screens me from the world it holds – that is, makes me invisible. And it screens that world from me – that is, screens its existence from me'.[12] For Cavell, this first ability to render the viewer temporarily 'invisible' is a crucial facet of cinema and his proposition leads him to later define the way in which 'movies reproduce the world magically...Not by literally presenting us with the world, but by permitting us to view it unseen'.[13] Cavell's conclusions here represent an acknowledgement that the world in film, the world beyond the screen, is a (fictional) world. The world beyond the screen might even appear as 'real' as the one we experience everyday but the key distinction is that we are not required to be part of the world beyond the screen – are not in any case able to be – and that gives the filmed world a special quality and an attraction that separates it from our experienced reality. Therefore, Cavell's description of the screen as a barrier between two worlds is fundamental as it symbolizes the ontological borderline between the two spaces.

Cavell tells us finally that 'The screen overcomes our fixed distance; it makes displacement appear as our natural condition';[14] his observations up to this point regarding the cinema's ability to grant a viewers' invisibility having prepared the way for such an appraisal. Writing thirty years later, Deborah Thomas would appear to concur with Cavell's position and further explore it in her analysis of spaces in Hollywood cinema.[15] Thomas asserts that:

> When I examine my own experience of watching a film, it feels to me as though I am positioned at the boundary produced by the screen (or by the extended virtual screen), not myself, but, rather, as a disembodied viewer, unreflected in mirrors, unseen by characters within the film, and taken out of my real body in the film theatre or in my easy chair at home.[16]

Thomas' critical preoccupation with spaces and meanings in American cinema serves to enhance Cavell's thesis by extending the terms of our relationship to the 'screened world' as it impacts upon elements within that world itself, such as mirrors and other characters within the film, thus establishing new areas of interrogation between the spectator's world and the world of the film. Thomas' sense of disembodiment or unreflectedness in relation to the film world correlates emphatically with Cavell's sense of displacement, but her invocation of that sensation also speaks of the spectator's freedoms and limitations in relation to the film world. As Thomas asserts, 'we will find ourselves in a privileged position, as film spectators, to take account of effects which are the result of editing or camera position or the composition of the image, of which the characters, as characters, will never be aware'.[17] This clearly situates the viewer in a position of assumed authority in relation to the inhabitants of the film world (and leaves us well-placed to embark upon the interpretative criticism of films). But this authority is flawed as, at the same time, Thomas is also conscious that 'we lack [the characters'] freedom to walk around within these spaces and choose their own viewpoint. The fact that we are given access to the film's geography, architecture and décor from a predetermined set of positions inevitably shapes what we, as spectators, see, and influences what we make of it'.[18] This assertion brings us back to Cavell's notion of the photograph possessing only a section of the world, not the world itself: there will always be parts of any world that are not seen. And Thomas maintains here that the same, or something similar, is true of cinema. We are screened from the film world not only by the screen that Cavell saw as a barrier but also by the 'predetermination' inherent in our experience of it.

However, like Cavell, Thomas is also interested in the fact and properties of the cinema screen and, similar to Cavell again, sees it as 'what both characters and spectators come up against as the limiting boundary of their respective worlds'.[19] Thomas' repeated use of the word 'boundary' in her argument is particularly useful, as it reminds us not only that a border between audience-world and character-world exists, but also that this border is in itself bordered by the confines of the screen. We are not only limited by our separateness from the film-world, symbolized by the screen-as-boundary, but also by that screen's boundaries: the section of the world we are permitted to see. Again, this relates not only to Thomas' concept of predetermination, but also to Cavell's theory of the implied world outside of the camera's scope for capture. Thomas proceeds to further contemplate how the screen-boundary between film world and real world operates and, particularly, the ramifications of the camera's mobility for the film audience, explaining:

> Thus, if we construe the screen as a transparent plane of rectangular shape between us and the narrative world, then even if we were to watch a film whose camera was continually circling around within the spaces of the narrative world, it would be as if our imaginary screen were turning on its axis while moving through space like a mobile revolving door, with us condemned to remain forever on the opposite side from the action.[20]

This extends some of Branigan's earlier assertions regarding the two-dimensionality of the screen and the three-dimensionality of the image. Thomas reminds us that the cinema screen does not work simply as a static window onto the film-world, with that world moving in front of it, but is actually a very unusual type of 'imaginary screen' that moves discriminately through the film-world, as the camera moves and changes position. Not a window at all. Such emphatic freedom is evident as the camera demonstrates its ability, in some films, to adopt positions that seem to replicate or resemble character point of view as a matter of course. There are any number of positions that the camera can adopt, and any number of movements it can perform. In thinking along these lines, we are reminded again of Cavell when he tells us that 'The fact that in a moving picture successive film frames are fit flush into the fixed screen frame results in a phenomenological frame that is indefinitely extendible and contractible, limited in the smallness of the object it can grasp only by the state of its technology, and in largeness only by the span of the world'.[21] Microscopic and telescopic lenses are not conventionally used in film-making, but there exists an indefinable variety of shot distances and types that constantly challenge our vocabulary founded upon definitions of long, medium and close-up shot. Likewise, it would appear that theoretically there is nowhere in the film-world that is out of bounds for the camera: it has the potential freedom to look anywhere.[22] That fact of it 'choosing' to look in particular places, at particular times, constructs the audience's understanding of a film's world.

V.F. Perkins provides a further distinction to concepts of a film world by considering in more precise terms its relationship to the real world. This line of enquiry occurs in his book *Film as Film*, published in 1972, which itself presents a wide-ranging discussion of the form and nature of movies, and a persuasive argument concerning the kinds of criteria we might employ in order to understand and evaluate achievement.[23] In a section entitled 'Form and Discipline', Perkins makes a number of observations that effectively knit together the established realist and formalist debates, which have traditionally been ideologically opposed to one another, and in doing so encapsulates the nature of the relationship between the world on the screen and the real world. Even recent contributions, such as Irving Singer's *Reality Transformed*, published in 1998, have entered into the debate between the two camps.[24] Although Singer now terms the divide as existing between 'classical' film theorists, he nevertheless seeks to resolve the differences once again between the realists who 'emphasize that film records properties of the physical world that lends themselves to the photographic process' and the formalists who 'call attention to the technical means by which a film-maker goes beyond the real world in order to express his or her artistic vision'.[25] In *Film as Film* Perkins argues that:

> The photographic narrative film occupies a compromise position where a fictional 'reality' is *created* in order to be *recorded* [emphasis in original]. Here the relationship between reality and illusion, object and image, becomes extremely complex; any attempt to isolate either in a 'pure' state becomes correspondingly inept.[26]

The product of this position is the suggestion that it is neither profitable nor desirable to mark the line too heavily between reality and illusion in films. In Perkins' terms, the two states of illusion and reality are fundamentally interrelated, with the narrative film recording and creating its reality simultaneously. However, he does not perceive a conflict here, thus dissolving the 'battle lines' between realist and formalist debates. The dogmatism of the either/or position is effectively rejected in favour of 'and'. It is interesting that Perkins' conviction that the relationship between reality and creation is more complicated actually serves to clarify the terms of the debate. One of the founding principles of Perkins' argument in *Film as Film* is the concept of synthesis, most influentially the principle of the synthetic relationships between elements in film that create meaning and significance. (Perkins is justifiably drawn to films that achieve this with the greatest skill and subtlety.) When discussing the relationship between reality and creation in film, he again invokes a concept of synthesis, stating that:

> The fictional film exploits, where purer forms attempt to negate, the conflict between reality and illusion. Instead of trying exclusively either to create or to record, the story film attempts a synthesis: it both records what has been created and creates by its

manner of recording. At its most powerful, it achieves a credibility which consummates the cinema's blend of actuality and fantasy.[27]

Here, Perkins makes clear that it is the nature of the fictional film itself that renders a firm distinction between reality and illusion inappropriate. The synthesis between reality and illusion in the film-making process is encapsulated in terms straightforward enough to evoke the naturalness of their blending together. Perkins' assertions enrich the debate concerning the film world by providing a crucial account of the ways that audiences understand the world in film: not as a world imagined entirely by the film-maker but as one that borrows and integrates elements from the world we already know into its fantasy. This is true of all films and will presumably remain true so long as film-makers remain members of human society. These distinctions extend Branigan's model of audience comprehension based upon the formal qualities of the cinema screen. Taking both theses into account, we arrive at the notion of audiences understanding worlds in film as worlds not only through a cognitive ability to make the two-dimensional three-dimensional but also because of the film world's relationship to our own: the ways in which it relates to a reality that we already understand through experience. For Perkins, there is no profit in articulating a position based upon cinema's ability to either capture reality or create illusion, as the realists and formalists have traditionally sought to do: the world presented in a film necessarily incorporates and relies upon both reality and illusion.

The scope of *Film as Film* is broad and, although the debate concerning the formal nature of the world in film informs Perkins' conclusions, it is a strand that forms part of a much wider argument that cannot be fully related here. However, Perkins returns to the subject once more in his article 'Where is the World?: The Horizon of Events in Movie Fiction'.[28] The essay 'sets out both to show that the fictional world of a movie is indeed a world and, by means of a few concrete examples, to sketch some of the ways in which it matters that a fictional world is a world'.[29] This statement of intent provides us with a useful definition for the narrative world in film by calling it a 'fictional world', but also extends the existing terms of the argument, suggesting not only that the fictional world *is* a world but also that this *matters*. This is in partial response to film studies' lack of attention, in the main, to the fictional world, but also to the ways in which the fictional world is dismissed (as a 'loose metaphor' for example[30]) or taken for granted.[31] We might return to Irving Singer's work to find the kind of broad dismissal to which Perkins alludes. Singer expresses the belief that:

> ...it would be bizarre for us to look at a Hollywood movie about a town in the old west and to infer that in one direction there really were ranch houses of the nineteenth century, in the other an actual saloon, up the hill a graveyard populated by people who lived and died in that period, and so on. If we are not shown these bits of reality, we give no thought to them, and they are not part of our aesthetic suppositions. Though the photographic image will show us what the sets look like, as mediated by the camera used in the shooting of the film, we know they only represent a town that could have existed a hundred twenty years ago. We would not assume that the town itself exists beyond the frame. We might not see the sets as the hollow and insubstantial constructions

that they are, but neither do we take the cinematic images as anything more than a portrayal of some town that *may* have once existed [emphasis in original].[32]

This assertion is actually made in response to Cavell's theory of the implied world, which we have already visited here, and effectively dismisses the notion that we can think of the film world extending beyond the parameters of the frame. Singer's account of the world matches the 'loose metaphor' misconception with which Perkins takes issue and therefore dismisses notions of the fictional world *as a world*, the supposition reached by each of the theorists thus far and crystallized by Perkins. Singer's break from that position is exemplified in his choice of language, seeing the world on the screen as a 'portrayal' of somewhere that 'might' have existed, rather than somewhere that does – a fictional world – and extends beyond the section the camera has captured for us. Singer seems to collapse two different arguments into his conclusion. In one sense, he is correct in asserting that we do not watch a western in the assumption that this film was made two centuries ago, that all of the characters can be found in the record books, that their deeds occurred at some point in our world history exactly as they are shown in the film and so on. But some of the characters *could* be found in record books, and some of the places *can* be found on any map of America, so the relationship is significantly more complex than Singer suggests, as the real and imaginary combine within a film's fictional world (and we will later see how Perkins attends to those complexities in his own discussion).

Singer then takes these facts in order to detail our dismissal of anything that occurs outside of the frame: 'If we are not shown these bits of reality, we give no thought to them, and they are not part of our aesthetic suppositions'. It is an extraordinary critical leap that he makes here, from a rejection of the film world as the 'real' world to the rejection of it as a world at all, and the conclusion has been reached by invoking a different argument regarding our knowledge that the film's world is disparate in some ways to our own. In the fictional worlds that films create, to use Perkins' terminology, a consideration of the areas outside of the frame is often crucial to our understanding of the areas framed for us. It would be a very particular type of film that constantly made us aware of the artificiality of its sets, and certainly not one that represented a conventional trend in film-making. Yet, even if the film did make us aware in this way, we could still legitimately suppose that beyond the film's 'artificial' set a world exists and extends, just as it would do in reality. Thus, Singer's suggestion that we close down opportunities for this kind of conjecture when watching a film is flawed on a number of levels. If it were really true that 'we would not assume that the town itself existed beyond the frame' what degree of meaning or significance could a film hope to achieve, given that we would constantly remind ourselves that none of it is real, and where could be our enjoyment in this?

To pursue this further, we might take a short example from a particular film. In *Rosemary's Baby* (Roman Polanski, 1968) we are shown a party where a group of Rosemary's female friends visit her and her husband's apartment, in part to celebrate her pregnancy. During that party, Rosemary (Mia Farrow) shares some of her fears and anxieties with her friends, regarding the pain she is experiencing during her pregnancy and the serious doubts she has regarding her obstetrician. In fact, her fears and anxieties extend beyond this as she is unsure whether she has been impregnated as part of a satanic ritual involving her neighbours (she was unconscious at the time of conception). Her obstetrician was recommended by these neighbours and in a later scene, when it becomes clear to her that he is involved in their apparent plot, she runs out of his waiting room and into a phone box. In this state of panic, she telephones her previous obstetrician with her fears. It is a plausible response, but why telephone the previous obstetrician? Why not the friends who we saw earlier? They exist somewhere unseen in the film's world, presumably have telephones and apartments; presumably could provide refuge. We have not seen these locations, have not seen the friends since they visited Rosemary, but the fact that they exist somewhere unseen in the film world is crucial to our understanding of Rosemary as we see her in this scene. Possibilities for her reluctance to contact them present themselves. Perhaps she is apprehensive about approaching her friends. Perhaps they are not as good friends as she might like them to be. Perhaps she seeks a figure that is the exact reverse of the new, sinister obstetrician, and so returns to her previous doctor. Perhaps she can only think about the welfare of her unborn child and so, desperate to secure its well-being, contacts someone who can provide that security. Perhaps contacting the original obstetrician represents a return to a time before the interference of her neighbours (and her husband) who press-ganged her into visiting the new doctor, so her phone call marks an act of overdue defiance, of taking control in spite of hysteria. Equally, the previous obstetrician was recommended to her by her friends, so Rosemary's desire to return to him may represent a reconnection with them, albeit one step removed; retaking their advice after a period of trauma.

There are, no doubt, many more possibilities than those listed here and it may be that even further scrutiny of the film might never provide definitive answers to such conjecture (a measure of the film's achievement does not hinge upon its ability to provide conclusive answers). Our concern here, however, is that each of these possibilities rests upon the acknowledgement of a world outside of the camera's scope, our acceptance of the friends as being people occupying spaces outside of those we have been shown in the film, their significance carrying over into those instances when they are not in the camera's view, outside of its frame. The knowledge that there are zones beyond our view that Rosemary might make contact with but chooses not to shapes our understanding of her character, her situation and ultimately the film. In *Rosemary's Baby*, it is particularly important that the phone booth scene takes place within the city, where methods and communication and travel are different from those found in a desert, or in a forest. Likewise, it becomes crucial that the city exists in the 1960s rather than the 1860s, where the character would be faced with a significantly different set of decisions and opportunities in terms of whom to contact and how to contact them. Contrary to Singer's theory, therefore, we find ourselves thinking constantly about the spaces outside of the frame and construct them as real with the film's fictional world. In this way, characters' actions have consequences within the complex world they inhabit, to the extent that we can think of them in terms relating to our understanding of human behaviour, rather than as merely simulated 'representations' of people.

Perkins effectively meets Singer's claims head-on in those passages of 'Where is the World?' where he turns his attention to Fritz Lang's *You Only Live Once* (1937). Perkins concerns himself with a sequence in which the central pair, Eddie (Henry Fonda) and Joan (Sylvia Sidney), are heard to enter a car and drive away in an off-screen space whilst the camera stays with Father

Dolan (William Gargan) and Whitney (Barton MacLane), the lawyer, to capture their conversation.[33] Through a detailed analysis of the sequence, Perkins suggests that the off-screen action functions at least as importantly as the on-screen. Perkins is alert to the fact that a real car almost certainly did not exist in the studio when the sequence was filmed, but he warns that: 'we should not fall into thinking that the off-screen space is in any special sense fictional or imaginary. That would oblige us to see the on-screen image as non-fictional or real. On-screen and off-screen are equally fictional and imagined; seen/unseen and heard/unheard draw many of the relevant distinctions'.[34] In Perkins' terms, then, off-screen cannot be seen as more 'fictional' than on-screen because they both feature and function within the film's fictional world. To construct a hierarchy of significance based only on distinctions of on-screen and off-screen thus becomes meaningless. Self-evidently, such a conclusion directly challenges Singer's earlier conception. Perkins goes further and actually returns the debate to Cavell's earlier concerns regarding the camera's ability to capture only a part of a world, stating that: 'We are offered an assembly of bits and pieces from which to compose a world. Fragmentary representation yields an imagined solidity and extensiveness. The malleability of the image is in a reciprocal relationship with the seamlessness and continuity that the image can evoke in our minds'.[35] We might also relate this formation back to Thomas' notion of the 'predetermined' way in which audiences experience the film world, with a particular view being selected for us over other potential perspectives.

That question of 'predetermination' would perhaps be synonymous with certain aspects of viewpoint that Perkins highlights earlier in his essay. This discussion occurs in relation to another of Perkins' 'concrete examples', Orson Welles' *Citizen Kane* (1941). When addressed to this film, Perkins' argument resonates with Cavell's concept of displacement and Thomas' notion of disembodiment (or unreflectedness) as he discusses the incineration of Charles Foster Kane's sledge, Rosebud, at the end of the film. Perkins observes: 'That we can be present as an audience to witness the absence of witnesses is an index of the separation between our world and the world of the fiction'.[36] In Perkins' terms, our separation from the world of the film imbues the viewer with a freedom to witness those events that cannot be seen or understood by any other character within that world. *Citizen Kane's* finale provides a particularly emphatic demonstration of this, and in doing so offers a further sense of the ways in which our disembodiment and displacement as viewers allows us to experience worlds wherein the absence of any character's viewpoint is not a limiting factor. Perkins makes a similar point also in relation to *Citizen Kane* when he describes a particular gliding camera movement as 'taking a course unrelated to anything human. Its movement is not performable by any wingless being'.[37] The experience and understanding of characters within the film world is therefore not a prerequisite to our experience and understanding as viewers. (Indeed, this is particularly true of the camera movement Perkins describes which takes in seemingly endless crates and assortments of Kane's possessions, their proliferation helping to create the defining tone of the film's final act: the burning of the sledge called Rosebud.) The question of viewpoint is of interest here, and Perkins himself navigates this in his discussion when he later asserts that: 'The camera's looking escapes some of the restrictions on our sight: those that follow from the fact that, for us, eye and ear always have to go with body. The movie can explore the opportunities of unembodied viewpoint but it can never escape the necessity of viewpoint itself.[38] This goes some way to explain our general inclination of referring to the camera's 'gaze' or to suggest that the camera 'watches' even when the viewpoint or perspective is in no way attributable to a character in the film. This anthropomorphic tendency indexes our need to attach viewpoint to views provided in film and thus, as Perkins elucidates, the movie's intrinsic connection to viewpoint itself.

Perkins further finds *Citizen Kane* to be a rich source for discussion when outlining the fictional world's relationship to a society we experience in our everyday lives. He states that the film's final sequence:

> ...climaxes the anomaly that places *Citizen Kane* both in and beyond our world, our 1941 world. Of course this is our world. It shares our economy, our technologies, our architecture, and the legal systems and social forms that yield complex phenomena like slum landlords, divorce scandals, and fame. Its history is our history of wars and slumps and the rise of mass media. Its notorious people (e.g. Adolf Hitler) and its decisive events are the ones we know.[39]

This details the complex fusion between real and fantasy that Singer's earlier claims failed to properly address: that film fiction can, and predominantly does, take place within a world that we recognize as our own. To return to an earlier example: in Polanski's film, before Rosemary had rushed out of the doctor's surgery, she had picked up an old copy of *Time* magazine bearing the question 'Is God Dead?' This undoubtedly has certain ramifications for Rosemary, given her extraordinary position, but we also recognize the magazine, indeed the headline, from our culture. Our understanding of this moment relies partly upon our knowledge and experience of the world, and the film has thus re-emphasized its notion of Rosemary belonging to our world, our 1968 world. However, as with his argument in *Film as Film*, Perkins is keen to detail the problems that lie in over-emphasizing the correlation between the fictional world and the real world. He addresses this in relation to *Citizen Kane* again, stating:

> But of course its world is not ours. Kane is famous throughout that world, and we have never heard of him nor of Jim Geddes, his political rival. Susan Alexander's celebrated fiasco at the Chicago Municipal Opera House involves an occasion and a location without reality for us. Everyone there and nobody here knows about the construction of a new Xanadu (their Xanadu) in Florida (our Florida). These are some of the aspects that mark the world as fictional. They do not thereby negate its worldhood.[40]

So the world in film is a complex amalgamation of real and fantasized elements, but crucially the existence of both does not compromise our definition of the fictional world as a world.

The Nature of Worlds in Film

Discussing the event of the world in film has led us naturally to work concerning the nature of the world as it appears in film. Indeed, Perkins' debate in 'Where is the World?' integrates a consideration of film form and the nature of film narrative. This is particularly evident later in the piece as he describes those moments when characters apparently look out at the audience from the film world, thus instigating an extraordinary relationship between audience and the fictional world through the 'barrier' of the screen.[41] In this instance, narrative and form combine to produce effect. In fact, Perkins lays out some of the conditions that films adhere to and some of the characteristics they display in a section of *Film as Film*.

Perkins uses the example of Dusan Vukotic's *Play* (1962) to demonstrate the extent to which worlds created in cinema can overcome objections on the grounds of rationality by establishing a credibility of their own. In Vukotic's film, two children draw pictures, which then come magically to life and engage in a battle with each other. The drawings become more and more audacious as the battle escalates. Perkins concerns himself not with the quality of the film, but with its 'method and effect'.[42] He points out that the rational explanation for the film's occurrences would be that these events take place in the characters' minds, yet he asserts that this is not the order of logic that the film presents. Rather, the boundaries between imaginary and real have become dissolved, allowing the characters to interact with their creations not *as though* they were real but because they *are* real. As Perkins tells us, the film 'puts the real boy and girl on exactly the same level as the animated drawings'.[43] And of particular interest to Perkins is the fact that we accept this abandonment of everyday rationality, accept the brand of fiction that the film proposes, apparently without question.

Perkins' argument in *Film as Film* takes into account the presence and influence of the film-maker, who controls the shaping of the film's world. But he is careful to acknowledge that the film-maker does not have unlimited freedom with regards to the choices he or she makes, insomuch as each choice must be consistent with those already made. Moments of emphasis must be balanced within the parameters already established, if over-assertion is to be avoided. Perkins suggests that the film-maker's aim 'is to organize the world to the point where it becomes most meaningful but to resist ordering it out of all resemblance to the real world which it attempts to evoke'.[44] In terms of aesthetic composition, this means that symbolic elements must be located coherently within the film's fictional world: if a source-less red light was shone onto a character's face each time they flew into a rage, or green light used to represent their envy, then the film would have exceeded the boundaries of its own fictional world and thus compromised the credibility of its fiction. Perkins makes this point in relation to John Huston's *Moulin Rouge* (1952) which contains an instance of a room 'that change[s] colour in sympathy with its occupant's mood'.[45] Nothing in the film's fictional world could account for this phenomenon and, instead, Huston has employed the effect at the expense of the world he created or, as Perkins puts it, 'broke[n] down the essential structure of his picture's relationship and thus destroyed the world within which his hero existed'.[46] Whatever kind of world the film proposes, it must operate according to the logic of that world, rather than imposing meanings upon it. Perkins refers to these meanings directly as '*asserted* meanings, crude juxtapositions...both blatant and unclear, like over-amplified noises bellowing from a faulty loud speaker [emphasis in original]'.[47]

In *Film as Film* and elsewhere, Perkins is concerned with matters of style and meaning in film, but it is these very matters that impact upon narrative structure in film. I would go further to contend that the criteria he employs relate directly to a study of cinema's alternative worlds. On the one hand, he demonstrates through the example of *Play* that a film is able to create rules of possible occurrence that do not follow the rational logic of everyday existence, that 'the cinema's magic is powerful enough to overcome purely rational objections'.[48] The advent of an alternative world in a film therefore need not compromise the credibility and coherence (Perkins' terms) of the fictional world *per se*. According to Perkins' argument, we are positioned to accept them as easily as we might accept that a child's drawing can come to life in a film. The alternative world, whether it is 'other', 'potential' or 'imagined', then expands the boundaries of the fictional world, rather than destroying them. As we will discover, the films contained within this study display great strategic care in negotiating the expansion with logic and reason, supporting the fiction they propose. Perkins provides a crucial account of what is required, stating that: 'As an illusion-spinning medium, film is not bound by the familiar, or the probable, but only by the conceivable. All that matters is to preserve the illusion'.[49] Thus, a film can never compromise its credibility by including an event that is unfamiliar or improbable according to our laws of reason, but only by including an event that is inconceivable according to its particular laws. This, surely, would present useful criteria when embarking upon a study of alternative worlds in films if we are concerned with whether the advent of the alternative world is supported by the logic of the film's fiction, rather than whether we find it more or less probable. No criteria can be applied in which finding a village that wakes for one day every hundred years (*Brigadoon*) can be more plausible than repeating the same day over and over again (*Groundhog Day*). As with Vukotic's *Play*, we are likely to accept either instance as long as they are supported according to the film's brand of fictional logic. As Perkins asserts:

> On one level cinematic credibility is no different from that which we demand of other story-telling forms. It depends upon the inner consistency of the created world. So long as this is maintained, the premises are beyond question...But the created world must obey its own logic. There is no pretext, whether it be Significance, Effect or the Happy Ending, sufficient to justify a betrayal of the given order. In a fictional world where anything at all can happen, nothing at all can mean or matter.[50]

So the advent of the alternative world does not threaten credibility, but the arrangement of that world might. In *The Wizard of Oz*, for example, it is acceptable to us that Oz should be colour and Kansas black and white. But those two states must behave according to worldhood[51] that the film establishes. Lighting must be located within those worlds: when a beam of light shines upon Dorothy's face as she sings in the Kansas farmyard, it is shown to be a ray emanating from the sun as it briefly appears between the clouds. Likewise colour. In Oz, the Wicked Witch of the West (Margaret Hamilton) has a green face not to symbolize any feelings of envy she may experience (although this is surely an aspect of her character), but because, according to that world's laws, green is her skin's natural colour. In Oz, water can melt a witch, whereas no person can be melted with water in Kansas. The film is quite clear in its diegetic distinctions. As long as these features are motivated by the worlds that the film creates, we can have no difficulty in accepting them.

Along these lines, Deborah Thomas provides an interesting continuation of some of Perkins' themes, and consequently contributes to our understanding of how worlds in films operate. She discusses two films in order, John Ford's *My Darling Clementine* (1946) and Nicholas Ray's *Party Girl* (1958). During her analysis of the latter, Thomas makes the observation that:

Where the presentation of the visible world in Ford's film is a harmonious one which reconciles its conflicting elements (at least once the Clantons are dead) so that the narrative world by the end of the film is a fitting one for Wyatt Earp to inhabit, it is not so clear that Vicky and Tommy will find a place to nurture their romance, even when Rico, Louis and the others are dead. The world of *Party Girl* is much more overtly repressive, misogynistic, and self-serving, and those on the right side of the law are just as complicit as those on the wrong.[52]

Thomas draws attention to the ways that the attitudes and behaviour of characters can contribute to the tone of a film's world. This, in turn, affects our expectations of that world. Perkins listed the Happy Ending as one feature that cannot 'justify a betrayal of the given order'. If we apply this to Thomas' account of *Party Girl*, we can see that there are certain conditions inherent in that film's world which effectively rule out the possibility of an ultimately happy ending. Ray has placed certain ideological limits upon the world he has created, and Thomas' doubts as to whether a happy future together can possibly exist for Vicky and Tommy respond to those limits. Both Ford and Ray's films develop and sustain a tonal order that shapes audience expectation and retains the story's credibility.

A reversal of tone, from dark to light, or from complex to facile, can stretch that credibility, yet our disappointment in those cases is testament to the powerful way in which films shape our expectations by shaping their tonal structures. A breach of the established order is a jolt to our senses. (As Perkins makes clear, a case of this occurs when a film imposes a 'happy' ending that is manifestly out of keeping with the actions and attitudes of the characters previously, something that often elicits marked dissatisfaction amongst audiences.) This is different, I think, to the advent of an alternative world, which represents an expansion of the film's established order rather than an unmotivated reversal of it. Even if a character says that a place cannot exist, and it then turns out to be real, it was only ever a character within the film that gave this viewpoint, not the film itself. Thus, the credibility of the film's coherent fictional world has not been compromised.[53]

Thus far, we have detailed the ways in which various critics have described our propensity to consider the world outside of the camera's frame. Inherent in Thomas' comments regarding *Party Girl* and *My Darling Clementine* is the suggestion that often we also consider the world of the film after the film itself has ended. Based upon the evidence presented to us during our 'disembodied' encounter with the world, we formulate certain hypotheses as to how the characters might behave in the future when we view them no more.[54] This might suggest that we, as viewers, expand the film's fictional world not only spatially by speculating upon the zones outside of the camera's frame, but also temporally, by speculating upon events before and after the time frame in which we watch the film. Many films encourage this temporal expansion by making reference, with varying explicitness, to unseen events that occurred before the time period in which the film takes place. (The narrative of Douglas Sirk's *All I Desire* (1953), for example, hinges on events that occurred in an unseen past, and Perkins discusses this film in detail in his essay, 'Where is the World?'[55]) Following this line of argument, we might conclude once again that our understanding of the fictional world in film is never restricted to the events captured by the camera's 'gaze' but, instead, that we readily construct a world outside of those spaces selected for us, and construct stories that reach beyond the story that we witness as it unfolds on the screen. Thus, as our speculations can extend spatially beyond that which is represented on screen, so they might expand temporally beyond the moments of the characters' lives that are shown to us in the film's duration.

The Prospect of Alternative Worlds in Film

Perkins' argument regarding credibility and coherence has provided the beginnings of criteria against which alternative worlds in film might be judged. But it is useful now to turn attention towards those debates which connect more directly with the notion of alternative worlds in film.

Peter Wollen's article 'Godard and Counter Cinema: Vent d'Est' seeks, in one sense, to champion the film-making of Jean-Luc Godard by establishing his divergence from the 'values of old cinema' and examining one film of his, *Vent d'Est* (1970).[56] To illustrate the contrast between Godard's cinema and the 'old Hollywood-Mosfilm, as Godard would put it', Wollen sets out schematically what he perceives to be the seven cardinal virtues against the correspondingly oppositional virtues that Godard promotes. According to Wollen, this second set would themselves be cardinal sins for Hollywood cinema. This, he sees, as Godard's 'counter-cinema'. The two lists read as follows (with Hollywood's virtues on the left and its cardinal sins on the right):

Virtues	Cardinal Sins
Narrative transitivity	Narrative intransitivity
Identification	Estrangement
Transparency	Foregrounding
Single Diegesis	Multiple Diegesis
Closure	Aperture
Pleasure	Unpleasure
Fiction	Reality

Wollen makes it explicit once more that his discussion is also an endorsement of Godard's approach, concluding his list of distinctions thus: 'I should say that my overall argument is that Godard was right to break with Hollywood cinema and to set up his counter-cinema and, for this alone, he is the most important director working today'.[57] This statement also serves to reassert in emphatic terms the dichotomy that Wollen is keen to highlight: Godard versus the Hollywood cinema. It is not possible or necessary to address each of Wollen's distinctions within the context of our discussion here but, keeping in mind my move towards a study of alternative worlds in films, we are bound to find ourselves drawn to Wollen's concept of *single diegesis* versus *multiple diegesis*, and the ways in which he attributes one category to Hollywood cinema and one against it.

Wollen provides a clearer definition of what he means by these terms: 'A unitary homogenous world vs. heterogeneous worlds. Rupture between different codes and different channels'.[58] If we apply this terminology to the study of alternative worlds in film, we see that each of the films presents different manifestations of heterogeneous worlds, in that they harbour more than one world order. Yet, each film creates a relationship between the two worlds, thus unifying them in the story and evading arcane rupture. The relationship that the film maintains between the disparate worlds creates meaning and significance. The creation of meaning and significance, surely, is not merely the aim of Hollywood cinema, or even cinema itself, but a standard objective of storytelling. However, even though the narratives of films can involve alternative worlds, those distinct worlds still exist in one, over-arching, fictional world: the world of the film. To suggest otherwise would be absurd: no film can overreach the confines of its own world; it refers to elements outside of the world it presents, but in doing so incorporates them into its own world. In this sense, alternative world films – including those made in Hollywood – present heterogeneous narrative worlds within a homogenous cinematic world. (We have already attended in detail to analyses of the form and nature of that over-arching world.) This is different to Wollen's argument that:

> In Hollywood films, everything shown belongs to the same world, and complex articulations within that world – such as flashbacks – are carefully signalled and located.[59]

The point regarding flashbacks is generally true, but difficulty arises when Wollen seeks to assert that everything in Hollywood films belongs to the same world. Everything in a *film* belongs to the same world – the world of the film. Dual or even multi-narrative worlds can easily coexist in Hollywood films, as much as they can anywhere else: just as they can in any other national cinema, just as they can in any story.

Jane Feuer revisits some of Wollen's arguments in her study of the Hollywood musical.[60] This occurs in a section entitled 'Dream Worlds and Dream Stages', and it is self-evident that this chapter concerns itself more with the creation of these states within the Hollywood musical than with Wollen's propositions or, indeed, a wider consideration of alternative worlds in films. When discussing *An American in Paris* (Vincente Minnelli, 1951) and *That's Entertainment!* (Jack Haley Jr., 1974), Feuer finds that both films 'acknowledge levels of fantasy in musicals'. She continues:

> Each film places a secondary, more stylised fictional world into a primary, less stylised fiction. The secondary, the unreal, the dream world, holds at bay the imaginative excess to which musicals are prone.[61]

For Feuer, dream sequences provide opportunity for musicals to explore a stylized mode, thus complementing the 'imaginative excess' that she regards as a constituent feature of most musical films, and certainly most Hollywood musicals. The Hollywood musical would thus seem well suited in nature to the placement of another, more stylized, fictional world in its narrative. So Feuer is able to pair the unreal world – the dream world – with the genre of film-making she analyses. When addressing Wollen's argument, Feuer in fact sees a correlation between the Hollywood musical and the cinema that Wollen champions (the cinema that Godard is associated with) in stating that: 'Both the Hollywood musical and the modernist cinema use dual worlds to mirror within the film the relationship of the spectator *to* the film. Multiple diegesis in this sense parallels the use of the internal audience [emphasis in original]'.[62] This not only dismantles the boundary between Hollywood and Godard that Wollen marks out, but also extends Wollen's concept of multiple diegesis by speculating upon the way that it recreates the relationship of the audience to the film. For Feuer, just as the showing of a film represents a world created – or placed – within our world, so the 'second fictional world' created in the Hollywood musical creates, or places, a world within its world. Any alternative world in a film, therefore, could be seen to imitate the alternative world we experience when we watch a film. This conceivably relates back directly to the accounts of the world in film, as experienced by the audience, which we have visited and evaluated in this chapter in the work of Branigan, Cavell, Perkins and Thomas. Crucially, however, the relationship between audience/film and film world/alternative world is one of resemblance rather than reproduction: characters in these films step across from world to world in films, whereas we would be misguided if we thought we could step into the world of a film. Feuer, however, is concerned more with the advent of *dream* sequences in Hollywood musicals than alternative worlds in general. Consequently, her debate returns to this topic as she asserts that:

> In dream sequences the parallel between the dream in the film and the dream that is the film is rendered most explicit. The Hollywood musical creates dream sequences within musicals in order to obliterate the differences between dreams in films, dreams in ordinary life, and dreams as the fulfilment in ordinary life of the promises offered by the movies.[63]

Feuer recasts the notion of the dual worlds in films mirroring the relationship of the spectator to the film by having the film act as a kind of dream itself, thus making the dream section a dream within a dream. This perhaps relates to a long-established tradition amongst all sorts of critics to see the film experience as 'dream-like', observable at least since Hortense Powdermaker's (often misinterpreted) notion of Hollywood as 'The Dream Factory' and probably before.[64] Feuer sees that films have the power to collapse the distinctions between the dreams they present, the dreams we have, and our dreams that are fulfilled as we watch films. However, we might find reason to doubt whether films actually possess the ability to perform such feats, and whether we would ever be receptive to such an attempt. Stanley Cavell has warned of the dangers in being too 'quick about equating films with dreams,' reasoning that:

> Most dreams are boring narratives (like most tales of neurotic or physical symptoms), their skimpy surface out of all proportion with their riddle interest and effect on the dreamer. To speak of film adventures or glamours or comedies as dreams is a dream of dreams: it doesn't capture the wish behind the dream, but merely the wish to have interesting dreams.[65]

For Cavell, therefore, a cursory consideration of the actual nature of our dreams reveals that film narratives are nothing like them at all (most film narratives at least) and the undisciplined use of the term 'dream' in relation to film can be misleading. To Cavell's list of 'adventures or glamours or comedies,' we could feasibly add musicals. While we might provisionally accept that the tone and form of the Hollywood musical complements the placement of a dream sequence within it, as Feuer earlier asserts, this is distinct from any idea of the film as a dream-like experience, and the dream sequence itself may well be far more lucid and structurally organized than any dream we could ever have.

Feuer's account of alternative worlds is guided by her interest in dream sequences and 'stages' as they occur in the Hollywood Musical. Given this generic bracketing, a logical point for expansion would be to consider how closely the potential for the creation of dream sequences and alternative worlds can be related to the Hollywood musical. Indeed, this study incorporates films that include 'a secondary, more stylised fictional world into a primary, less stylised fiction,' as Feuer terms it, but which do not belong to the musical genre. In fact, although film musicals feature as close studies in two chapters, in each case an equivalent close study is made of at least one film from a different genre that possesses a corresponding dramatic structure. This would suggest that the propensity for alternative world narratives is not necessarily restricted to the musical genre, but occurs across generic boundaries in film. Thus, my study expands the terms of Feuer's debate, one which is understandably centred upon musicals given the theoretical impetus of her overarching study, by tracing the relationships across genres in films that include alternative worlds within their narratives.

Deborah Thomas also draws attention to film's ability to maintain two distinct worlds and, consistent with the thrust of her own critical interests, she locates this around the issues of spaces and meanings. For example, Thomas describes a scene in John Sayles' *Lone Star* (1996) in which an elderly man named Hollis (Clifton James) talks about Charlie Wade (Kris Kristofferson), who was sheriff in the town many years ago:

> ...the camera moves to a basket of tortillas on the table while Hollis withdraws his hands from the frame on the left, and Wade's hand reaches towards the basket from the other side of the table (to remove some money hidden amongst the tortillas as Hollis describes Wade's susceptibility to bribes), with a younger version of Hollis just out of shot and revealed through a cut as the scene proceeds. Although all the on screen events – both past and present – are diegetic, their apparent co-presence goes against the film's diegetic logic (this is not, after all, a science fiction film about time travel). It is as if a larger imaginary space – a cinematic space – is being evoked which past and present can somehow momentarily cohabit.[66]

Thomas' analysis reveals the film's ability to show both a present and a past to exist continuously, with firm temporal distinctions disabled through the expressive use of the tortilla basket as a link between the two states. Thomas' suggestion that it is as though a 'cinematic space' is being evoked which past and present 'can momentarily cohabit' is useful as it relates back to the notion of an overarching film world in which disparate narrative worlds can feasibly exist and, to use Thomas' term, can cohabit. Thomas' observations might prompt a rethink of what we take to be a film's diegetic logic and, indeed, the malleability of those logical codes. The sequence in *Lone Star* does represent a break from the film's established diegetic logic, as

Thomas describes it, and the move from the world of the present to the world of the past is not as clearly indicated as it might be in a science fiction film (where a time machine would be the standard device for transportation). Yet, the move from present to past in the scene does not translate as particularly aberrant. In fact, Sayles makes the linking of past and present appear natural through the style of the sequence and, crucially, the continuity of Hollis' voice between states.

We are returning, then, to Perkins' earlier observations regarding Vukotic's Play and our willingness to accept a film's brand of fantasy and temporarily discard our own laws of rational explanation, as long as the fantasy remains credible and coherent according to the film's rules of fantasy. In one sense, Sayles' linking of past and present in a single shot merely relies upon, and possibly extends, the ways in which time and space become malleable in film narratives generally, and in storytelling generally. Indeed, we might see Sayles' visual transfer from present to past as a particularly inventive use of the flashback, a convention with a long-established history in cinema and, again, storytelling more generally. It is unlikely, therefore, that such a transition would lead us to accuse the film's director of having abandoned all narrative sense. Indeed, an earlier film like John Brahm's The Locket (1946) demonstrates the extent to which we can willingly follow a series of intricate flashbacks, as the film's narrative presents a kind of Russian Doll structure of character memory in which we almost forget whose recollection we began with. If we are to accept the notion of diegetic logic, then we also have to accept that this is not a fixed marker; that a film possesses the ability to alter and expand the terms of its logic at any time. As we find with Lone Star, the manner in which this is undertaken can go some way to reduce any sense of rupture or disorientation. Thomas' concept of a larger 'imaginary space – a cinematic space' is useful because it is suggestive of a wider boundary that will also remain intact – can only remain intact. So, although the film's narrative may harbour different frames of time and space, these divergent states will always be framed within the widest boundary of the 'cinematic space'. Within that frame, any number of events or complications is possible. Thomas' observations are pertinent to a study of alternative worlds in films insofar as she implicitly suggests that a film can contain as many worlds as it sees fit; it will only ever expand the limits of the film's overarching world – its diegetic boundary – rather than defy its own diegetic logic.

According to this formulation, it is even possible for a character to become caught between worlds. Thomas describes the complicated moment in Vertigo (Alfred Hitchcock, 1958) when Scottie (James Stewart) kisses Judy (Kim Novak) in her hotel room after she has completed her transformation back into Madeleine: 'Suddenly he finds himself back in the stable where he had kissed Madeleine...earlier in the film'.[67] This moment is potentially problematic in terms of the film's diegetic logic because 'What we have is not precisely a flashback, since Scottie looks wonderingly at the surrounding stable from what seems to be a vantage point outside its space and time, yet he remains nonetheless immersed within the scene'.[68] Thomas states that, as in Sayles' film, two separate diegetic spaces cohabit in the shot, yet this time the central character becomes aware that something is amiss:

Scottie is bewildered by what appears to be his literal physical transportation – as his present self – out of the present time and space in which he thought he was located (in the hotel room), so that the scene does not come across as a flashback, nor as an effect fully determined by an inner fantasy which swamps his consciousness. Instead, his partial awareness that something is amiss may reveal a glimmer of awareness that he is in a film whose world is being manipulated from elsewhere.[69]

For Thomas, this sequence is extraordinary not only because it contains two worlds within a single scene, or because the blend would seem to index Scottie's 'inner fantasy which swamps his consciousness'. The sequence also seems to reference the crafting of the film world through Scottie's bewildered reaction to the effect. It is almost as though Scottie were with us (the audience) for a brief moment, but also within the moment, and acknowledges very briefly that events, even those pertaining to his own inner fantasies, are out of his hands. The sequence performs a more audacious leap from past to present than the equivalent in *Lone Star* by moving the present characters seamlessly into their past. Rather than locate this move purely as a product of Scottie's mind, the film draws attention to the extraordinary development through Scottie's reaction to the occurrence: his astonishment. Thomas suggests that Scottie becomes aware of himself as a character within the film, and we might speculate as to whether this effect is similarly startling as the moments of direct address that Perkins is interested in towards the end of 'Where is the World?'[70] Yet, the suggestion that Scottie could conceivably acknowledge 'he is in a film whose world is being manipulated from elsewhere' – even for a fleeting moment – requires further elucidation as it seems to expand the dramatic and diegetic potential of the film beyond Thomas' initial account of it. The moment of Scottie's unsettlement is potentially unsettling for an audience because *it is as if* he was acknowledging his placement within a fictional world, and thus that he is in the film itself. However, this relationship is dictated by our awareness as an audience, rather than emanating from Scottie's awareness as a character. The moment of resonance that Thomas describes occurs as a character within the fictional world makes an unexpected connection with the audience outside of that world, but it perhaps pushes the moment's impact a little too far to suggest that the character themselves becomes aware of this to any discernible extent. Certainly, however, Thomas is right in asserting that: 'it is difficult to find words to describe accurately what is happening both in narrative and cinematic terms'.[71]

In contrast to Thomas' description of the complexity of multiple worlds in narrative cinema, David Bordwell, in an article entitled 'Film Futures', aims to convey the relative narrative simplicity of a group of films containing alternative versions of the same world.[72] The article describes the 'forking path' plots of four films: *Blind Chance* (Krzysztof Kieslowski, 1981), *Too Many Ways to Be No. 1* (Wai Ka-Fai, 1997), *Sliding Doors* (Peter Howitt, 1997) and *Run Lola Run* (Tom Tykwer, 1998), considering the bearing of folk-psychology upon these stories of parallel worlds. Bordwell begins with Jorges Luis Borges' story 'The Garden of Forking Paths', in which a sage Ts'ui Pen devises a novel whereby a character, rather than choosing one possibility over another at moments of decision, chooses all the routes of possibility simultaneously, thus creating several futures, several times, that themselves fork again, creating ever more futures and times. Bordwell's purpose for detailing the novel's plot is to note that the infinite complexity of Borges' narrative never occurs in films. Rather, the 'exfoliating tendrils of Borges's potential futures have been trimmed back to cognitively manageable dimensions, by means of strategies characteristic of certain traditions of cinematic storytelling'.[73] The result is that a limited choice of two or three potential paths is presented in the films rather than the 'infinite, radically diverse set of alternatives evoked by the parallel-universes conception'.[74] Bordwell contends that this limiting of choices corresponds to 'a more cognitively manageable conception of what forking paths would be like in our own lives'.[75] Here, the concept of folk-psychology is invoked, whereby we all can imagine a moment in which a choice one way or the other would have widely divergent consequences. Bordwell suggests that the films' narrative structure relates to the viewer's knowledge and experience, and traces this 'moment of choice' through each of the four films' narratives, titling them 'what-if plots' accordingly.[76]

Bordwell's assertions clearly relate to notions of dual and multiple worlds in film, as articulated variously by Wollen, Feuer and Thomas. In identifying the tendency for 'forking path' film narratives to contain only a small number of potential worlds, Bordwell in fact highlights the propensity of these films to create resonance between one world and another, reversing or revising key details in order to communicate the weight and purpose of certain decisions and directions. Films containing dual or multiple potential worlds thus achieve significance though comparison. It would be interesting to see whether this kind of resonance and coherence would or could be sustained across a larger number of potential worlds, although I can think of no film that readily explores this. Without such an example, however, it becomes difficult to conclude with Bordwell that: 'As film viewers, we like the number of parallel universes to be *really* little [emphasis in original]'.[77] With apparently no film containing a plethora of potential worlds, we are ill placed as audience members to voice a preference, and it is unclear what our criteria for such a preference might be.

Bordwell acknowledges that one film, *Groundhog Day*, represents something of an exception to his central thesis by 'proliferating a great many futures for its repellent protagonist'.[78] However, he points out that the film places limits upon this 'proliferation' as it 'presents those futures as very short-term alternatives, and it multiplies redundancy around its forking point (the clock radio's wake-up song) and the parallel events in the repeated day'.[79] This is certainly true on a surface level, and the film also does not allow the proliferation of potential worlds to expand geographically as the film's protagonist is confined to the town of Punxsutawney due to a snow storm. However, although these limits are placed on the potential world in a way that restricts *Groundhog Day*'s narrative expanding in quite the way that Ts'ui Pen's does, the film remains sufficiently ambiguous about the number of days Phil (Bill Murray) spends in his cycle of potential days to allow for our speculation to exceed the boundaries of what is actually shown to us. There seems to be a deliberate attempt to show Phil performing very difficult tasks – ice sculpting, concert-standard pianoforte – that could not be mastered in the actual run of repeating days shown to us. We are entitled to ask how long he has spent in the parallel world. What else did he do there? And, of course, these questions cannot be satisfactorily answered. (Kristin Thompson's observation that the total number of days is forty-two, a suggestion offered to her by Bordwell, simply does not account for the periods of learning implied but not depicted by the film.[80]) Therefore, although on one level the film represents a linear narrative progression that Bordwell alludes to, this collapses as it makes explicit the fact that an inordinate number of days were also experienced, but we never witnessed them. However, as Bordwell rightly points out, the film does not depict Phil walking from new world to new world, but restarting in the same world each time. Thus, the film can be said to create resonance between the different versions of the same world recast over and over again, a notion I pursue in the section of this study entitled 'Potential Worlds'.

The concept of resonance between worlds remains unexplored in Bordwell's account of the films, as he naturally concentrates on a general description of narrative events to form a wider comparison of their traits. We might consider that this approach risks reducing the films to a series of plot lines, thus resisting detailed analysis in favour of overarching description. Clearly, this amounts to a contrast of methodological approaches and we have to account for Bordwell's aim of sketching out a sub-genre of film in a relatively short space for discussion. Yet, there is the sense that the reductive strategy has avoided a consideration of how these worlds are made important in the films, or how the actions of the characters are made significant in the worlds they inhabit. Those matters of importance, significance and resonance surely influence our appreciation of the potential worlds the films create (certainly in the best films of the type) and may therefore be central to our understandings and evaluations. Bordwell's conclusions help to identify a strand of alternative worlds observable in narrative cinema, but room is left for more rigorous analysis of the branch of narrative cinema described. The ways in which alternative worlds are shown to matter in film will, necessarily, constitute a central concern within the following chapters.

Notes

1. Edward Branigan *Narrative Comprehension and Film* London: Routledge, 1992.
2. Ibid. p. 33.
3. Ibid.
4. Cf. Ian Christie *The Last Machine: Early Cinema and the Birth of the Modern World* London: BFI Publishing, 1994, p. 15.
5. A later film, *The Countryman's First Sight of the Animated Pictures* (R. W. Paul, 1901) would seem to play on the fun of this effect by having a country 'yokel' in the film, watching an image of a train approach and reacting in the melodramatic fashion befitting one who thinks the train might race out beyond the screen and plough into him.
6. Branigan, p. 33.
7. Terms such as 'familiar' and 'unremarkable' might seem to question the validity of Branigan's assertions, suggesting that he merely revisits a concept obvious to anyone who has seen a film. In response to this, I might recall a comment made by Richard Dyer in his influential article 'Entertainment and Utopia' (Richard Dyer *Only Entertainment* second edition London: Routledge, 2002, pp. 19–35) that 'because entertainment is a common-sense, "obvious" idea, what is really meant and implied by it never gets discussed'. Just as Dyer looks beyond the 'common-sense' usage of the term 'entertainment', so Branigan might be seen to look beyond the common-sense experience of cinema-going to examine at a more precise level the processes that are at work there.
8. Stanley Cavell *The World Viewed: Reflections on the Ontology of Film* enlarged edition London: Harvard University Press, 1979 p. 20.

9. Ibid. p. 21.
10. Ibid. pp. 23–24.
11. Ibid. p. 24.
12. Ibid.
13. Ibid. p. 40.
14. Ibid. p. 41.
15. Deborah Thomas *Reading Hollywood: Spaces and Meanings in American Film* London: Wallflower Press, 2001.
16. Ibid. p. 114.
17. Ibid. p. 10.
18. Ibid. p. 9.
19. Ibid. p. 109.
20. Ibid.
21. Cavell, p. 25.
22. The camera's ability to 'look' anywhere is theoretically true. However, in practice restrictions have regularly been placed upon its freedom to view, not least through official and unofficial censorship in the cinema. Thus, areas of the filmable world have remained out of bounds.
23. V.F. Perkins *Film as Film: Understanding and Judging Movies* New York: Da Capo Press, 1993.
24. Irving Singer *Reality Transformed: Film as Meaning and Technique* London: MIT Press, 1998.
25. Ibid. p. 1.
26. Perkins *Film as Film* p. 61.
27. Ibid. p. 62.
28. V.F. Perkins 'Where is the World? The Horizon of Events in Movie Fiction' in John Gibbs & Douglas Pye (eds.) *Style and Meaning: Studies in the detailed analysis of film* Manchester: Manchester University Press, 2005, pp. 16–42.
29. Ibid. p. 16.
30. Ibid.
31. Ibid. p. 22.
32. Singer p. 47.
33. Perkins 'Where is the World?' p. 23.
34. Ibid. p. 25.
35. Ibid. p. 26.
36. Ibid. p. 19.
37. Ibid. p. 17.
38. Ibid. p. 20.
39. Ibid. p. 19.
40. Ibid. p. 20.
41. Ibid. pp. 35–36 The use of 'barrier' here relates back to Cavell's earlier terminology, rather than being a term offered in Perkins' argument specifically.
42. Perkins *Film as Film* p. 63.
43. Ibid.
44. Ibid. p. 70.
45. Ibid. p. 122.
46. Ibid. pp. 122–123.

47. Ibid. p. 119

48. Ibid. p. 63

49. Ibid. p. 121

50. Ibid.

51. 'Worldhood' is a term that Perkins employs throughout his discussion in 'Where is the World?' Although he invites any suggestion of a better word, worldhood certainly emphasises a definition of the fictional world as a world (p. 39).

52. Thomas p. 31

53. V.F. Perkins gives an account of the dangers inherent in assuming that a character's voice is the film's voice in his article 'Must We Say What They Mean?: Film Criticism and Interpretation' *Movie 34/35* pp. 1-6. This article is a partial response to a section of David Bordwell's *Making Meaning: Inference and Rhetoric in the Interpretation of Cinema* (London: Harvard University Press, 1989) in which Bordwell takes Dorothy's statement 'There's no place like home' to be the film's defining message. (p. 8).

54. Gilberto Perez outlines the strong impact of a film which conversely allows for no speculation upon how its characters progress after the film has ended. The film is Buster Keaton's *College* (1927) and Perez explains that after the completion of the plot's various machinations there 'follows a very peculiar epilogue. No sooner are the newlyweds out of church than a dissolve transports us many years later to the middle-aged couple in their home, sitting among their several children; this in turn swiftly gives way to the couple in their advanced years, abidingly sitting at home beside each other; this in turn to the closing shot of their adjacent graves' (Gilberto Perez *The Material Ghost: Films and their Medium* London: The Johns Hopkins University Press, 1998, p. 92). This startling end is particular to what Perez terms Keaton's 'unsentimental' notions of the romantic, but it also stands out from most narrative films, where the invitation to speculate on the characters' futures is by and large left open.

55. Perkins 'Where is the World?' p. 28.

56. Peter Wollen 'Godard and Counter Cinema: Vent d'Est' Afterimage, Fall 1972, reprinted in Leo Braudy & Marshall Cohen (eds.) *Film Theory and Criticism: Introductory Readings 5th Edition*, New York: Oxford University Press, 1999, p. 499.

57. Ibid.

58. Ibid. p. 502.

59. Ibid.

60. Jane Feuer *The Hollywood Musical* London: BFI Publishing, 1982.

61. Ibid. p. 68.

62. Ibid.

63. Ibid. p. 73.

64. Hortense Powdermaker *Hollywood: The Dream Factory* Boston: Little Brown, 1950.

65. Cavell p. 67.

66. Thomas p. 102.

67. Ibid.

68. Ibid. p. 104.

69. Ibid.

70. Perkins 'Where is the World?' pp. 35-36.

71. Thomas p. 102. Further useful discussion of the sequence can be found in Charles Barr's BFI Classic on the film (Charles Barr *Vertigo* London: BFI Publishing, 2002), William Rothman's chapter on *Vertigo* in *The "I" of the Camera* (Cambridge: Cambridge University Press, 2004), or in Andrew Klevan's *Disclosure of the Everyday: Undramatic Achievement in Film* (London: Flicks Books, 2000). Klevan's approach utilizes Cavell's earlier work on the film in *The World Viewed* whilst Rothman's account intersects with the Cavellian notion of the unknown woman, the subject of his book *Contesting Tears: The Hollywood Melodrama of the Unknown Woman* (London: The University of Chicago Press, 1996).
72. David Bordwell 'Film Futures,' *SubStance* vol. 31, no. 1, 2002.
73. Ibid. p. 91.
74. Ibid. p. 90.
75. Ibid.
76. Ibid. p. 94.
77. Ibid. p. 92.
78. Ibid. p. 103.
79. Ibid.
80. Kristin Thompson *Storytelling in the New Hollywood: Understanding Classical Narrative Technique* London: Harvard University Press, 1999, p. 379.

PART ONE: IMAGINED WORLDS

2

Imagined Worlds

'There's no world. It's all in that gentleman's mind'.

Professor Duvernois (*Abre los ojos*)

G.A. Smith's 1900 film *Let Me Dream Again* opens with a static two-shot of a man and a woman sitting behind a table. The man sits to the left, dressed in an evening suit, his thinning hair smoothed over his shiny head. He smiles repeatedly with a bawdy enthusiasm for the young woman beside him. She sits to the right of the frame and is dressed ostentatiously in a white lace bodice and large white ruff that is studded with soft black material bobbles. She wears a white pointed hat that also bears three black bobbles and her outfit is finished with a black eye-mask.

The carnivalesque quality to her costume contrasts with his more formal attire and lends her character traces of mystery and exoticism, explaining somewhat the allure that has overtaken

Let Me Dream Again

Let Me Dream Again

her leering companion. The couple laugh and smoke together, she removes her mask and they start to embrace passionately. Suddenly, however, the image slips out of focus, and when clarity returns we find that we are viewing a different scene. The man remains in the frame, but he is now in bed and dressed in his nightgown. To the right of the frame, the young woman has been replaced by an older, less attractive female that we take to be the man's wife.

Thus, we realize that the encounter with the first woman was merely a dream and now the man has returned to reality once more. The visual match of the man and the woman's positioning in each shot (as well as the spatial resemblance of the bedspread surface to the now-disappeared table) creates a rhyme between reality and illusion. In the restored reality, the man's wife responds with markedly less enthusiasm to his embraces and removes his hands from her. She continues to scold him vigorously and he responds with a series of exaggerated facial contortions that communicate his horror and discontent at the dream being replaced by reality: his dream-girl replaced by his wife. The film ends with the two turning their back on each other, turning directly to the camera in a brief comic flourish, and then away again.

Given the rapid, transnational development of cinema in its early years, it would be difficult to ascertain whether *Let Me Dream Again* was the first example of a dream sequence in a film. Indeed, with so many films having been lost from that period, a judgement of any kind is made at least precarious. (Leslie Halpern, however, is apparently oblivious to this difficulty when she states confidently but erroneously that 'The earliest documented dream sequence – a prophetic dream appearing in a circular inset called a dream balloon – was used in Edwin S. Porter's 1903 film *The Life of an American Fireman*'.[1]) Nevertheless, Smith's film stands out as an effective early use of the dream sequence technique in cinema. The disparity between reality and illusion is emphatically used to create the film's visual humour; the spatial resemblances inherent in the placement of actors and set in both scenes serve to highlight the divergent qualities of the dreaming and waking states. The man's revelation is played for its humour, with the actor's exaggerated expressions of revulsion and loathing constructing his character as a figure of ridicule, rather than attempting to elicit any sympathy from the audience (quiet disappointment or reflection would, perhaps, produce a different effect). The film's comic impact relies upon Smith's decision to begin in the dream state, rather than showing the man falling asleep, then dreaming and then waking up. Thus, the audience is temporarily deceived into confusing reality with illusion: taking the dream to be waking life.

The sudden revelation of Smith's film perhaps has its dramatic origins in the Magic Lantern shows that went before (and can be seen as a precursor to) the birth of cinema. Some lantern slides, for example, would feature two sheets of glass, with different images painted on each: the first image would be projected and then the second slid over the top, to show a change (a butterfly emerging from a cocoon, for example) or to create a new and sometimes surprising scene (a cave becoming a palace, for example). These 'slipping' or 'slipper' slides follow the basic narrative structure of movement from one state to the next that we recognize in Smith's film as he shifts from the dream world to the real world.[2] Recalling the conventions of the Magic Lantern shows, the film achieves a degree of surprise and amusement as an audience realizes that one thing is really something else. Smith's film succeeds in creating a *relationship* between

Dream of a Rarebit Fiend

the two states – dreaming and waking – by establishing a direct contrast between them, inviting the audience to recognize the shortcomings in the central character's life that are temporarily alleviated in his dream.

The dream sequence device became widespread in films of the period, directly resembling the format Smith favoured, or else varying or extending it. A variation can be found in Edwin S. Porter's *The Dream of a Rarebit Fiend* (1906), based upon Winsor McCay's comic strip of a year earlier. Porter begins his film by showing the protagonist gorging himself on rarebit and beer, staggering through the streets of New York (swaying wildly due to his intoxication) before retiring to bed and entering a nightmare state in which his bed flies inexplicably over the city skyline.

The drunk is finally skewered on a church steeple before he awakens. Thus, Porter provides an explanation for the fantastic events of the man's dream by making clear that they are just the fabric of a dream, brought on by the excessive consumption of rich food and strong drink. Structurally, Porter's film expands the pattern of the dream sequence film to three stages: awake, sleeping and waking again. Unlike Smith's film, it is not necessary for Porter to trick the audience into confusing dream with reality. Rather, his film revels in the visual special effect of a man sailing through the night air on his bed frame, allowing for this spectacular occurrence through the framing logic of the dream, which we understand as surpassing the physical order of real life.

That dreams and dreaming were represented in these early films should not surprise. Ian Christie tells us that 'Dreams had long served artists as an excuse for fantasy and a means of exploring the forbidden and the impossible. Now early cinema inherited this tradition, and amid its early dream scenarios we find the first fantasies of flight and interplanetary travel, as well as comic dreams of wish-fulfilment and poetic justice'.[3] In line with Christie's observations, Smith's and Porter's films find opportunity to explore the forbidden and the impossible respectively through the device of a character's dream. (These interests correspond with a cornucopia of other films from the early period of cinema that did not include dream sequences but still dealt with the fantastic, such as George Méliès' *Journey Across the Impossible* (1904) which involves a train voyage into outer space, and the illicit in works like Porter's notorious *The Gay Shoe Clerk* (1903) in which a salesman is encouraged by his female customer to sensationally raise the hem of her skirt as he fits her boots.) The films each reconcile the dilemma of representing a character's inner thoughts by placing the camera at an objective distance in relation to the individual as they experience their dream. Thus, the effect is created not so much of either character merely having a dream, but rather of existing within a dreamed 'world', their actions captured by the camera just as they are in the films' real fictional worlds.

There are practical reasons for placing the camera at an objective distance to the character in each case. The joke of Smith's film relies upon character and audience mistaking the dream for reality and, thus, it is important for each state to bear a clear spatial resemblance within the frame in the ways I have described earlier. The visual effect of Porter's protagonist travelling through the air is achieved by superimposing him over shots of the cityscape, thus ruling out the possibility for any subjective character viewpoint to be portrayed on technical grounds. Nevertheless, it is significant that each film presents dreams as a visually accessible space, a discrete environment in which characters exist and interact as they do in the world, rather than restricting themselves to the basic truth that the dreamer usually experiences their dreams from their own subjective point of view. By lifting the constraints of first-person subjectivity in dreaming, the films allow their audiences a perspective on the events of the characters' dreams and, indeed, those characters' behaviour within their dreams. Thus, the concept of the mind's eye is only loosely adhered to as we occupy a viewing position within the character's dream world, independent of their personal perspective and viewpoint.[4]

The implied suggestion, therefore, is that even from an early stage, cinema was committed to portraying a fantasy of the dream experience rather than providing an accurate account. We might expand upon Cavell's assertion, raised in the previous chapter, that 'To speak of film adventures or glamours or comedies as dreams is a dream of dreams: it doesn't capture the wish behind the dream, but merely the wish to have interesting dreams'[5] by suggesting that even filmed dream sequences themselves are dreams of dreams, happily unrelated to less sensational constraints of realistic representation. Thus, among the multitudinous dream sequences observable in narrative cinema, a great many present the dream as a stable, logical and discrete environment that possesses few of the inconsistencies, perplexities or banalities of real-life dreaming. In this sense, they function in the films as 'worlds' in their own right, contained within the wider fictional world of the film. The dreamer, most often, then functions as a character in that world, to the extent that we may even temporarily forget we are still watching their dream at all.

A complex version of this occurs in Buster Keaton's *Sherlock Jr.* (1924). In this film, Buster has been wrongly accused of the theft of his fiancée's father's pocket-watch and has been banished from their house. His attempts to shadow the real thief, another suitor to his fiancée, have failed and he ends up back at his job as a film theatre projectionist. (Buster's desire to be a detective is explicitly revealed in the film's first scene as we discover him reading the book *How To Be a Detective* when he is supposed to be sweeping the theatre.) Whilst screening *Hearts and Pearls: or, The Lounge-Lizard's Lost Love* Buster falls asleep and, through a double exposure technique, a partially transparent 'dream' Buster rises from the slumbering body and watches the film being projected.[6] As he looks, the actors on the screen turn away from the camera and return as real faces from Buster's life: his fiancée, the caddish suitor, her father and a hired hand. Buster leaves the projection booth and attempts to enter the film being screened in his dream, but he is pushed back into the auditorium by the caddish suitor. He enters the film again, but the scene suddenly changes around him to a garden, then a busy street, then a cliff, then a lion's den, then a desert railroad and so on. Naturally, these changing scenes provide Buster with opportunities for spectacular physical interaction with his surroundings: he falls off a bench

Sherlock Jr *Sherlock Jr*

in the garden scene, is almost run over by cars on the street, has to warily escape the lions in their den, almost falls from the cliff in that scene and nearly gets mown down by a freight train in the desert, for example.

Bruce Kawin notes that 'Throughout this sequence the image has included the screen, the proscenium, the musicians, and much of the audience, with the camera rear and center, more or less where the projection window ought to be; indeed...this *is* the view from the projection booth, and the image is the dream-field of the projectionist [emphasis in original]'.[7] Kawin's remarks regarding point of view can certainly be traced within the visual representation of the scene (and correspond with the author's wider commitment to an event in film narration that he terms 'mindscreen').[8] But the presence of the film theatre within the frame also lends stability to the dreamed world, rendering it constant and coherent whereas the film within the dream is significantly less predictably fixed.

While the scenery in the projected film changes indiscriminately, the locale of Buster's dream – the film theatre – remains constant, so that his turbulent journey though the different scenes references to a greater extent film form, comedically exploring the consequences of editing and montage for Buster's character (something he might reasonably dream about given his close professional association with the cinema). The alternative would be to have the film theatre location change suddenly, in the way that scenes can change unpredictably and confusingly in ordinary dreams yet, in retaining the features of the theatre such as the proscenium arch, the audience and the orchestra within the frame, the film avoids such a disturbance, imbuing the dream space with a consistent spatial logic that ordinary dreams may not possess.

When the montage of images has completed, the film screen fades to black. An expanding iris shot brings us back to the scene of the original movie, *Hearts and Pearls*, as Buster is re-imagining it with those real faces still replacing the film's original cast. The camera tracks in, causing the film screen to fill the frame, and so the theatre disappears from view.

Sherlock Jr

From this point on, until Buster wakes again in the projection booth, his version of the film within his dream dominates *Sherlock Jr.*'s narrative, with no further reference being made to the film theatre surroundings. In this 'dreamfilm', Buster reinvents himself as a famous sleuth, Sherlock Jr., and through a series of hilariously extravagant manoeuvrings solves the mystery of some missing pearls, thus correcting his lack of success in solving the real life mystery of the missing pocket watch (in fact his fiancée is solving that crime while Buster sleeps by acquiring the description of the man who pawned the pocket watch and matching it to her other unscrupulous suitor). As the film-within-the-dream progresses, we might have cause to forget that this is in fact a character's dream as, in Kawin's words, 'the image looks no different from that of any third-person film'.[9] Yet, despite the film-within-the-dream 'expanding' to become a narrative in its own right, this narrative has still been carefully placed within the wider narrative of Buster's dream, so that we are clear we are watching his dream of stepping into the film he is screening and becoming the alter-ego Sherlock Jr. Although ambitious and unconventional (even, I think, by contemporary standards), the creation of a film within Buster's dream within the film does not threaten the internal logic of *Sherlock Jr.*'s fictional world. Indeed, it even serves to make sense of the spectacular stunts that Buster performs in that imagined world such as walking through a mirror and jumping through a fence, as well as allowing for the repeated miraculous appearances of his helpful sidekick (the theatre manager, now transformed in the picture).

In this sense, two divergent orders are established between the real world and the imagined world in *Sherlock Jr.*, with the boundaries of possibility and expectation significantly expanded in the latter realm. Yet, there is a causal logic to the imagined world that maintains coherence and stability, qualities that are not necessarily prevalent in dreams that we experience ourselves, and allows Buster's 'dreamfilm' to be followed as though it were another 'third-person film'. Furthermore, a relationship is made tangible between the imagined world, in which Buster is a successful detective, and the real world where he is a failure, thus creating a resonance that keeps us mindful of the character's reality as we witness his fantasy. As with the earlier films *Let Me Dream Again* and *Dream of a Rarebit Fiend*, we view the character within their imagined world, seeing Buster's actions within his dream rather than sharing his visions through the replication of his point of view.

Sherlock Jr. clearly presents a more complex case than the earlier films mentioned, and part of its fun is the self-reflexive use of cinematic codes and devices. Ira Nayman's essay 'Films, Dreams and Stolen Pocketwatches' rightly focuses upon this self-reflexivity as he suggests that 'the stolen pocket watch is not the main purpose of *Sherlock Jr.*....in fact, it is only the set-up for what the film is really about: an exploration of the differences between the cinematic world and the real world'.[10] Nayman's point regarding the pocket watch is justifiable given that the film resolves the issue fairly undramatically by having the fiancée solve the mystery a third of the way through the film. Yet, although clearly motivated by the form of *Sherlock Jr.*, Nayman's focus upon the relationship between film and reality risks bypassing the patent fact that Buster *dreams* that he enters a film, rather than *actually* entering it (as a character does in Woody Allen's *The Purple Rose of Cairo* (1985), for example). So there is an inaccuracy when Nayman concludes that 'In *Sherlock Jr.*, Keaton demonstrates that film logic doesn't have the kind of linear causality which he was careful to have in most of his other works...there is a scene where Keaton jumps through the stomach of his sidekick, as well as the brick wall he is standing against. This shot comes totally out of the blue, without set-up or explanation, and with no attempt at rational explanation. That's film'.[11] As a rational explanation for the moment of Keaton jumping through the stomach and the wall, 'that's film' is not quite adequate in this case. The apparent occurrence of an impossible event is related not so much to film logic as to dream logic, being as the jumping incident takes place within Buster's dream of a film. Crucially, an attempt at rational explanation for the impossible event has been made, and made quite explicitly: this event takes place within the wider structure of Buster's dream. Therefore, we understand that a different spectrum of possibility exists, based upon the elastic logic of dreams and dreaming. In this way, we can legitimately suggest that the film succeeds in presenting a coherent imagined fictional world alongside its real fictional world, methodically explaining the transition from one state to the next, defining a marked change in the boundaries of possibility, and creating resonance between the two states through the transformation of Buster's character from hapless amateur detective to super sleuth.

Kawin suggested that we can follow Buster's 'dreamfilm' as though it were 'any other third person film' and we might say the same of a number of other dream sequences in films, whereby we view characters from an objective position as they experience and explore their dreamed spaces (and certainly this is the case in the three films discussed in detail after this chapter). A significant reason for the absence of point of view restriction in the filmed dream sequences discussed may be the general impracticality and unattractiveness of sustained first-person perspective in film. George M. Wilson draws attention to some of the problems inherent in Robert Montgomery's *The Lady in the Lake* (1947), for example, which attempts to show the whole of the film's events through the 'eyes' of its central character, Philip Marlowe. Wilson remarks that the film:

> gives the impression that there is a camera by the name of 'Philip Marlowe' stumbling around Los Angeles and passing itself off as the well-known human being of the same name. The film has a number of faults, but the basic difficulty appears to be this. We do not and probably cannot see tracking or panning shots as corresponding to the continuous reorientation in space of the visual fields of people such as ourselves. Despite what textbooks on editing...often claim or seem to claim, we do not see a straight cut, even within a scene, as representing the phenomenology of a shift in a perceiver's visual attention. For these and, no doubt, other reasons, it may be that it is only in very limited sorts of context and style that a shot is construed as someone's field of vision. It is a genuinely open question whether the type of extended, direct subjectivization of the image track which occurs in *The Lady in the Lake* is a feasible alternative of film narration at all.[12]

Wilson here lays out the disparities between the nature of camera movement/editing and our understanding of human visual experience. The attempt to replicate the qualities of human vision for any sustained period, as in the case of *The Lady in the Lake*, becomes merely an exercise in illustrating those discrepancies, making plain the differences between the camera's field of vision and 'the visual fields of people such as ourselves' with every new scene. Wilson goes on to suggest that films in which 'a certain central character appears in segments throughout the film, and the action is only partially, if at all, seen through his or her physical point of view' are more successful as 'Features of the projected image or the *mise en scène* are used to depict or symbolize or reflect aspects of the way in which the character perceives and responds to his or her immediate environment'.[13] Those instances represent a choice on the part of the film-maker to align the audience temporarily with a character's viewpoint (although not necessarily attempting to see the world 'through their eyes') to convey a sense of their interior emotional or intellectual perspective at an important moment in a narrative.[14] Part of Wilson's argument is the suggestion that it is neither desirable nor necessary for a film to attempt to literally show the world from a character's field of vision in order for us to understand their point of view. The same is true in dream sequences. In *Sherlock Jr.* we can without difficulty appreciate that the events in Buster's dream are a product of his subconscious imagining without having to witness the sequence exclusively from his visual perspective. Crucially, the strong visual pleasure of Keaton's energetic performance would also be completely lost in such a representation, thus destroying the film's purpose and effect. Following Wilson's reasoning, such a project might actually serve to undermine the plausibility of the imagined world due to the camera's inadequacy in replicating the human field of vision. Likewise, in accordance with Wilson's assertions, given that Buster's dream occupies a large portion of the film's narrative an insistence upon first-person perspective might risk the kinds of difficulties that beset *The Lady in the Lake*.

The dream sequence in *Spellbound* (Alfred Hitchcock, 1945), famously based on designs by the Spanish surrealist painter Salvador Dalí, appears to solve some of the problems (in technical terms at least) associated with representing the world of a character's imagination in the first-person perspective. Structurally, the film depicts John Ballantine (Gregory Peck) recounting his dream in a makeshift therapy session with psychiatrist Dr Constance Peterson (Ingrid Bergman) and her former mentor, Dr Brulov (Michael Chekhov). Within this structure, the film alternates between images from Ballantine's mind as he remembers the dream (the transitions cued by the camera zooming swiftly towards his head as he speaks and cross-fades to the remembered dream images) and shots of him sitting in Brulov's study, retrospectively discussing the dream's events with his two companions. This pattern prevents the dream image from dominating the frame for any sustained period, re-emphasizing its formal unusualness and restating its divorcement from the visual appearance of everyday reality. As substantial parts of the dream are shot from Ballantine's viewpoint, the alternating structure also avoids protracted periods of first-person perspective that Wilson defines as problematic (and in the case of *Lady in the Lake* 'spectacularly disastrous').[15]

However, the camera is used to replicate the human field of vision in *Spellbound*'s dream sequence, which might still incur the kinds of difficulties Wilson draws our attention to. Yet, the imagined world in *Spellbound* possesses a surrealistic, warped visual quality, due to the sets originating from Dalí's designs and reflecting aspects of his hallmark artistic genius.

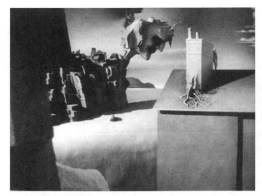

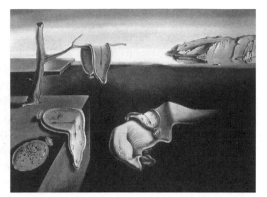

Spellbound   *The Persistence of Memory*

Thus, although it might be argued that the camera quite poorly reproduces the nature and quality of human sight through the use of drifting, fluid tracking shots and a series of zooms, this point-of-view style resists become disconcerting as it coheres with the odd, near-hallucinogenic composition of the imagined world as Ballantine remembers it (and as depicted in Dalí's designs). Thus, as Hitchcock's camera movement suggests mobility distinct from the restrictions of ordinary physical laws, such an occurrence does not present a challenge to our sense of coherence and conceivability as we watch the surrealistic dream images. The dreamed world is defined as a discrete space replete with a logical order distinct from ordinary reality as presented in the film's fictional 'ordinary' world; the strange, suspended movement of the camera-as-eye within that world serves to reinforce this notion.

The placement and use of the imagined world in *Spellbound* does become problematic for different reasons, however. In a key article, Andrew Britton voices his dissatisfaction with the film's treatment of the dream, explaining that

> Apart from the sequence in which a voluptuous, scantily-dressed girl appears, kissing the players in the casino in turn, and identified by Ballantyne [sic] as Constance (a sequence which Brulov dismisses wearily as "plain, ordinary wish-fulfillment"), the dream images are made to coincide point-for-point to 'real' events, as if they were empirical clues. The film purports to be an explication and justification of psychoanalysis, and yet the fundamental Freudian thesis that a dream represents the fulfillment of a wish is mentioned only to be dismissed as comparatively trivial, and replaced by an inverted version of the *pre*-Freudian thesis that dreams "could be used for practical purposes" (Freud's words) – here, not to foretell the mystery of the future, but to unravel the mystery of the past [emphasis in original].[16]

Britton lucidly identifies the film's uneasy blending of Freudian psychoanalytic processes - the interpretation of dreams itself constituting one fairly obvious example - and its insistence that the dreamed events should pinpoint in coded terms the events that Ballantine experienced in reality: once the code is broken, the riddle is solved exactly. Britton takes this to be an entirely specious application of Freudian theory and, in response, constructs a counter-reading of the dream as an

Oedipal dream, providing evidence from the film itself to support his revisionist account. The intricate complexities of this counter-argument, and indeed its justification within the film's plot, are not a central concern here. Rather, it is crucial to note that Britton's critical reservations are based upon his rejection of the kinds of resonances the film seeks to establish between the imagined world and the real world. The direct correlation that is drawn between dreamed and real events, as though the former could contain 'empirical clues' that accurately explain the latter, is out of step with the film's enthusiasm for psychoanalytic practices, and so the plausibility of the film's plot is fundamentally compromised. Thus, in the case of those films that construct relationships between the imagined world and the real world, there is an implicit requirement to make those relationships coherent but also credible. This is not the same as making the relationships or resonances obvious: it might be that a little more thought is required so that we can properly understand what a character's dream tells us about their life. I would suggest that this is one of the lasting pleasures of such films, and that we may in fact welcome the challenge of further contemplation.

The following two chapters present case studies of films that contrast the real world with the world of a character's imagination in ways similar to the films discussed here. *The Woman in the Window* and *The Wizard of Oz*, for example, create extended dream sequences like *Sherlock Jr.* and, although the characters do not dream of stepping into a film as Buster does, their dreams take the form of discrete, coherent narratives that have a stable plot and structure unlike the peculiar, volatile nature of real dreaming. Like *Let Me Dream Again*, the two films withhold the information that we are watching a character's dream, eliciting surprise - to substantially varying degrees - at their conclusions. As with *Sherlock Jr.*, the dreams of each character address a sense of lack they experience in their everyday lives, loosely corresponding with the widely held Freudian idea that 'the dream represents a wish as fulfilled'.[17] By way of a contrast, *Eternal Sunshine of the Spotless Mind* intersects images from the imagined world with sections from the real world as its central character dreams, in much the same way as *Spellbound* returned from images of Ballantine's remembered dream to the room in which he sat as he recounted it. *Eternal Sunshine of the Spotless Mind*'s imagined world shares some of the surrealistic qualities (and pleasures) of Dalí's dreamscape, which itself might be traced back to the wild fantasy of Porter's *Dream of a Rarebit Fiend*. Like the over-consumption of rarebit and beer in that film, *Eternal Sunshine of the Spotless Mind* provides a framing logic for the wild eccentricity of its character's imaginings. Unlike *Spellbound*, the film avoids any direct application of scientific accounts of dreaming, such as Freudian psychoanalytic theory, and instead presents a fantasy of science that can only be judged according to its own fictional logic, rather than compared against any established factual methods or theories. In this sense, it sidesteps the kinds of contentions Britton raises in relation to Hitchcock's film.

In discussing each of the films, *The Woman in the Window, The Wizard of Oz* and *Eternal Sunshine of the Spotless Mind*, I am concerned with exploring the resonances created between the character's imagined worlds and the real worlds that they temporarily take leave from. My investment in the films hinges upon their use of a character's imagined world to show up certain truths about their real lives: to shed light upon what we understand those characters to be. Arising from my discussion in this chapter, I am inclined to trace this tendency of the films back to the earliest example I cited, G.A. Smith's *Let Me Dream Again*, which showed us, in a matter of seconds, a character's dissatisfaction with his real life as he dreamed of an enticing alternative.

Notes

1. Leslie Halpern *Dreams on Film: The Cinematic Struggle Between Art and Science* Jefferson, North Carolina: McFarland & Company, 2003, p. 9.

2. The cinematic technique that Smith employs to perform this shift also constitutes something of a speciality for the period. As Barry Salt explains: '[a] unique occurrence in these years is the use of a focus-pull to give an out-of-focus blur on a medium shot of a man kissing a beautiful woman, then a cut to another out-of-focus blur which pulls in to a medium shot of the same man in bed kissing his ugly wife, from whom he recoils when he realises that he has been dreaming...there were to be no other examples of this device for a couple of decades, transitions in and out of dreams being done with dissolves from Zecca's Pathé remake of this film as *Rêve et réalitié* (1902) onwards to *And the Villain Still Pursued Her* (Vitagraph, 1906)'. Barry Salt 'Film Form 1900–1906' in Thomas Elsaesser (ed.) *Early Cinema: Space Frame Narrative* London: BFI Publishing, 1990, p. 39.

3. Ian Christie *The Last Machine: Early Cinema and the Birth of the Modern World* London: BFI Publishing, 1994, p. 34.

4. Both Smith and Porter's films in fact take their place in a period of the cinema where film-makers of all nationalities regularly explored the nature of viewing and viewpoint, often for voyeuristic means in films such as Pathé's *Par le trou de serrure* (Peeping Tom), made in 1901. Indeed, Smith integrates a series of close-up point of view shots from a character's perspective as they look through a magnifying glass in his film *Grandma's Reading Glass* (1900).

5. Stanley Cavell *The World Viewed: Reflections on the Ontology of Film* London: Harvard University Press, 1979, p. 67.

6. Buster's translucent alter-ego is variously described by critics as a 'ghost', which accurately depicts the look of the entity that emerges from his sleeping form, but is somewhat misleading as an account of what is actually taking place in the scene: Buster is safely asleep, he is not dead or in any way near-death.

7. Bruce F. Kawin *Mindscreen: Bergman, Godard and First-Person Film* Princeton, New Jersey: Princeton University Press, 1978, p. 52.

8. The term 'mindscreen' extends beyond the scope of this study. Kawin describes it thus: 'A mindscreen presents the landscape of the mind's eye, much as subjective camera presents what is seen by the physical eye...There are many instances in which the contents of a character's mind are displayed on the movie screen (or in which the movie screen behaves like a mind), and not all of them are intended to approximate dreams [emphasis in original]. The mind may wander, or dwell on a memory, or be in the grip of a hallucination, or think through a problem. And beyond that, a character may envision a story while in the act of relating or hearing it' (Bruce F. Kawin *How Movies Work* London: University of California Press, 1992, pp. 74–75). It should be clear that Kawin is dealing with the mind's eye in a much broader sense and, indeed, his study incorporates films like *Citizen Kane* due to the subjectivity of its narration. As I investigate 'imagined' worlds alongside 'potential' and 'other' worlds in film, my criteria is somewhat divergent to Kawin's and thus not concerned with the wider uses of mind' eye narration in films. In the context of my study, 'dream sequence' is also a perfectly acceptable term in relation to the imagined world.

9. Ibid.. p. 59.

10. Ira Nayman 'Films, Dreams and Stolen Pocketwatches,' *CineAction!* No. 67, November 2005, p. 40.

11. Ibid. p. 42.

12. George M. Wilson *Narration in Light: Studies in Cinematic Point of View* Baltimore; London: The Johns Hopkins University Press, 1986, pp. 86–87.

13. Ibid. p. 87.

14. One film that Wilson cites in relation to this is Nicholas Ray's *Bigger than Life* (1956) in which the camera corresponds to Ed Avery's (James Mason) viewpoint as his vision of the world becomes profoundly affected by the cortisone drug that he is taking. The film dramatises his altered perception through the warped angles and colours in shots that resemble his demented point of view.

15. Wilson, p. 86.

16. Andrew Britton 'Hitchcock's *Spellbound*: Text and Counter-text,' *CineAction!* No. 3/4, Winter 1986, p. 80.

17. Sigmund Freud *The Interpretation of Dreams* Joyce Crick, trans., New York: Oxford University Press, 1999, p. 98.

3

MAKING IT HOME

The Wizard of Oz (Victor Fleming, 1939)

The Woman in the Window (Fritz Lang, 1944)

Two Dreams

In Kansas, a young girl wakes from her dream. The last she remembered, she was in a faraway place, surrounded by an assortment of strange but dear friends. Farewell tears still wet on her cheeks, she had closed her eyes and murmured the words 'there's no place like home' again and again in the hope that they would return her home. When her eyes next open, she is in Kansas once more, at home and in bed. Although confused and adamant that the world she just left was real and no dream, she takes in her surroundings. Faces which appeared in that other world are here now: the wizard is just a man; the lion, tin man and scarecrow are just farmhands. Finally, somewhat resolutely, she utters those words once more: 'there's no place like home'. The screen fades to black.

In Gotham, an assistant university professor is awoken by the firm shake of a hand on his shoulder, the calling of his name, and by the chiming of a nearby clock. He is at first disoriented, perhaps because he never expected to wake up again. The last he remembered, he had taken an overdose of sleeping medication as a final resort to escape capture for manslaughter. But now there is no medication, no crime, and he is back safely in his club. It was all just a dream. He rises, finishes his drink, and takes in his surroundings: his pen is back in his top pocket, no longer a damning piece of evidence; the man he thought he murdered is now passing his hat at the desk; the cunning blackmailer is now the amiable doorman. Reality is restored once more.

These are the final moments of two films released within five years of each other, *The Wizard of Oz* and *The Woman in the Window* respectively. As will become clear, these films differ greatly in terms of style and tone. In both, however, the dreams of the characters, Dorothy Gale (Judy Garland) and Professor Wanley (Edward G. Robinson), represent the major part of the story. When each character awakens again to reality, both experience instinctive and understandable feelings of relief: Dorothy had, after all, stated and restated her desire to return home and Wanley must surely cherish his escape from what seemed like certain death. Indeed, it would be difficult to argue that any emotions felt at the conclusion of both films should not include relief of some kind. However, as the dreams fade for each character, there is the possibility that the memory of the dreams might also fade, that the experiences, which turned out to be imaginary, might soon be forgotten now that a return to reality has been negotiated. Wanley practically runs for his life when, in the film's closing sequence, he is faced with a female bearing only the merest hint of resemblance to a character he conjured in his dream. Back in Kansas, Auntie Em has already begun to brush away any talk of Oz ('we dream lots of silly things...'). Life goes on.

Having been given privileged views of the characters' imagined worlds as well as their real worlds, we are well placed to evaluate what potentially is lost in such a sudden abandonment of their respective dreams. Our special position, involving an intimacy that could never be enjoyed in real life, provides us with the ability to appraise whether the character's immediate embracing of reality is an instance of instinctive relief obliterating the importance of the fantasy. We can ask whether their impulsive joy at being part of their real world once more actually makes them blind to some of the harsher realities that those worlds previously contained, realities that are perhaps easier to suppress than confront (but which presumably still exist). Those truths concerning the characters' real worlds might threaten the durability of the joyful relief they both experience at having reality restored once more. The fact that they dreamt of leaving at all (in different ways) should tell something. To follow this line of argument is to investigate whether, despite the immediate relief of the characters, the films themselves make their dream lives especially significant, with important lasting ramifications, rather than merely frivolous diversions or, much less, easy get-outs from potentially convoluted dramatic cul-de-sacs.[1] The existence of a real world and a dream world in the stories provide opportunity for comparison between those two states. Scrutinizing the dreams of Dorothy Gale and Professor Wanley therefore constitutes a fruitful approach as those characters' dreams are shown to contrast in certain important ways with their real lives. Throughout this chapter, I will maintain that the characters' fantasies re-focus our attention upon the shortcomings of their respective realities. Consequently, in these films, dreams matter profoundly *as dreams*.

Lonely Spaces

The *Wizard of Oz* begins in a world of sepia from the outset; even the roaring MGM lion has been tinted in coffee-brown shades. As the credits begin to roll, motifs based around the theme of freedom are played out. The musical score is an overture and, within the conventions of that established form, exhibits a particular kind of tonal freedom as it moves from a foreboding rendition of *Ding Dong the Witch is Dead* to an epic, romantic *Somewhere Over the Rainbow*, then subsides into the carefree celebration of *It Really Was No Miracle* before merging into a rendition of *Come out, Come out* which itself moves from a soft, slow, seraphic chorus into a climactic, grandiose burst of volume and power. The images that accompany this overture are also imbued with an unrestricted quality. Clouds pass behind the letters of the credits, giving the impression that the words are sailing through the sky themselves.

The Wizard of Oz

Equally, there is the sense that the camera has been placed within the clouds, moving with similar ease through the skies. In the absence of solid ground or any horizon within the frame, our view is temporarily liberated from certain rudiments of ordinary human existence. The effect elicits a sensation beyond everyday experience. As well as establishing aspects of mobility and freedom, the images constitute the film's first fantasy, ensuring that we start in a make-believe space unreachable in reality.

A gentle fade to black cues expectations of proceeding action, but instead a eulogy to the enduring charm of L Frank Baum's story appears, written in the clouds like the credits earlier. The overture continues over this section, but less strident now than the previous crescendo of *Come out, Come out*, before dwindling slowly and finally fading away to nothing. A concluding pluck of harp strings and another fade to black punctuate a move from the film's introductory sequence to its story, marking the transition with the briefest moment of darkness and silence. A short pause for breath before the storytelling begins.

When sound and vision are restored we are somewhere quite different. There is a path passing through two fields and into the distance, but that description could hardly suffice. The world is still monochrome, and the sepia tint of the image has drained the life and colour from the surroundings, making leaves and grasses look withered, dry, half-dead. Any shrubs and trees are spindly and feeble, starved of vitality. The dark wooden lines of telegraph and fence posts divide up the stark landscape, but the barren scene stretches out beyond these boundaries, as the dusty fields and dirt track reach out into hopeless oblivion. Even the sky, so recently a site of freedom and movement, has transformed into an ominous, foreboding feature. The clouds, a painted studio background, are low hanging, heavy and oppressive now, meeting the desolate landscape at the horizon. Land and sky converge to form an imposing picture of stillness and gloom.

When discussing this vista, Salman Rushdie draws attention to the lack of 'realness' in this 'soft focus' studio-set depiction (suggesting that a realistic depiction of Kansas, complete with its poverty, might have compromised the ensuing leap into fantasy).[2] This assertion is useful when we consider that an attempt at depicting reality has been resisted in favour of a more impressionistic rendering. The features of this scene have been constructed for a specific purpose. The move from the opening titles to this landscape bring us down to earth literally, but the overwhelming bleakness of the landscape also guarantees an emotional descent, a lowering of mood as we are figuratively brought back down to earth.

In this environment, the most striking visual features are actually the fence posts and telegraph polls as they rise up vertically against the horizontal plains, dull yet distinct against the

The Wizard of Oz

scene's grey hues. Their status as points of interest is quickly compromised, however, as a young girl runs into the foreground of the scene with her dog, her movement alone striking a contrast with the staid surroundings. Indeed, she exhibits a particularly uninhibited style of travelling: running, turning and spinning to look about and behind her. As she twirls and skips, her bunches of hair swish around her face and her arms sway to and fro, enhancing and extending her unrestrained style of movement. The fluency and vitality of her motion is complemented in a lively section of music that actually pre-empted her entrance, beginning just before the fade up from darkness before this scene as though tracing her progress even before she enters the frame. The music becomes a soundtrack to the girl's exuberance, conveying those aspects of her character displayed through her style of movement. The quality of the music also recalls the film's overture, continuing the themes of freedom and release that were found there and making them synonymous with this character. In this monochrome world, colour cannot signal vibrancy, so that quality is conveyed through movement and sound. Amid the dusty stillness, the young girl is a breath of fresh air, yet she is not divorced from her surroundings: we might also notice the way in which the fencing either side of the track visually hems her in, containing her movements in a way that is not so much repressive as restrictive.

The girl, of course, is Dorothy. As she bobs to the ground, we cut to a closer shot of her that enhances details such as her pinafore dress, her tightly bunched hair and her small black dog, which she calls 'Toto'. Such features secure her identity for anyone who knows her story. Dorothy's bob down is also a turn backwards, back towards the camera, and towards us. In combination with the closeness provided by the change from long shot to medium close-up, this movement initiates the first brief moment of intimacy between character and audience and, likewise, between performer and audience, for this girl is also Judy Garland. There is another story, then: the story of an actress, to which this film, with its portrait of youth and innocence, forms a somewhat painful prologue in a life almost characterized by lost innocence and disillusionment. On screen, actress and character are always there, but are like the separate colours in an iridescent fabric, where each shade emerges more clearly only as the light plays on the material's surface. It becomes impossible to say what singular colour such a material is, as it is made of the two shades. Likewise, both Garland and Dorothy exist simultaneously on screen, with each gesture and movement belonging to both actress and character. As V.F. Perkins has suggested: 'The camera's hanging on the moments of the character's life is necessarily taking moments from the actor's'.[3] Real world and story world converge in screen performance, as character and performer exist together.[4] Inevitably, critics tend to place emphasis upon either the character or the performer as a way of reading a film, depending on their particular argument. Although my interest lies with the storyworld of the film, and thus with Dorothy, it is not uncommon for *The Wizard of Oz* to be read in the context of Garland's personal story[5] (although a reading of this kind is historically specific, and it would clearly have been impossible for an audience of 1939 to carry out the same retrospective interpretation). Yet even with these definitions in place, it is still unrealistic to divorce performer and character: as I describe Dorothy's movement in this opening scene, and I am also describing a way of moving that Garland has adopted. The film displays both the fiction of a character and the document of a performance.

If at first we had taken Dorothy's exuberant style of movement to be indicative of cheerful abandon, this assumption evaporates with the move to close-up. From here, we realize that her energy was borne not out of delight, but out of anxiety. As she bobs down and turns, Dorothy gazes back along the track beyond the frame, searching the landscape that she has just crossed, eyes wide in fear. She clutches her little dog close: 'She isn't coming yet Toto...Did she hurt you? She tried to didn't she?' So Dorothy was not just running, but running away; her swinging and twirling around a way of ensuring that she was not being followed. If the fencing either side of Dorothy was a visually restrictive element, hemming her in, then this unnamed pursuer constitutes a repressive force. The revealing of Dorothy's anxiety is matched by a change in music: as she bobs down, the vigorous pace of the rising string melody subsides into soft accompaniment. Naturally, the quieting of the music coincides with the first lines of dialogue, but it also complements the low mood precipitated by Dorothy's apprehensive demeanour.

Dorothy concludes by saying: 'Come on – we'll go tell Uncle Henry and Auntie Em...Come on Toto!' It is delightful that Dorothy imagines she and Toto will tell the story together and her phrasing evokes a sense of make-believe, conveying the tenderness of her years and thus emphasizing her vulnerability within this situation due to her status in the world. Certainly, Dorothy feels unable convincingly to face the threat herself, and so the names of Uncle Henry and Auntie Em come to represent refuge for her: telling them will provide security against the threat. Furthermore, she seems to assume instinctively that they will understand. Spatially, an oppositional relationship is established within the scene: at one end of the path there is the cruelty of this woman countered by the safety of Uncle Henry and Aunt Em at the other. As Dorothy rises and turns to continue along the track and away towards home, she apparently moves towards the resolution of her troubles. The underscored music complements this upturn in mood by reverting back to the original lively theme that opened the scene when Dorothy speaks her final words and continues her journey.

We cut to a farmyard scene just as Dorothy hurries across the background of the shot. She runs between various elements such as fences, trees, a barn, a cow, a tyre-swing, a washing line and so on. This composition creates a matrix of horizontal and vertical lines, enhancing earlier notions of Dorothy being 'hemmed in' by her environment. Those features situated towards the foreground of the shot compromise her status within the frame. These imposing elements form a picture of stillness – even the tyre-swing does not sway – and Dorothy's swift movement is once more discordant with her surroundings. The space is also compartmentalized as fences divide the yard in the immediate foreground, the cow's grazing patch behind that, then the dusty track and finally the fields beyond. Everything is in its place. In contrast once again,

Dorothy moves across this formal arrangement as she runs, and crosses its boundaries as she enters the farmyard. She reaches Auntie Em (Clara Blandick) and Uncle Henry (Charley Grapewin) and, as she engages with them, it becomes apparent that they are ruled by a similar sense of proper place and order that pervades their surroundings.

The two are moving chicks from a broken incubator to hutches. They are almost mechanical in their activity: Auntie Em scoops chicks into her apron whilst counting before placing them into a hutch in the foreground; Uncle Henry puts them into his hat before placing them in a different hutch which is then taken and stacked in the background. The procedure revolves around order and repetition, putting everything in the right place to protect their livelihood. Dorothy threatens to break the efficiency of this production line as she excitedly tells the story of 'what Miss Gulch did to Toto'. She hangs close on Auntie Em's shoulder, unknowingly hindering her progress. At one point she picks up a chick and holds it close to her face, but Auntie Em takes it off her and counts it in the hutch with the rest: there is no room for sentiment here. Garland delivers her lines in a continuous, spill-over stream of words that not only conveys Dorothy's anxious enthusiasm to share her experience, but also contrasts with the dry, regimented order of the task being performed by her elders. Dorothy's advances are dismissed and rebuffed repeatedly until finally a sharp 'we're busy' from Auntie Em silences her. Dorothy murmurs a quiet, defeated 'oh, all right' and makes her way across the yard, leaving the scene of the chicken counting. Garland swings and touches her hands together in a gesture evoking the self-consciousness of a scolded child and, as she walks slowly away, a brief glance back towards the pair conveys Dorothy's deflation at her elders' dismissal of her emotions. Auntie Em and Uncle Henry's absorption in their task is understandable,[6] but it becomes clear that they occupy a world in which Dorothy struggles to be accommodated, both spatially and emotionally. In this scene, her uncle and aunt are located at a site of activity in which Dorothy effectively has no place. Their resistance to Dorothy is not vindictive (and the as-yet-unseen Almira Gulch provides a good example of a genuinely antagonistic force) but instead is borne out of a general incompatibility between them and their niece. This disparity is evident in Baum's original story, especially with Auntie Em:

> When Dorothy, who was an orphan, first came to her, Aunt Em had been so startled by the child's laughter that she would scream and press her hand upon her heart whenever Dorothy's voice reached her ears; and she still looked at the little girl with wonder that she could find anything to laugh about.[7]

The gulf between the characters is not made so dramatic in the film, but Dorothy's alienness to her elders is retained as they fail to understand what is important to her, and she merely disrupts what is important to them. Auntie Em and Uncle Henry become synonymous with their environment, caught up in the dry routine of the everyday, devoid of excitement or emotion.[8] It is to be expected, therefore, that Dorothy's particular blend of youthful exuberance should contrast as much with them as it does with her surroundings.

Leaving her aunt and uncle, Dorothy finds the three farmhands, Zeke (Bert Lahr), Hunk (Ray Bolger) and Hickory (Jack Haley) who are mending a wagon. She approaches Zeke with her

The Wizard of Oz

problem, but he has 'hogs to get in' and disappears. Hunk offers some advice, but she is reluctant to take it, as he is preoccupied with his work and questions whether she has any brains at all.[9] Dorothy approaches Zeke once more and, as he gives his advice, she begins to walk along a wall separating two pigpens, arms outstretched to balance. Suddenly, she topples into one of the pens and Zeke has to rush to rescue her, lifting her out and over the pen into the arms of Hunk and Hickory. Once Dorothy's safety is established, the group begin to tease a sweating Zeke over his apparent lack of courage.[10] This respite from work is soon ended, however, as Auntie Em arrives, threatening to sack the men and sending them brusquely back to their chores. Dorothy uses the moment to try to speak with Auntie Em about Miss Gulch and Toto but is shooed away again and told to 'find yourself a place where you won't get into any trouble'.[11] Auntie Em's advice is consistent with the presiding regime on the farm of putting things away in their proper place: chickens in their coop, pigs in their pen, farmhands to their chores, to create an ordered environment. Auntie Em instigates much of this ordering and here she attempts to compartmentalize her niece similarly, but finds she has no place for her. Her advice instead leads Dorothy to contemplate, famously, where such a place might exist.

The question of Dorothy's place within her world is raised repeatedly in this opening section as a succession of spaces and situations are shown to which she does not belong. Incongruous with her environment from the outset, she fails to penetrate Auntie Em and Uncle Henry's devotion to their location and duty and is effectively made to leave. From there she visits the farmhands but each are equally bound to their duties and zones: Zeke leaves her for his hogs, Hunk is busy mending his truck, Hickory has left to attend his 'contraption' and when returning to Zeke she falls foul of balancing between two spaces and has to be rescued. Each of the characters Dorothy encounters can be defined by a specific task they carry out in a specific location, and she passes between them, trying to engage them with her troubles, attempting to find a place to be heard and understood.

This, of course, prompts Dorothy to imagine a place far away from the world she knows. It is apt that at this moment the world around her should melt away: the crude clucks and grunts from the farmyard, which have been quite vociferous, quieten to nothing as the music gently swells and, as the camera settles into a close-up of Dorothy, the scene's background becomes unfocused and hazy, and so the realities of farmyard life and landscape are beginning to subdue.

Her song represents longing borne out of loneliness. In the lines leading up to it, Dorothy's voice begins to change; her speech becoming slower, more considered, until Garland's more resonant singing voice breaks in with 'Somewhere...' The effect is of Dorothy finding a different voice – an inner voice perhaps – as she moves away from the constraints and frustrations of the world around her and moves into song. 'Finding one's voice' is traditionally associated with freedom of expression, a freedom which Dorothy enjoys now. The moment is her first escape from the world into a realm of private fantasy, and Garland directs her focus almost exclusively out towards the skies, as though searching the clouds for anything beyond the confines of her dreary horizon. Our first view, of course, was of clouds before we were brought down to earth in Kansas. Dorothy's gaze upwards here references and reverses that initial descent, marking her psychological departure from reality. The particular magic of this scene is intensified as the clouds actually break, causing sunlight to pour across Dorothy's face, bringing the first smile to her lips since the film began. But the song's pleasure is tinged with sadness: Dorothy is happiest only when she has shut out her world, withdrawing into a private domain where it cannot touch her. When the song finishes, that world remains.[12] It is a world to which Dorothy barely belongs and it is no surprise that later when the cyclone hits, she is nowhere to be found.

This opening sequence asks what kind of world Dorothy, an orphaned child, has been adopted into. The equivalent pre-dream section of *The Woman in the Window*, however, focuses upon a man in middle age, and asks instead what kind of world he has created for himself. This film's tone is darker, as becomes apparent from the start. The opening credits are displayed off-square, diagonally, as though promising a narrative which itself is off-kilter and edgy in the noir tradition that was well-established by 1944 when the film was released. A vigorous, straining string arrangement accompanies these credits, again suggesting tense aspects to be revealed in the film's ensuing story. The transition between each set of credits is marked with a dissolve until eventually the screen fades to black. On the fade up, an engraved plaque sets the location, Gotham College, and this image cross-fades to a card framed on a plain wooden door, informing us that Assistant Professor Wanley is giving a lecture on 'Some Psychological Aspects of Homicide'. With those words, the subject is firmly established: the film declares its investment in both murder and the human mind. As we join the lecture Wanley is framed in a long shot as he proposes to the class certain qualifications to the Biblical injunction 'Thou shalt not kill', the most significant being that 'the man who kills in self-defence should not be judged by the same standards as the man who kills for gain', given that Wanley will later dream of killing in self-defence. Florence Jacobowitz has suggested that the film immediately links the professor with entrapment and the potential to kill.[13] Jacobowitz concentrates on Wanley's key qualification, but also on the 'horizontal bars of light and shadow cast across his face' as he lectures that constitute a 'motif of confinement'.[14] If we accept this, we might also observe the camera's gradual track forward that slowly confines the space around Wanley, entrapping him visually; or the way in which, in this tighter shot, he places his hand on a pile of books like the accused swearing their oath in a trial. Further to Jacobowitz's account, the prominence of the words 'Sigmund Freud' 'unconscious, preconscious, conscious' and 'id, ego, superego' written on the blackboard behind Wanley, occurring in this film about a dream, has inevitably prompted psychoanalytic readings.[15]

For different critics, themes of entrapment and references to psychoanalytic theory in this sequence pre-empt Wanley's dream, thus anticipating the film's future events. However, the opening scene also communicates something of his present situation. Particularly, it conveys aspects of Wanley's

The Woman in the Window   *The Woman in the Window*

somewhat diminished status within the world. The long shot of the lecture hall depicts him in a stark, isolated position alone at the front of the class, occupying only a small area of an expansive stage. The black and white shades of his suit blend with the chalked blackboard, the white panelling behind him and the black and white of the horizontal shadows that fall across the stage, lending an indistinct quality to his own appearance as he merges within the scene's monochrome composition. The use of long shot is particularly effective as it withholds a proper appreciation of Wanley's expressions and features, making him indefinite to us.

The scene could conceivably have opened with a close-up of Wanley as he delivers his lecture (the mounted sign in the previous shot already having established the location and occasion) thus immediately affording him a degree of prominence. But this kind of portrayal has been resisted in favour of a less distinct introduction whereby Wanley is merely one of a number of elements contained within the frame. Indeed, the writing on the blackboard might detract our attention, with the name of Sigmund Freud looming large over Wanley as he stands beneath it, casting a formidable intellectual shadow.

Edward G. Robinson's short stature contributes to his character's inferiority within the scene, just as elements of his performance contribute to the subdued manner of Wanley's introduction. Robinson delivers the lecture in a hesitant, disjointed manner, leaving unusual pauses between words and phrases that break the continuity and impact of his address. As he speaks, he paces slowly across the stage area, his gaze often dropping to the floor, breaking his connection with his audience and restricting the potential for any sustained focus. His hands, which could be used to emphasize or illustrate, are held behind his back, causing him to hunch over slightly, making him appear older than his years. Even when Wanley makes a gesture, touching the desk as he passes it, he leans his weight against it slightly in an awkward motion as though using it for support. This movement is again suggestive of Wanley behaving beyond his years, but also communicates a lack of assuredness in his physical movements that rhymes with the lack of confidence inherent in his vocal hesitancy and distracted manner. These aspects of Robinson's performance combine with the film's compositional style to present Wanley as a man without vigour, awkward in his own environment and somewhat adrift from his world.

Even as the film focuses in on Wanley, defining him as its subject, his status remains compromised. As the camera tracks slowly forward, sweeping over the heads of the students seated in the foreground of the shot and towards Wanley in the background, it picks out small flurries of activity as various grouped students turn and converse with one another. In one such instance, a student seated on the front row turns and talks with two peers seated behind him, so facing away from his lecturer.

The move towards Wanley could serve to prioritize and emphasize him within the scene but that process is undermined as the activity of the students – placed between him and the camera – suggests a degree of authority resting with them rather than him. It is his duty to talk to them but they choose whether or not to listen. The lack of interest exhibited by sections of the audience is apparently repeated in the editing of this scene. As Wanley begins a new passage with the words 'the man who kills in self-defence should not be judged by the same standards as the man who kills for gain...' the scene unexpectedly fades into silence and darkness, mid-sentence, as though we too had lost interest in the lecture once the crucial detail (crucial in retrospect at least) is delivered. The gentle fade avoids a truly stark disruption and instead the film exhibits a kind of apathy to what is taking place, slowly drawing away rather than sharply cutting. A pattern of representation is at work in this opening sequence, one that undermines any command Wanley might exert over both his audience within the film and the film audience. The visual composition of the scene compromises his status, denying him any immediate prominence within his surroundings. Furthermore, Robinson's performance combines with the reactions of the class to lessen the impact of Wanley's presence and speech, to the extent that when the fade to black cuts off his flow, we are not straining to catch his vanishing words.

Like Dorothy before, the question of Wanley's place in the world is raised in these opening moments. The representation of his character dilutes any dramatic impact, marginalizing him despite his position at centre stage. This marginalization continues as, having finished his work at the college, Professor Wanley says goodbye to his vacation-bound wife (Dorothy Peterson) and children at the train station. For Jacobowitz, this scene provides another 'context of confinement' and Reynold Humphries goes further, suggesting that Wanley's wife particularly is 'presented as both fussy and well meaning, treating her husband like a child who will have the greatest difficulty in surviving without her'.[16] Both accounts realize Wanley's unassertive role within the scene. Yet while his wife might appear domineering through her care for him, Jacobowitz's and, to a larger extent, Humphries' accounts risk inaccurately constructing her character as an antagonistic force whereas, more truthfully, her actions represent an ordinary pattern that married couples settle into. It would be unfair to overlook Mrs Wanley's gentle smile and sympathetic manner in an effort to overplay notions of her husband's entrapment. Rather than being confined in the situation, Wanley allows himself to be led, so his wife makes statements and asks questions that he merely responds to, resulting in his final promise that he will go out and not stay 'cooped up every night working all the time' according to her wishes. It is striking in this exchange that both actors convey a sense of rhythm and relaxed predictability in their responses to each other, as though this were the type of conversation that these characters have had many times before, with each taking the same roles they always have, and will continue to many times in the future. As a portrait of a middle-aged couple that have moulded each other into certain modes of behaviour over the years, the scene is effective to the extent that we might overlook its skilful construction.

As Mrs Wanley speaks to her husband, he lightly fans his face with his hat in a feminized gesture that somewhat undermines his masculinity in their relationship. His wife instead assumes a protective authority over him, and likewise instructs their children to kiss their father in the absence of his self-assertion. As his son says 'so long Pop!' Wanley repeats 'so long!' in a similarly playful tone. The direct repetition of his son's phrase echoes the childlike aspects prevalent in his interactions with his wife, further illustrating the ambiguity of his position within his family. As the group moves towards the barrier, Wanley first tells his children to look after 'mother', as though she were his mother too, before quietly saying to his wife 'watch these two won't you?' These instructions might constitute an exertion of authority, yet he simultaneously relinquishes responsibility for their care as he recognizes and trusts their ability to take care of one another without him. Just as Wanley's status within the lecture hall was diminished through a series of representational choices, so his position within his family is made indefinite through the course of his interactions with them. (And, as they depart, we might detect the first signs of a move for Wanley from a stable, comfortable environment which apparently runs itself with only minimal involvement from him, to a situation in which he is forced to make assertive choices and crucial decisions.)

Wanley has arranged to meet two friends, Doctor Michael Barkstane (Edmund Breon) and a District Attorney Frank Lalor (Raymond Massey), at his club. On arriving, he becomes momentarily mesmerized by the portrait of an attractive female in an adjacent shop window. His two friends arrive while he gazes into the window; Barkstane points towards Wanley and he and Lalor laugh knowingly. Wanley eventually breaks his gaze and catches sight of his friends. As he greets them Barkstane speaks first: 'flirting with our sweetheart?' He follows this with the line 'we've decided she's our dream girl' and Lalor chimes in: 'that's right, we saw her first'. In this friendly exchange, an understated alliance is revealed between the Doctor and the DA as they arrive together, stand together and refer to their union in terms like 'we,' 'us' and 'our'. Implicitly, Wanley is left outside of their partnership and this dynamic is maintained inside the club. In medium-long shot, Wanley and Lalor sit in armchairs either side of a coffee table whilst Barkstane occupies a sofa between them, yet he actually sits at the end nearest to Lalor, thus forming a physical union between the Doctor and the DA and meaning that, wherever the camera is placed, it can never visually associate Wanley with either of the two men.

Indeed, a preceding close-up of Wanley followed by a diametrically opposed medium shot of the two friends re-emphasizes the isolated position of the former and the solidarity of the latter. From this unified pose they politely scrutinize Wanley, making him more of a subject than a participant in the conversation, with Lalor particularly offering his friend the benefit of his professional advice and wisdom. Both men direct objects such as a teaspoon and cigar towards Wanley as they speak, as though emphasizing key points of their individual lectures.[17] Certainly, this accentuates an inequality between them and him, creating an imbalance of status which is furthered as Barkstane later advises: 'just you run along to bed like a good fellow and forget the whole matter', addressing Wanley as though he were a child.[18] When this line is spoken,

The Woman in the Window

the two men have crossed over to stand with Wanley, but he remains seated and so they tower over and talk down to him, thus maintaining the well-mannered authority they have exerted throughout their discussion. Again, even as the two occupy a shared space with Wanley, they remain united and dominant. Evidently, this final relationship is consistent with the structure of the film's opening sequence, in which Wanley has been dominated by the world around him. The film's achievement lies in its ability to express this theme of subordination within a conventional structure of establishment, without indulgence or overstatement.

Curious Companions

When Wanley's friends leave, he walks slowly to the bookcase, chooses a book and sits down to read. (The book he selects is *The Song of Songs Which is Solomon's*, a cycle of poems that in one sense is a celebration of married love, but also contains more erotic and salacious themes. In terms of the film's narrative pattern, it is an appropriate choice of title as Wanley is momentarily suspended between the propriety of a monogamous relationship and the suggestion of an illicit liaison yet to come.) As Wanley walks to his seat and reclines, murmuring lines from the book he reads, Arthur Lange's excellent score incorporates a musical motif that recurs throughout the film in various forms, always sensitive to changes in mood and tone. Here, it adopts a slower, thoughtful, quality as its two countermelodies strain softly against one another, creating a mood of quiet reflection. There is also resignation in the music's form: Wanley's resignation. Firstly to an evening spent in his club with a book for company, but also a wider resignation to 'this solidity, this stodginess... the end of the brightness of life, of spirit and adventure' that he remorsefully described to his friends earlier. As he walks over to the bookcase, he walks between other members of the club, all of whom are well in advance of his own years. The impression is given of Wanley walking through a museum containing various exhibited projections of his future existence, spanning out inevitably before him. Yet, he is there already. He has retreated to an environment that encourages exactly the sort of 'solidity' and 'stodginess' that he earlier lamented. He simply mistakes his cage for a sanctuary. Wanley's habit for 'losing himself in a book', as described by his wife, is explainable here as his way of postponing his world, an exciting but partial escape made safe by its fictitiousness. Tonight, however, he experiences an escape more lucid than the reading of a book. As the waiter brings another drink, Wanley signs and asks to be reminded when it is ten-thirty. The music dwindles as the image dissolves from Wanley reading to a shot of a chiming carriage clock showing ten-thirty, explaining 'Sometimes I'm inclined to lose track of time'. The same dissolve occurred earlier as he entered the club to demonstrate an ellipsis in time. Apparently, to Wanley and the audience, the same transition has occurred here, but the dissolve now marks a transition into the world of Wanley's dream.

On leaving the club, Wanley is again drawn towards the portrait that he gazed at earlier. As he peers now, the face in the picture is doubled as another face is reflected in the window of the shop. Wanley turns to find the woman in the picture, the woman in the window, standing beside him, smiling gently. The film has effectively brought this woman to life by representing her firstly as a soft-lined, two-dimensional, idealized figure of womanhood, secondly a sudden glimpsed reflection of a face on a window and thirdly a real person standing next to him on the street, her realness exemplified in vivid details such as her sequinned dress and feathered hat. It is a mysterious introduction and, in this scene, the woman proves equally difficult to read. Joan Bennett plays this woman, Alice, and delivers her lines with a calm assuredness, lingering seductively over words and phrases such as 'I was alone...I don't like to be' and 'long, low whistle,' infusing them with subdued innuendo. Yet, she also conveys an attentive sincerity, making it inappropriate to read her approaches as only predatory. Likewise, her vocal lingering also suggests intelligent consideration of her responses marked by the sophistication of her speech in lines such as 'I regard it as an unusually sincere compliment...' These divergent facets mingle to form an enigma. This ambiguity rhymes with her mysterious introduction and, similarly, with the sleek shimmering darkness of her sequinned dress, diamond earrings and feathered headdress that connotes seduction, sophistication but also danger. Alice's opacity complicates our understanding of her nature, her position and her intentions. Therefore, her offer to clarify matters for Wanley by suggesting 'I'm not married, I have no designs on you and one drink's all I'd care for...' does not succeed in making anything clearer for us, it merely extends the game she appears to play.

At this stage, Alice's nature is concealed to the extent that she might conceivably develop into the classical death-dealing *femme fatale*. Ironically, this possibility evaporates fully once a killing actually occurs. After drinks at a nightclub, she and Wanley go back to her apartment where they drink champagne and view some sketches of her (perhaps reflecting Wanley's desire to view this beautiful woman but with the legitimacy associated with looking at art). They are interrupted by a man whom Alice calls Frank (later revealed as Claude Mazard). Despite Wanley's assurances and Alice's fretful insistence, Mazard (Arthur Loft) immediately misreads their being together as less than innocent. He strikes Alice and, when Wanley intervenes, knocks him back onto the couch and begins to strangle him. Alice cowers in the corner, pleading with Mazard to stop, but to no avail; Wanley reaches out to a pair of scissors they were going to cut a champagne wire with, and Alice takes her chance, rushing the scissors to Wanley then standing back apprehensively as he stabs his assailant repeatedly in the back. Mazard rolls over dead. Rather than orchestrating this killing, as a *femme fatale* might do, Alice is visibly dazed by the sudden brutality of events as she stands clinging to the mantelpiece for support, breathless with shock. Indeed, Andrew Klevan suggests that, throughout the period immediately after the killing, her 'awkward and stilted movements suggest, at first, suspicious behaviour but then, as the scene develops, they indicate the genuine bewilderment and incapacity of someone who is unfamiliar with criminal activity'.[19] The coy assuredness of her earlier exchanges dissolves in the face of events. As Klevan intimates, there is a genuineness to Alice's behaviour now that reveals her earlier cool manner to have been a constructed act, a projection of an image she chose for herself but can sustain no longer as her world turns dark. Her mystery evaporates as she instinctively reacts with shock, dismay and fear, and any veiled threat she might have possessed has vanished. In terms of the character's function within the generic bracket of the American film noir, notions of Alice as *femme fatale* are compromised to the extent of being dispelled. Her show of seduction is also ended, inappropriate now and, as she leans into a chair, deflated by her trauma, she is suddenly careworn and remorseful, no longer interested in preserving the act of enticement.

The shift in tone of Wanley's dream is sudden, as the fantasy of attracting an alluring young woman melts into the fantasy of killing. The distinction between the two fantasies however, is that in Wanley's dream, his liaison with Alice apparently had few tangible consequences, whereas the killing of Mazard forces him to confront the implications and correct the situation. And so he becomes absorbed in the nightmare of culpability. He manages to dump Mazard's body but details such as his tyre-tracks and footprints, as well as his inability to conceal his knowledge of the crime, threaten to implicate him. And so the downturn continues as this imagined world becomes imbued with a ruthless logic that hinders his every move until finally he is defeated, and must engineer his own fatal escape. Significantly, although hopelessly implicated in this downward spiral, Alice does not become part of the world's stifling oppressiveness. It might be assumed that, with her role as dream-girl relinquished, Wanley's affinity with her would be lost. Yet, in replacing Wanley's fantasy of a woman with her reality, the film supplants Alice's distanced allure with the comfort of her companionship. Whilst all other elements in the film apparently conspire to bring Wanley down, Alice forms an alliance with him against the trauma that encircles and threatens to consume them. In contrast, figures from Wanley's real life reappear as darker incarnations in his dream: Lalor's shrewd and unremitting pursuit of Mazard's killer constantly threatens Wanley's safety and even the good-natured Barkstane becomes part of the predicament, prescribing a strong poison as sleeping potion to Wanley, which eventually kills him, and practically forcing him to visit the crime scene with Lalor. Later, we discover that both Mazard and an unscrupulous blackmailer called Heidt (Dan Duryea) are in fact the cloakroom attendant and doorman at Wanley's club.[20] Figures from the male domain of the club therefore become repressive forces that work against Wanley, hampering his every move. The transformations of the attendant and doorman are evidently works of his imagination, but the behaviour of the Doctor and DA in the dream merely continues their subdued supremacy over him in real life, intensified now as events close in around Wanley. It is somewhat poignant that even in dreaming Wanley resigns himself to a lower status within their friendship, so that the two men continue to dominate him in conversation and neither stop to ask him, an assistant professor of psychology, his opinions of the case. Although exaggerated through the dream's heightened anxiety, the DA and Doctor continue to behave in a manner consistent with real life and thus, subconsciously, Wanley acknowledges his own inferiority in relation to them.

Alice, a partially fictitious creation (partially, for there must be a woman somewhere that looks like Alice and sat for the shop-window portrait that Wanley was drawn to) and the only major female presence in the whole dream, counterbalances the dreamworld's repressive elements. She forms a tender and supportive union with Wanley amid their shared troubles and, as Jacobowitz recognizes, is 'the only empathetic character who cares for the protagonist and is finally the only one in whom the protagonist can confide'.[21] Similarly, Klevan pays particular

The Woman in the Window

attention to the inaccuracy of the DA's description of Mazard's killers: 'Now these two people, this man, this woman, sit hating and fearing each other, wondering how long it will be before the other is caught and blasts the whole story out'.[22] This, as Klevan elucidates, is the opposite of the relationship that Wanley and Alice share as they instead set about concealing Mazard's killing together and, when Heidt appears and attempts to blackmail Alice, show similar solidarity as they seek to find a resolution. After Heidt has visited Alice's flat and made his demands, she arranges to meet with Wanley that night. We join their conversation as they walk side by side along a deserted city sidewalk. A set of railings runs parallel to the sidewalk, forming a see-through barrier across the characters. In the context of current events, the horizontal iron rails act as bars of a cage, imprisoning the couple and challenging the freedom they experience as they walk casually together. It is not unreasonable to suggest, as Tom Gunning does, that the fencing 'all too clearly evokes jail bars'.[23] This symbolism involves a fatalism that undermines the characters' current attempts to overcome their troubles. However, the framing of Wanley and Alice together behind the railings also encompasses the extent to which they share their dilemma, shouldering the burden equally and honestly rather than betraying one another. This mutuality is expressed in visual terms. They keep pace with each other as they walk; when Alice stops momentarily, Wanley instinctively slows to a halt, turning towards her and waiting; when he makes a move to carry on, she responds and walks in time with him once more. They move as a unit, naturally cohesive and wordlessly coordinated. Both are dressed darkly and in the twilight the streetlamps pick out brighter features about their persons, making them luminous. The effect causes the two to be mirrored as the light catches corresponding patches on their bodies: their faces, the tips of their hats, Wanley's white shirt and Alice's exposed neckline, her jewelled brooch and his folded pocket-kerchief. This patterning of light and dark further unifies the characters, reinforcing their solidarity. The bars in front of them emphasize their potential entrapment, but their harmonious appearance stresses their companionship despite their predicament.

The presence of the fence bars brings to mind 'the horizontal bars of light and shadow' that were cast across Wanley's face in the opening scene. The theme of entrapment is expressed in the same terms, but Wanley's position has not remained constant. In the earlier scene he was alone, visually isolated and intellectually distanced from his seated audience. His situation is far more precarious now, but he faces it with a companion to whom he has a natural affinity. The pair's visual closeness is matched in their dialogue. Thoughtfulness and empathy for the other infuses their exchanges: when she reveals that she kept his monographed pencil and the blackmailer found it, he replies gently, 'oh well, it's done now,' when his reaction might have been stronger.[24] Perhaps his kindness is in response to Alice's explanation 'I wasn't sure of you then...I wanted something...' that places any wariness of one another in the past, emphasizing their present bond. They are equally considerate of each other's position: he puts her mind at rest over Heidt – 'I can't think of anything else you could've done' – and she makes it clear that she will contribute towards paying him off – 'I have a little and can raise a little more' – which leads Wanley to compliment her 'you're very fair, Alice'. Their cordiality transcends the murkiness of their predicament. Wanley suggests that paying off Heidt will not resolve anything and, at this point, the style of the sequence changes. The couple emerge from the iron railings and the camera moves to a closer shot as they pause once more. Wanley proposes three methods of dealing with a blackmailer in three different ways: firstly he is stationary when suggesting that 'you pay him and pay him till your penniless,' the second option to call the police is given as he begins to walk on, leading Alice, and finally as he delivers the crucial third alternative 'or...you can kill him,' he carries on walking out the frame, leaving Alice to follow. The emergence from the barred railings could represent a temporary reprieve as the couple seek to deal with the blackmailer. Yet also, as the barrier is removed, the characters are prioritized in the frame once more, especially as the camera moves into close-up. The concentration upon the couple heightens the drama of Wanley's words especially – complemented by a rise in the underscore – strengthening his authority within the scene. Alice remains silent as she listens to his advice and he leads her as he holds her attention. The film makes time for the impact of his words, fading only once the final line has been delivered and thus increasing its power. A subtle shift has occurred from the responsibility being shared between them to Wanley providing a potential solution, with Alice remaining attentive. Klevan suggests that the relationship is reminiscent of a 'clergyman...dispensing kindness or taking the opportunity to have a quiet word with one of the congregants'.[25] There is certainly evidence of this in Wanley's manner and the scene's pacing but, more importantly, the moment reverses Wanley's ineffectual lecture at the beginning of the film. Where he had a distracted audience, he has Alice's full attention here; where he had an inhibited style of delivery then, he delivers his advice with a drama and gravitas now; where previously the film cut inconsiderately away from his speech, it currently allows his final words to hang resonantly in the air as he walks on enigmatically. His companionship with Alice provides an empowerment denied to him in reality. The relationship is complicated as their alliance is forged in such a precarious situation and Wanley receives Alice's trust and respect in a moment where his thoughts turn to outright murder. Nevertheless, within this dark dilemma, Wanley encounters the warmth of friendship.

Dorothy's bond with her friends in Oz – Scarecrow, Tin Man and Lion – is more emphatic. Indeed, she instigates each friendship with a physical connection: lifting the scarecrow down from his post, tapping and oiling the Tin Man and even slapping the lion on his nose. Dorothy's introduction to each of the characters is marked by song and dance and, in each case, the new friend links arms with her and carry on their journey along the yellow brick road in unison, singing and dancing as they go in a gesture of joyful solidarity. Their union is arguably less complicated than Alice and Wanley's, in that they are innocent of any crime and stand against a tyrannical force, The Wicked Witch of the West (played by Margaret Hamilton and doubled with Miss Gulch in Kansas). Yet, like Alice and Wanley, Dorothy enjoys a mutuality with her friends: she will help them to get a brain, a heart and courage and they will help her get to the Emerald City, to the Wizard of Oz, and home. With each new companion, Dorothy receives further help and support, a pattern that reverses the run of events back on the farm where she encountered rejection from each individual she turned to. In Kansas, Dorothy existed at the edge of a predetermined regime, but in Oz the world revolves around her, from the moment her house lands on the Wicked Witch of the East, and the trio's unquestioning acceptance of her friendship encapsulates her elevated status. Of course, their actions run against the unhelpfully dismissive attitudes of their equivalents back home, Hunk, Hickory and Zeke. Dorothy's line to Scarecrow and Tin Man 'Oh, you're the best friends anybody ever had! And it's funny, but I feel as if I've known you all the time – but I couldn't have could I?' refers to the pair's alter egos in real life. But her words also highlight the distance between them and their Kansas counterparts: Scarecrow and Tin Man are almost unrecognizable as Hunk and Hickory not only because the actors are radically changed visually in the different roles but also because the characters act so differently towards Dorothy. Her line comes after Scarecrow and Tin Man have both pledged to help her in spite of the Wicked Witch's dangerous pursuit of them, and their allegiance makes them 'the best friends anybody ever had'. Logically, Hunk and Hickory's earlier unhelpfulness towards Dorothy's dilemma with Miss Gulch marks them as far inferior by comparison.

Dorothy's companions in Oz are a magical group: Scarecrow and Tin Man brought inexplicably to life and both, along with Lion, imbued with the power of speech. For all three, speech and movement translate into song and dance, creating effervescence beyond the limits of ordinary life. Indeed, emotion and action are abundantly heightened and exaggerated in Oz, so that joy and fear are experienced more frequently and passionately than was ever the case in Kansas. Dorothy was out of place there, more fervent than those around her, eventually resorting to expressing her emotions in song, just as her three companions in Oz will do later. In this way, music provides a link between Dorothy to Oz. The link is strengthened as Dorothy's short daydream of a place faraway takes the form of a song and she later dreams of a faraway place full of music. And, of course, Oz is full of colour. The film departs from the laws of reality by having its central character dream in colour when she herself inhabits a monochrome world. It would seem that Herman Mankiewicz, an early screenwriter for the film, was the first to insist on the colour definition between the two states. Regarding the Kansas prologue, he noted 'this part of the picture – until the door is flung open after Dorothy has arrived in the land of the Munchkins – will be shot in black and white'.[26] Mankiewicz's insistence upon this colour contrast apparently relates to his warning to the studio about Dorothy and Toto in the prologue: 'Only one thing is vital – neither of them dares to be gray'.[27] Mankiewicz was no doubt responding to Baum's original characterization of Kansas as overwhelmingly 'grey' and his emphatic colouring of Oz with elements such as the emerald city and the yellow brick road. Additionally, Mankiewicz's comments reveal the extent to which colour is used representationally rather than realistically in the film, to illustrate the dulled mood of Kansas in contrast with the emotional vitality of Oz. (Of course, the use of colour to convey symbolic meaning rather than merely represent a realistic world is hardly special to this film and can be observed in great abundance across the history of colour cinema.) In this context, colour exemplifies the vibrancy of Dorothy's imagination, as she provides her own escape from her dry, stifled reality into a rich and vigorous world.[28] Although Oz makes a show of its own colourfulness relentlessly (the ruby slippers, the horse of many colours, the poppy fields, the witch's green face etc.) Dorothy never makes explicit reference to it, or to the colourlessness of Kansas – or to her colourlessness in Kansas for that matter. (In fact, in saying initially to Toto 'we must be over the rainbow' she locates Oz as a product of her imagination, just as she imagined a place over the rainbow earlier.) In this sense, we might regard colour as representing the power of Dorothy's imagination in this film, emphasizing the extent to which her creativity simply had no place in Kansas.

Dorothy's desire to return home would appear to stem from a sense of duty to those back in Kansas. Particularly, it seems tied up with her anxiety over Aunt Em. Before the cyclone, Dorothy had run away with Toto and ran into Professor Marvel (Frank Morgan), a travelling showman (doubled with the Wizard in Oz). In a trick to send the runaway child back home, Marvel pretends to see Aunt Em in his crystal ball, overcome with grief at Dorothy's disappearance 'putting her hand on her heart...dropping down on the bed!' Afraid, Dorothy runs back to the farm, a pattern that is continued in Oz as she persistently attempts to return home. When locked in the witch's tower, awaiting death, Dorothy sees an image of her aunt appear in a large crystal ball, mirroring Marvel's 'vision' earlier. In this vision, Auntie Em frantically searches for Dorothy before the image cruelly transforms into the Wicked Witch, mocking Dorothy's anguish. Significantly, Aunt Em's concern for Dorothy occurs in two spurious forms: once in Marvel's trick-vision and once in the 'trick-vision' of Dorothy's dream. Yet, in reality, her search for her niece is soon ended as she allows herself to be first into the storm cellar when the twister hits. Consistent with her earlier actions, Aunt Em's pragmatism has obliterated sentiment. So Dorothy's alarm is based upon a false understanding, yet she clings to it throughout her journey in Oz, even at the end. When the Wizard's balloon departs without her, her trio of friends share her distress and are themselves overcome. Tearful, they stand around her, laying comforting hands upon her and bowing their heads in sorrow for her.

Tenderly, quietly, Lion says: 'Stay with us then Dorothy. We all love you. We don't want you to go'. Dorothy says he's very kind, but 'this could never be like Kansas. Auntie Em must have stopped wondering what happened to me by now'. The tangibility of this group's affection for Dorothy is thus contrasted with the fragility of the bond between Dorothy and her aunt: here she is loved and wanted, there even Dorothy acknowledges that she might be forgotten already. It is unlikely that Aunt Em, or anyone else in Kansas, could muster words like those spoken with such honest compassion by the Lion. Oz, indeed, could never be like Kansas, but Dorothy's sense of duty to her home has reversed the value of each.

Glinda, the Good Witch of the North, (Billie Burke) appears magically and tells Dorothy that she always had the power to go back to Kansas, but had to learn it for herself. When asked, Dorothy says that she has learnt 'that if I ever go looking for my heart's desire again, I won't look any further than my own backyard; because if it isn't there, I never really lost it to begin with!' Up to the delivery of this line, a reprise of *Somewhere Over the Rainbow* had underscored the scene, but with these words it is lost. It is appropriate that this theme so synonymous with Dorothy's dreams of a better place should die out at the moment she herself promises never to dream of anywhere else ever again. Seeing Dorothy surrounded by the emotional warmth of her companions, we must feel that the price for returning home is unfairly set. Knowing that this is Dorothy's dream, it has to be concluded that she has set *herself* an unfairly high price. We may feel a sense of loss in realizing that her rich imagination might be lost to her from now on

The Wizard of Oz

through this self-denial. Indeed, it seems as though Dorothy says what she thinks she is meant to feel (she asks Glinda for approval afterwards) rather than what she actually experiences. Scarecrow responds: 'But that's so easy' and he may easily have said: 'That's *too easy,*' for there is an unnatural convenience to Dorothy's words that represses any genuine sentiment. Genuine sentiment is certainly expressed, however, as she realizes she must say goodbye to her friends. The farewell is infused with unabated emotion as Dorothy embraces each in turn: mopping Tin Man's tears away as he tells her his heart is breaking, stroking Lion's mane as he says that without her he would have no courage, and finally putting her arms around Scarecrow's neck, whispering 'I think I'll miss you most of all'. She kisses each companion on the cheek, but they are inconsolable, tears flooding down their cheeks, heads bowed in emphatic grief. Underneath the scene plays a gentle reprise of *If I only had a Brain/ Heart/The Nerve* that nostalgically recalls Dorothy's first discovery of each friend and the bond that has brought them all to Oz with her. This is what she gives up now. The underscore intensifies the sadness of the scene, emphasizing that the joy Dorothy's companions have brought to her, and she to them, is nearly at an end, never to be recovered. She kisses this world goodbye and, in doing so, marks a break with her childhood, preparing the way for a return to the adult world where dreams and fantasies have no real place. If she is to belong there, then childhood castles in the air will have to be left behind so that she might begin to resemble the adults that surround her in Kansas. The end of the dream thus signals the drawing to a close of her childhood years.

Glinda takes over proceedings and once Dorothy has tapped her heels together three times, the three companions disappear from the frame, never to be seen again, as the camera moves to a close-up of Dorothy's face. It is as though each tap eliminated one character at a time. Behind Dorothy, Glinda is performing a kind of hypnotism; waving a wand around her head in circular motions and making her repeat the words 'there's no place like home' over and over again. Of course, Glinda is Dorothy's creation and so, as V.F. Perkins notes, she is hypnotizing herself to accept this dogma.[29] The camera frames her utterances in close-up, and so it is easily discernible that, even as she speaks this creed, tears for her friends still sparkle on her cheeks. If returning to Kansas seems too easy, leaving Oz behind seems all at once unbearably difficult.

Waking Up
Dorothy's return to Kansas is signalled violently by the clumsy crash of her house as it twirls and hits the ground, momentarily obliterating our view. Not for the first time in this film, matters are brought back down to earth and, once again, we are in the monochrome world of Kansas. A close-up of Dorothy fills the screen as she murmurs those same words 'there's no place like

home' over and over again. A pair of hands places a compress on her forehead and a voice says 'wake up honey'. We cut to a wider shot and the camera pulls back to reveal Dorothy's room; she is in bed, Aunt Em sits patting her hands and Uncle Henry stands behind his wife. Perkins remarks that 'no one is sufficiently moved by Dorothy's recovery to do more than pat her hand'[30] and, certainly, her guardians' behaviour is characterized by an emotional restraint and rigidity. Indeed, when Aunt Em looks as though she might be reaching with affection to touch Dorothy's face she merely removes the compress in a gesture of ordered practicality so abundant in her character earlier. Uncle Henry never moves from his spot and when a visiting Professor Marvel enquires about Dorothy's health, he cheerfully replies 'we kinda thought there for a minute she was going to leave us' as though she were one of their cooped chicks. When Dorothy sits up to tell Uncle Henry that she did leave them, Aunt Em places her hands on the young girl's shoulders and restrains her in a repressive gesture that cruelly mimics the warm embraces Dorothy received just moments ago in Oz. In fact, the whole scene is a reversal in tone from those final farewells as tears and kisses become hand-pats and firm words. Aunt Em responds to Dorothy by saying 'you just had a bad dream,' but this dismissal is quite wrong: Dorothy's dream was wonderful to her. The strains of *Somewhere Over the Rainbow* underscore this section, as though reminding us of the power of Dorothy's dreams, but that power is diminishing now, as she struggles to make anyone listen to her account of Oz, and so the melody mourns the loss of her dreams as it recalls her now-repressed desire to escape the confines of her world. She is greeted with a series of patronizing nods and smiles, as though everyone assembled were temporarily indulging this nonsense. Their lack of interest causes Dorothy to change focus:

> Oh, but anyway, Toto, we're home – home! And this is my room – and you're all here – and I'm not going to leave here ever, ever again because I love you all! And...oh, Auntie Em, there's no place like home!

On paper, these words read like an emphatic declaration of joy. Yet, given the nature of the world Dorothy has returned to and the manner of the inhabitants that face her, the statement amounts to a lowering of expectation, the death of dreams. Her sentiment is undermined by the reality of her surroundings, and also by her own actions. As she declares her love for those around her, Dorothy clutches Toto close to her, hugging him in a gesture that emphasizes the lack of unabated physical comfort she has received from anyone on recovering from her apparently life-threatening injury. Once more, she turns to her little dog for affection. Her action is framed in a close-up that also partially captures Aunt Em, sitting motionless beside Dorothy, offering no warmth of contact. Contrasted so clearly with the series of affectionate, heartfelt farewells in Oz, this scene becomes a bleak, emotionally barren portrayal of Dorothy's life in Kansas. As nothing in the final scene suggests that her future there will be different, her promise to 'never leave here ever, ever again,' becomes a guarantee of Dorothy's perennial loneliness.

It becomes difficult for us to accept Dorothy's final statements because, as Perkins elaborates, 'what we make of them...depends on the way we understand them to function in a context that has been elaborately constructed. If *The Wizard of Oz* secures conviction for Dorothy's last words, it must have found ways of characterising them as authoritative'.[31] As we have observed, this is not so. Through its depiction of Dorothy's home-life, the film has effectively called into question her relief in returning, so creating a mood that jars with the sentiment of her words. The neatness of a happy ending is thus rendered unsatisfactory, as we are led to question whether Dorothy is aware of her environment's shortcomings or whether, indeed, she is tricking herself into believing that she could be forever happy there.

Contrastingly, when Professor Wanley wakes up again, restored to his own world once more, we are likely to share his sense of relief. In his dream, his plan for Alice to poison their blackmailer has failed and Heidt has left, demanding yet more money. Alice shares the news with Wanley by telephone. This is surely the pair's lowest point: their plans are ruined and their lives are forever marred, yet they manage to retain the respect and consideration for each other that has characterized their relationship. Blame and anger never creep into their exchanges and instead Alice's wholehearted apology 'I'm sorry...I don't know what else I could have done...I was so scared...' is met with a remarkably tender reassurance from Wanley: 'I'm sure you did all that you could...we're just not very *skilful* at that sort of thing'. Wanley's use of the word 'we' emphasizes the bond between the pair as they share the ordeal, but he also adopts the role of counsellor, providing kindly support for Alice once more. Yet, when she asks in desperation 'What can we do now?' Wanley realizes his own limitations, acknowledging that he doesn't know and that he is 'too tired' to think about it anymore. With these words, he lets his receiver-hand fall to his lap in an unusual gesture of resignation and defeat. As he lets the receiver drop, he lets Alice go. Realizing that he is not up to the task of protecting them both ('too tired', he repeats) Wanley seems to decide then that he is not for this world, that he could never make himself or Alice safe within it. If he is to give it up, as he does imminently, he must give her up too.

So he replaces the receiver, lingers on photographs of his family on the side table, and slowly rises from his chair. The move suggests purpose, yet Wanley's anguished expression also suggests that a happy solution has not been reached. As he walks to the door, Arthur Lange's underscored motif emerges once more, soft and slow now to rhyme with Wanley's mournful acquiescence. We follow his progress at a respectful distance as he makes his way along a hallway corridor into the bathroom. Cutting to that interior, we watch Wanley pour a glass of water, take out the sleeping medication and begin tipping sachets of powder into the glass. He performs this task with a dulled sense of routine, as though enacting some inevitable duty. On realizing that he is constructing his own death, we also notice that something has died in him already, that his calm and kindly manner has evolved into silent solemnity. Having attempted to gain control of his fate and failed, Wanley seems to accept that he is ill-fated in this world, and thus relinquishes his life. A cut away to Alice's neighbourhood reveals that Heidt has been shot by the police and found in possession of items belonging to Mazard, which he had stolen from Alice. The police conclude that Heidt was Mazard's killer. Alice rushes back to telephone Wanley with the good news, but she is too late. She can't get through to him and so frantically asks the operator to try his number. We cut to Wanley's phone ringing and ringing, unanswered. The camera pans out and pivots right to reveal Wanley slumped in his chair, the glass tumbler held loosely in his right hand: the poison has been taken. He makes a faint attempt to reach the receiver, but his hand falls limply back down and he sags again. The camera moves into an extreme close-up of Wanley's face as he stares into nothingness, the telephone still ringing in the background, until finally his eyes close and his head tilts to the side. The ringing fades away. He is dead.

Inexplicably, a hand shakes his shoulder, a clock chimes grandly in the background, and he stirs, apparently brought back to life. We pull back to reveal Wanley sitting in his club and a waiter standing over him saying that it is ten-thirty, the time he asked earlier to be reminded of. The past events are revealed to have been a dream. The mood is thus lifted, and the underscore now has a lighter, more resolved tone. Wanley's own mood is similarly lifted as, after initial bemusement, he rises from his chair and discovers that he used the figure of the cloakroom attendant to embody the figure of Mazard in his dream. Likewise, outside Heidt is really the doorman. The film has moved into comedy now, reversing the anxiety of Wanley's suicide, and thus plays upon the relief he now experiences, so his reactions at seeing the two men and their reactions to him are played for laughs. We are bound to feel a natural relief at seeing an innocent life saved.

The film has one more joke left as Wanley risks another look at the picture in the window next door. There follows an almost-exact replication of events at the beginning of Wanley's dream, with identical motifs occurring such as the number of shots, the underscored music, the camera positioning, Robinson's positioning, the quality of the lighting and so on. Astonishingly, a woman's face again appears reflected alongside the portrait in the window. However, a sharp, shrill female voice cuts through the delicate soundtrack asking: 'Pardon me. Would you give me a light?' We cut to a woman with tightly curled blonde hair, heavy make-up, wearing a garishly patterned dress, a mink shawl draped across her shoulders, the tails and bodies of the animals hanging around her arms and body. She holds out a cigarette in her right hand, the large jewel of a heavy ring sparkling on one of her fingers.[32] Wanley looks in horror before running into the night, shouting 'Not for a million dollars!' as he goes. The film, whose mood has been getting steadily lighter since Wanley woke up, finishes with outright comedy. Yet, the humour is surely short-lived as Wanley runs back to a world already shown to contain so many constraints. The lighter-less female strikes a harsh comparison with Alice, reminding us of her delicate sophistication but also the tender bond that formed between her and Wanley. He enjoyed no similar relationship in his real life, and the mirroring of Alice with this crude version highlights the limitations of Wanley's world, the extent to which that kind of companionship can only be imagined and never realized. This woman's approach bears the hallmarks of a cheap pickup in a way that Alice's never did: she became a tender and true friend in spite of their terrible dilemma. It is understandable that he flees now, just as his relief on waking up is appreciable. Yet, his cheerfulness is offset by the film's earlier negative depiction of his workplace, family and friends. Wanley's death at the end of his dream is, in Gunning's words, 'one of the bitterest moments in Lang's cinema, bereft of even the romanticism of the end of *You Only Live Once*'.[33] Indeed, our lingering upon Wanley walking slowly to the bathroom, blankly tipping the powder into the glass and finally losing consciousness in his chair, intensifies the bleakness of the scene, unsettling even after we realize it wasn't real. So, although the film clearly strikes a note of relief in showing Wanley's death to have been no more than a dream, there may still be a lingering sense of loss. It would seem that as Wanley 'dies' in his dream, the 'spirit of adventure' that he feared losing earlier finally dies with him. He turns his back on the imagined persona he created for himself, understandably startled by where it might lead, and consoles himself with a world of little comfort. He resumes a life in which, as we have been shown, the tenderness of his union with Alice can never be realized; in which he will always be inferior and, to a certain degree, isolated. Given this wider context, the comedic tone of the film's epilogue may be only ephemeral as we reflect on matters.

With each film, I have tried to demonstrate ways in which the dream sequences are important as dreams. The films are particularly appropriate for this enterprise as they devote an unusually large portion of their time to the dreams of their characters. In each case, I have maintained that a contrast is established between the imagined world and the real world and this contrast shapes the defining tone of the films. Both films show a disparity between the relationships their central characters experience in real life and those they establish in dreaming, thus highlighting the shortcomings of the characters' real lives through this inconsistency. Therefore, the apparent resolution of each film is tinged with sadness as the central characters wake up to a world in which their place is still unclear, compromised or precarious. Significantly, the characters imagine worlds distinct from their realities, and thus compensate for the respective shortcomings in their lives. As I have suggested, both Dorothy and Professor Wanley imagine companions with whom they enjoy closeness unparalleled in their waking lives. The fact that they imagine these scenarios for themselves indicates the extent to which their unacknowledged awareness of their respective situations weighs upon them.

There is no way of knowing how each character responds to their dreams after we leave them in their worlds. Once Dorothy has a moment alone after the crowd has left her bedside or once Wanley has slowed down to a reasonable pace on the New York street, they may find time to reflect on their dreams and speculate as to why they found themselves in such strange, but strangely comforting, circumstances. (It is initially tempting to say that Wanley would be better placed for this sort of analysis due to his age and academic position, but it's debatable whether experience and education works so conveniently.) All we can say is that the films have left us with no firm assurances that life is going to be much different for either individual. Having presented us with worlds radically dissimilar from the ones the characters ordinarily inhabit, the films conclude with a return to familiar routine and a resuming of everyday patterns that neither person quite fitted with when we first saw them in their worlds. We can imagine any ending we like for Wanley and Dorothy, but neither film has given us much hope to build upon.

Notes

1. Certainly, audiences and critics frequently think of Lang's film in these terms. Paul M. Jensen perhaps crystallizes this attitude when he states that: 'The ending is a cheat used to rescue the director, who had painted himself into a corner'. Paul M. Jensen *The Cinema of Fritz Lang* London: Zwemmer, 1969 p. 156.
2. Salman Rushdie *The Wizard of Oz* London: British Film Institute, 1992.
3. V.F. Perkins *The Magnificent Ambersons* London: BFI Publishing, 1999, pp. 67-8.
4. In common terminology, we perhaps distinguish between the real world and the story world when describing what actress and character are 'in': Judy Garland is in the *Wizard of Oz*, but Dorothy is in Kansas and later finds herself in the Land of Oz.

5. See Gerald Clarke *Get Happy: The Life of Judy Garland* London: Time Warner, 2002, or Gerald Frank *Judy* London: W.H. Allen & Co. Ltd., 1975.

6. The hardworking ethos of Auntie Em and Uncle Henry can be further understood when we take into account the film's historical context within the period of the Great Depression. Although Baum's description of Dorothy's home depicts a barren, lonely place, there is a sense that the film creates an environment reminiscent of the Dust Bowl landscapes of thirties America, where farming livelihoods were under constant threat. The underlying anxiousness of Auntie Em's frenetic activity particularly seems to reference this period of hardship and desperation.

7. L. Frank Baum *The Wizard of Oz* London: Penguin Books, 1994, p. 3.

8. Baum actually makes the characters synonymous with their environment through colour, imbuing them with the same 'greyness' that infuses their world. Ibid.

9. This reference, like many spoken by the three farmhands in this section, pre-empts Hunk's appearance as the Scarecrow in Dorothy's dream later; Zeke appears as the Lion and Hickory as the Tin Man.

10. This, clearly, establishes the chief characteristic of Zeke's alter ego in Oz, the cowardly lion. Another scene was deleted from the final cut of the film, in which Hickory encourages Dorothy to 'have a little heart' thus establishing his link to the heartless Tin Man in Oz. (Noel Langley, Florence Ryerson & Edgar Allan Woolf *The Wizard of Oz* London: Faber & Faber, 1991, pp. 36–7).

11. Elisabeth Bronfen provides an interesting comparison between Auntie Em's view of 'trouble' and the way in which it is perceived in Dorothy's imagined world of Oz. Bronfen notes that 'Having arrived in Oz, [Dorothy] will do nothing other than get into trouble, as well as cause trouble for the witches who get in the way of her desire. Yet in Oz she is not reprimanded for her tendency to get into trouble; she is instead hailed as a national hero. Her journey through Oz thus allows her to abreact her aunt's reproach in such a way that the rebuke uncannily coincides with its opposite – recognition – and the threat of punishment transforms into praise'. (Elisabeth Bronfen *Home in Hollywood: The Imaginary Geography of Cinema* New York: Columbia University Press, 2004, p. 81). This account is crucial, I would maintain, as it acknowledges a fundamental ideological discrepancy between Dorothy's world in Kansas and the world of Oz she imagines, thus emphasizing the tone of the latter as Dorothy's dreamed reaction against the structure and mood of the former.

12. In fact, it immediately invades once more as, with the last chord of Dorothy's song fading away, we cut sharply to the fearsome Miss Gulch riding her bike, accompanied by her brisk, imposing, theme tune.

13. Florence Jacobowitz, 'The Man's Melodrama: The Woman in the Window and Scarlet Street' in Ian Cameron (ed.) *The Movie Book of Film Noir* London: Studio Vista, 1992, p. 153.

14. Ibid.

15. See for example, Reynold Humphries *Fritz Lang: Genre and Representation in his American Films* London: Johns Hopkins University Press Ltd., 1982, p. 100. Humphries takes issue with critics that have previously ignored the psychoanalytic references on the blackboard, but I wonder whether their obviousness in fact makes his serious reading of them problematic. It would be unusual in a film that expresses its themes through a carefully constructed style to present its crucial element so blatantly, in written form and underlined. The mention of Freud here reminds me of the way Lang playfully uses Freudian language and symbolism in a later film, *Secret Beyond the Door* (1948). Such references in that film are made boldly, drawing attention to themselves in a way that becomes entertaining, especially during a party scene where guests come out with phrases such as 'I got rid of gallons of repressed poison', 'my subconscious is a booby trap' and recite Freudian passages by

heart such as 'the murder of a wife or a girlfriend has its unconscious roots in a hatred for a mother'. Taken seriously, the blatant expression of these Freudian themes lacks Lang's usual sophistication, but taken lightly they might indicate a sophisticated sense of humour.

16. Humphries pp. 102–103.
17. Wanley also gestures with his cigar, but he holds it between his two forefingers in a manner that is less direct, less domineering, than that of his two friends.
18. Jacobowitz p. 155.
19. Andrew Klevan 'The Purpose of Plot and the Place of Joan Bennett in Fritz Lang's *The Woman in the Window*,' *Cineaction!* No. 62, 2003, p. 16.
20. Here we are reminded of Buster's casting of real figures into the dream-film of *Sherlock Jr.* We might reflect that, although Wanley does not dream of stepping into a film narrative, he is casting a narrative of his own, casting faces in the story he creates and directing their actions, albeit subconsciously, as though he were in charge of a private movie.
21. Jacobowitz p. 154.
22. Klevan p. 16.
23. Tom Gunning *The Films of Fritz Lang: Allegories of Vision and Modernity* London: British Film Institute, 2000, p. 301.
24. Klevan p. 19.
25. Ibid.
26. Michael Patrick Hearn 'Introduction' in Langley, Ryerson & Woolf, p. 9.
27. Ibid.
28. Bearing in mind that Oz is a product of Dorothy's imagination might help to understand some of that world's inconsistencies. Immediately, for example, we might question why Munchkinland looks so luscious considering it was under the power of the tyrannical Wicked Witch of the East (Rushdie, p. 42) or why the Munchkins are able to direct Dorothy to the Emerald City, but cannot take her there (V.F. Perkins, 'Where is the World' p. 40). I would contend that these inconsistencies result from the make-believe processes of Dorothy's young imagination, revealing an unsophisticated creativeness that overlooks such details. We might compare this to Wanley's educated, clinical but less extravagant mind that constructs a meticulous and intricate world where every detail is potentially crucial.
29. V.F. Perkins 'Must We Say What They Mean?: Film Criticism and Interpretation,' *Movie* 34/35 (Winter 1990), p. 2.
30. Ibid.
31. Ibid. p. 3.
32. Given the context of the Production Code's stringency, this seems to be the closest resemblance to a streetwalker that could feasibly be permitted.
33. Gunning, p. 303.

4

RETURN TO INNOCENCE

Eternal Sunshine of the Spotless Mind (Michel Gondry, 2004)

The Woman and the Window and The Wizard of Oz both include the epistemological twist (inherited, as we have seen, from a tradition of films like Let Me Dream Again) of presenting a world that we take to be something real but, in fact, turns out to be imagined. Until the final revelation that Professor Wanley has only imagined a life containing killing, blackmail and suicide, Lang's film suggests that the dream is merely a continuation of the character's real world as it resists making the breakpoint between reality and fantasy explicit. It is a narrative structure evoked, and elaborately revised in Alejandro Amenábar's 1997 film Abre los ojos (and in Cameron Crowe's ill-judged remake of 2001, Vanilla Sky), in which the real life of the central character, César (Eduardo Noriega), is spliced together with an imaginary existence after he has died and been cryogenically frozen for 150 years. In Amenábar's film, waking up from the dream has dramatic implications for the central character: César will find himself 150 years in the future, part of a foreign world he doesn't know or recognize with all of his close companions now dead.

Whereas The Woman in the Window and Abre los ojos both present imagined worlds that are temporarily confused with a continuation of ordinary reality, Dorothy's dream in The Wizard of Oz might be taken as a transition into an extraordinary reality: another world. Thus, until the final explanation of Oz as a dream-creation, the film could plausibly belong within the third category of films in this study, those containing Other worlds. Unlike those films in the previous chapter, Eternal Sunshine of the Spotless Mind[1] does not withhold the knowledge that its central character is asleep and makes it explicit that we visit the world of his imagination for portions of the film, thus avoiding the same narrative twist. However, although circumventing a trick of that kind, the film does possess a complex narrative order that requires an operation of attempted reconstruction on the part of the audience to appreciate the nuances and relationships played out in the story. Some of these complexities will be detailed in the following discussion of the film, such as the opening which takes place in the present before a title sequence, about seventeen minutes in, takes us, unannounced, back into the characters' immediate past. This chapter engages with that attempt to reconstruct Eternal Sunshine's events into a conventional narrative thread, as I lay out some of the themes that I take to be central to an understanding of Gondry's film.

Playing

In that beginning section before the main titles, a man and a woman make their way across a frozen lake. She leads him out onto the ice, reassuring him that 'it's really solid this time of year' but his first step is nervy and he loses his balance slightly, leaning over awkwardly to correct himself, saying cautiously 'I don't know...' She encourages him further, holding out her hand to him and repeating 'c'mon, c'mon' while he voices his unease with a strained, apprehensive 'yeeh' as he treads uncertainly. His outward apprehension is tamed as her string of 'c'mons' become softer and quicker, as though she were gently coaxing a small timid animal. And finally he is on the ice with her and they walk together, her fluently but him stiffly, his nervousness still dictating his movements.

As they walk he summons the courage to look up and, struck suddenly by the scene, says to her 'It's so beautiful'. A cut to the view he beholds illustrates the quiet splendour of the frozen landscape: the frosty floor made luminous white by the glow of an unseen moon, the blue-blackness of the sky above dividing the scene horizontally into halves of light and dark, a trail of car-lights moving weightlessly in the far distance emphasizing the couple's temporary remoteness to the world that still exists beyond their private domain. She returns his sentiment – 'Isn't it...' – before running past him and out onto the main part of the ice, giggling to herself. As she picks up speed she squeals, ignoring his warnings not to go too far, and slides along the smooth surface before landing flat with a hard bump. She gets up, moaning loudly 'Oh! My ass!' while he pads unsurely on the spot. She shouts again to him to 'c'mon' but, wanting to go back, he asks 'What if it breaks?' elongating the vowel sound in 'breaks' and slightly raising the pitch of his voice to turn his question into a small whine. Repeating his question back to him, she asks further 'Do you really care right now?' and walks over to him, hand outstretched says softly: 'Come here...please'. At this he relents and shuffles his way over to her. Meeting him, she guides him along the ice at a slight pace, allowing him to slide as she had done, but supported by her. As he slides she exclaims 'Slidey slidey!' and he responds tentatively 'This is good,' as though still unsure even of his own enjoyment.

We cut to a wider shot as she says: 'Let me show you this one thing...' and lies down on the ice. From here, she flaps her arms and legs once in a motion closely resembling the way in which children make angels in the snow. Lying still again, she beckons him to join her with a now familiar 'c'mon' and, after a short conversation concerning the thickness of the ice, he lies down next to her. An overhead shot captures the two lying side-by-side, gazing up at the sky, the dark outline of their bodies distinct against the brightness of the frozen floor. Immediately to the left of the couple is a star-shaped fracture in the solid ice, a feature of the *mise en scène* that acts as a metaphor for the fragility of their newly forming relationship here: there may be cracks in what supports the couple in this moment or, indeed, they might rest on a firmer foundation.

It is worth noting here the extent to which this shot particularly recommends itself for an interpretation of the relationships between elements contained within the frame. The fixedness

Eternal Sunshine of the Spotless Mind

of the camera's position is rare in a film comprizing a series of fluent, handheld camera movements that often attempt to capture the pace and rhythms of events from the characters' lives. The stillness of this shot, however, reveals it to be a deliberate composition that invites further consideration and conjecture. The symbolic weight of the image may contribute to its being used in the majority of the film's promotional material and, indeed, it has become an iconic representation of the relationship between this couple.

Down on the ice, she half-gestures upwards with her hand, saying 'Show me which constellations you know,' thus initiating the time-honoured ritual that lovers engage in. He murmurs hesitantly before confessing 'I don't...know any,' perhaps indicating his uncertainty over whether to engage in this traditional game that declares a couple's romantic cohesion. She gently taps his thigh twice and asks the question again, this time putting a firmer emphasis on 'know' as though temperately suggesting that he had misunderstood what she took knowledge to mean. This time he accepts with 'okay' but shuffles his feet and brings them awkwardly together as though still insecure about what is being asked of him. A second 'okay' is more resolute and suddenly he finds inspiration, proclaiming 'Oh! Here's Osidius' and pulling his hand out of his pocket to point up at the sky with a little authority before stuffing it back into his jacket. When she asks 'Where?' he pulls out the other hand to demonstrate the 'swoop and a cross' of 'Osidius the Emphatic', leaning gently into her as he traces the shape of the constellation in the night air. She laughs at his description, delighting in his response to her invitation, and chooses to extend the moment by saying 'You're full of shit, right,' causing him to reiterate: 'Nope. Osidius right there. Swoop and cross'. After this, he smiles and relaxes while she playfully whacks him with her hand and, through her laughter, says 'Shut the fuck up'. His smile remains for a second before the screen fades to black.

In the conventional chronology that the film muddles but that we cannot avoid reconstructing, this moment on the ice occurs near to the end of this couple's story, despite appearing near the start of the film. The two involved are Joel Barish (Jim Carrey) and Clementine Kruczynski (Kate Winslet). Two years into their relationship which has encountered a familiar catalogue of small difficulties, the volume of which has made them tragically significant, Clementine elects to have all memories of Joel removed, a magical process[2] carried out by the scientific research company, Lacuna Inc. Discovering this, Joel resolves to have his memories of Clementine likewise erased but, with the operation underway and him asleep, he realizes his actions are a mistake and tries desperately to cling on to the memory of her by journeying back across his unconscious landscape with 'her' (his imagined reconstruction of her) in an attempt to conceal her from the relentless glare of Lacuna's mind-wiping technology. Joel imagines Clementine's last words to him in this dreamscape to be 'meet me in Montauk', the place where they first encountered each other two years ago.

Importantly, although Joel's explicit goal becomes saving his memory of Clementine, he doesn't properly achieve this aim. Instead, the mind-wipe is carried out to the Lacuna employee's satisfaction and apparently he remembers her no longer. We might see this as contrasting somewhat with the theoretical and somewhat pervasive description of Hollywood narratives being driven primarily by goal-oriented protagonists, with those narratives effectively completing with the protagonist's accomplishment of their goals.[3] Whether we subscribe to this assessment of Hollywood cinema or not, it is certainly true that *Eternal Sunshine* challenges the expectation, providing a narrative that rejects rudimentary problem-solving structures.

The following day, Joel awakes and, driven by a force he cannot comprehend, skips work to make his way to Montauk where he meets Clementine once more. Due to Lacuna's interventions, they do not recognize one another as lovers, but something residual in both their memories seems to draw them together, just as it drew them both to Montauk (suggesting that Lacuna's methods are not infallible, a notion that will recur throughout this discussion). Drinks at Clementine's follow and the next evening they journey with each other to the frozen lake in the scene described above. The film jumbles the chronology of these events by showing Joel and Clementine meeting after the memory-wipe process, then flashes back to the night of the memory-wipe, before resuming the day of Joel and Clementine's meeting and progressing on past their visit to the frozen lake. (In addition, because the memory-wipe process is said to operate by working backwards through the memories one wishes to erase, the events of Joel's dream are revealed to us correspondingly in reverse order.)

One of the pleasures of this re-ordering of time is that certain resonances occur in reverse. For example, before they had the memory-wipe, Joel and Clementine visited this frozen lake and so they actually *revisit* it in the scene I have described, again indicating that the memory-wipe process is fallible as people repeat memories and experiences that should be completely forgotten to them. This revisiting occurs at the beginning of the film, of course, and so when we see Joel's remembrance of their first visit in his memory-erasing dream-state, we effectively look back to make the connection with a moment that really occurs in the couple's future.[4] The film's re-ordering of time equally allows us to appreciate and enjoy Joel and Clementine's relationship as though they were meeting for the first time just as, without their memories, they enjoy and appreciate each other as if for the first time. Away from the traumatic disintegration of their relationship in the past we, like them, are initially free to appreciate their coming together now.

The film reflects this newness by representing their Montauk reunion in a bleached-out *mise-en-scène*, conveying the blankness of a fresh start and echoing the blank pages of Joel's journal that no longer contain his memories of the past two years spent with Clementine (the pages having been removed by Lacuna as part of the memory-erasing procedure), requiring him to start again from today. This tonal blanching is particularly evident at the moment in which Joel and Clementine first glimpse each other on a beach. In this scene, the foamy wash of the sea, the lifeless buildings, the stretch of smooth sand and the still, formless sky all possess a stark whiteness, as though the colour had been drained from the world. In this environment, Joel and Clementine briefly catch each other's eye and the impression is again created of these two meeting without the backdrop of history or hurt, effectively against a blank canvas: her standing out in a bright orange hooded top with deep blue jeans and him likewise distinctive in a dark overcoat and knitted beanie hat. As they stand, the only two occupants of the beach, it is as though the world had become suspended for them, providing a hermetic space for their fresh start. It is significant to note that both seek out this empty, people-less place, as though acknowledging the new beginning they have each been afforded. Yet, despite the emptiness, they have actually returned to the spot where they both met for the first time (an event we see later in Joel's dream-memories), thus simultaneously referencing their act of togetherness, the closeness they once experienced. Again, further evidence is provided that the break Lacuna promised them has not been made cleanly, that their own residual attachment to the memories of one another compromises the success of the procedure. It is from this point that their reunion begins, culminating in their revisiting the frozen lake.

The charm of their meeting at the beginning of the film stems from a curious innocence inherent not only in their shared situation – believing that they have never met before – but also in their particular way of behaving together. In the episode at the frozen lake described above, each displays aspects of a childlike manner that is captivating in its speciality but also indicative of the brand of emotional and intellectual affinity existent between the characters. Joel's wariness as he makes his way across the ice and his consistent fear of it breaking depicts a particular vulnerability that evokes a childhood state: nervous, apprehensive, in need of reassurance. This impression is furthered as he grabs on to Clementine's hand for support, just as a child might reach out for physical reassurance. His turning the question 'what if it breaks?' into a whine by stretching and raising the word 'breaks' makes plain this childlike aspect of his behaviour by mimicking the intonation of a junior. Likewise, his wobbly style of walking on the slippery surface brings to mind the toddling motion of a young child whose physical balance is not yet fully developed. This impression of youthfulness is completed by Joel's use of simplistic monosyllabic sounds like 'woah', 'yeeh' and 'oh' to communicate his fears and worries, denoting a partial return to a more simplistic, instinctive mode of language used mostly in childhood.[5]

Clementine's demeanour is also childlike, but different in tone to Joel's. Unlike him, she displays an enthusiasm for the ice, skidding recklessly along its surface before landing on her 'ass'. Like

Joel, however, she uses a series of short, simplistic exclamations – 'whee!' when she skids, 'ow!' when she falls – that not only recreate the language of childhood but also express her exhilaration at being on the ice, rather than lack of confidence as they did in Joel's case. Although opposite to Joel's apprehension, her unbounded joy is similarly representative of a childlike attitude, encapsulating a reprieve from the weight of adulthood and a return to a more innocent sense of rapture. Her exclamation: 'Oh! My ass!' is unreserved and unguarded, cohering with childhood naivety, but also matching Joel's whine of 'What if it breaks?' in tone and delivery. The phrase 'slidey slidey' similarly lacks sophistication, conveying her delight in the feeling of speed and movement across the ice. Clementine's movement as she lies down on the frozen surface, closely resembling a child's angel-making in snow, reinforces and accentuates the allusions to youthful play inherent in her behaviour up to this point. If Joel acts like a nervous child who is unsure of his surroundings, Clementine encapsulates the adventurousness of infancy as she revels in her environment, making use of it for the purposes of fun and imagination. It is useful to reflect that another option is available to her in this scene: to behave maternally towards Joel in order to combat his nerves. Yet, she resists engaging with him on those terms by providing that kind of comfort, eager instead for them to play together rather than one of them facilitate the play for the other. In this sense, they are always children together or, rather, always adults finding time to be children.

Congruent to her own playful behaviour, Clementine asks Joel to use his imagination as they lie together on the ice. Her request for him to name constellations is not in fact an invitation to draw upon his actual knowledge of the solar system – as he makes clear, he has none. Rather, it is an invitation to invent a relationship between the stars, to create a story in the skies. In this sense, her asking is an appeal for unbridled imagination. Joel initially misunderstands, perhaps through an insecurity brought about by his being tested on the spot, but then grasps the challenge and invents his constellation, 'Osidius the Emphatic'.[6] Clementine's words to him – 'you're full of shit, right' – read as her testing his resolve, checking his willingness to preserve the illusion. His holding firm in spite of her interjections thus becomes indicative of his succeeding at her game by indulging in the kind of childlike imagining she took him to be capable of. His response is a rejection of wisdom and knowledge, traits associated with adulthood and growth. The way in which Joel understands Clementine's request displays the unspoken affinity that exists between the characters as they both indulge in a mode of behaviour that effectively rejects the trappings of adulthood in favour of a return to childish sensibilities and, as it turns out, fantasies.

Our attention remains upon the two characters' relationship with each other through the lack of a cut away to show the sky that Joel points to and describes. In addition to this, the overhead shot of the couple seems to mimic the conventional post-coital shot of the man and woman lying side-by-side gazing upwards. It is significant to note that the film replaces the act of sex between two adults with the event of two adults lying down and making up names for stars. It is as though their relationship relies upon a connection with childhood but also a subtle avoidance of the affirmation of adulthood through sex. The film avoids any overtly sexual scenes between the couple, leading us to question whether a condition of their remaining childlike with one another is that they wordlessly sacrifice sexual desire, something that would define them as adult.

The childlike behaviour of the central pair in this scene brings to mind a series of comments Stanley Cavell makes when describing a genre of film-making he terms 'the Hollywood Comedies of Remarriage'.[7] Cavell's definition of this genre is founded upon his experience of 'a film made in Hollywood between 1934 and 1949' and involves firstly the genre being 'the principal group of Hollywood comedies after the advent of sound and therewith one definitive achievement in the history of the art film' and secondly 'that the genre of Remarriage is an inheritor of the preoccupations and discoveries of Shakespearian romantic comedy'.[8] Certain characteristics of the remarriage comedy endure across periods and nationalities of film-making, a fact Cavell acknowledges as he makes reference to a film such as Smiles of a Summer Night (Ingmar Bergman, 1955), which exists both outside of Hollywood and the fifteen year period between the thirties and forties that he offers for consideration. The proliferation of the remarriage comedy's defining traits across borders and ages is perhaps testament to the potency of Cavell's claims, in turn providing opportunity for a number of classical and contemporary films to be related back to his central thesis. Indeed, Eternal Sunshine constitutes a recent example of a film that has occasionally been related to the genre of the Remarriage Comedy.[9] It may be that the comparison is made in order to immediately raise the status of Gondry's film by placing it alongside the masterpieces contained in Cavell's generic bracket, as well as to emphasize its tangible thematic correlation to those films. In the latter instance, it does not require too great a leap of imagination for one to form a thematic relationship between a film like Eternal Sunshine, in which two characters become fundamentally divorced from one another only to reconcile again and embrace the reality of each other, and a film like The Awful Truth, for example, which features a divorced couple, played by Irene Dunne and Cary Grant, whose efforts to prevent each other remarrying results in their symbolic 'remarriage'.[10]

When describing The Lady Eve, Cavell notes a particular characteristic of the remarriage genre that I wish to dwell upon here as a means of understanding some of Eternal Sunshine's themes and concerns. Cavell asserts that:

> Almost without exception these films allow the principal pair to express the wish to be children again, or perhaps to be children together. In part this is a wish to make room for playfulness within the gravity of adulthood, in part it is a wish to be cared for first, and unconditionally (e.g., without sexual demands, though doubtless not without sexual favours). If it could be managed, it would turn the tables on time, making marriage the arena and the discovery of innocence.[11]

In the episode on the frozen lake, the film seems to provide in fairly straightforward terms a space for Joel and Clementine to express their mutual desire to act like children together (knowing all the time that they are not). The extent to which the gravity of adulthood has been suspended is encapsulated in their shared willingness to play together. Within this, the burden of knowledge and experience is revoked and Joel is free, at Clementine's request, to construct a reading of the stars that bears no relation to conventional astronomy. The couple's pursuit of childhood enjoyment in the scene symbolizes a more general rejection of the adult world that they enjoyed in their (now-forgotten) life together. Childish pleasures emerge in the couple's shared rituals such as a game they play where they each hold a pillow over the other's face and the 'victim' pretends to suffocate and the 'killer' in turn feigns concern; and similarly in a game they play while parked outside the drive-in movies, where they each provide increasingly ridiculous soundtrack voices to the film they watch. In the scenes we see from Joel and Clementine's life together, this resistance to maturity seems to be the strength of their union. Indeed, as we retrospectively piece together events in the reverse-ordered remembrances of Joel's dreaming state, their relationship appears to break down precisely under the weight of adult concerns. When we linger on these scenes from Joel's memory, we discover that neither Joel nor Clementine appears equipped to contend with the demands of playing adult roles, as opposed to their fluency when playing childlike roles together, a fact which leads to their estrangement from one another.

Fighting

This is perhaps most apparent in a bitter sequence that Joel remembers as the last time he saw Clementine. (According to the time-reverse structure of his dream-remembrances, this episode from the end of his relationship with Clementine occurs at the beginning of his subconscious recollections.)[12] In this scene Clementine arrives back from some undefined place at three o'clock in the morning, apparently drunk, to find Joel waiting up for her, reading a book. As she walks unsteadily into the lounge from the kitchen, the camera quickly pans left from her in a swooping motion, zooming in to capture Joel in close-up, sitting in an easy chair, his open book forming a barrier between him and Clementine. Joel's anxiety is made clear to us as the rapid tapping of his fingers on the book's hardcover betrays his underlying emotional response to Clementine's actions. The proximity of the camera to Joel as he pretends to read begins a pattern of scrutinizing close-ups. This allows for the intimate observation of slight traits and expressions, such as Joel's tapping fingers, that convey something of the character's interior thoughts and emotions. Moreover, the succession of close-ups confines the space that the pair occupies, collapsing its dimensions to create a sense of entrapment that comes to symbolize the condition of their relationship at this juncture, whereby each feels equally constrained by the other.

Their exchanges in this sequence are charged with sour recrimination as they trade accusation and counter-accusation. Immediately Joel is cast in an adult role as he glances disdainfully across at Clementine and says pointedly 'It's three o'clock'. He infuses the words with a disapproving tone that replicates the style of delivery a weary parent might choose to address an errant child. When Clementine confesses that she 'kinda…sorta' wrecked Joel's car, he concludes that she was driving drunk and labels her 'pathetic', causing her to retort that she was only 'a little tipsy' and demand he doesn't call her pathetic. He responds 'Well it is pathetic. And it's fucking irresponsible. You could have killed somebody'. With these words, Joel effectively reinforces a role in excess of his years, a fact referenced as Clementine later calls him an 'old lady', an unattractive term that he returns by calling her a 'wino'. In using these particular descriptive words for each other's behaviour, Joel and Clementine redefine each other as both old and unappealing to one another. Indeed, their grown up-ness is a defining characteristic of both their behaviours in this scene. While Clementine initially begins as a kind of chastened teenager, she soon turns on Joel with the venomous analysis: 'Face it Joely, you're freaked out because I was out late without you…and in your little wormy brain you're trying to

Eternal Sunshine of the Spotless Mind

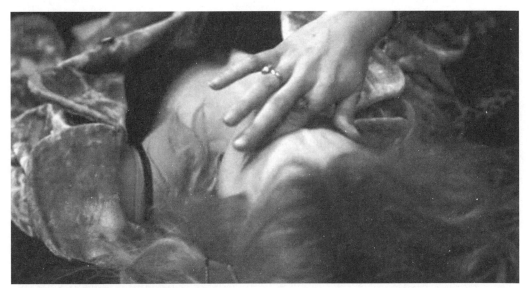

Eternal Sunshine of the Spotless Mind

figure out "did she fuck someone tonight?"' Thus, while Joel had previously taken the adult role in the argument, Clementine succinctly claims that position for herself, turning the attention from her misdemeanours to Joel's psychological state. Her patronizing use of the term 'Joely' and her demeaning description of his 'wormy little brain' illustrates the extent to which she attempts to reassert her status in the argument and diminish his concerns by suggesting they are merely the by-product of his pathetic jealousy.

It becomes clear that Joel and Clementine engaged in a different sort of game in this scene, one in which each attempts to cast themselves as the older and more knowledgeable in their argument. Furthering the destructive reach of the game, when Clementine reclaims authority with her proclaimed knowledge of his jealousy, Joel responds with a declaration of knowledge regarding her behaviour, replying: 'No. See Clem, I assume you fucked someone tonight. Isn't that how you get people to like you?' This merciless retort reproduces the terms of Clementine's earlier pseudo-psychoanalytic statement regarding his jealousy, but also advances the potential to hurt by suggesting that Clementine's infidelity is not a product of his imagination but fact.[13] Unlike the play between the two that we observed at the frozen lake, this game has a malevolent agenda, reliant upon which player can inflict the greatest degree of emotional harm on the other. Whereas the game of naming stars relied upon a suspension of real knowledge and fact, this game involves a contest of who possesses the most knowledge of each other in the relationship and whose vindictive statements can ultimately be taken as fact. The destructive nature of the game is encapsulated in the sharp, recriminatory tone with which Joel and Clementine address each other: him acerbic and intolerant, her incredulous and sneering. Their language is imbued with an adult inflection that was markedly absent from the sequence on the frozen lake, where a series of childish sounds at times took the place of emotional articulation.

The film succeeds in accentuating these distinctions between the two scenes by making Joel's remembrance of this tense encounter to be the first time we see him and Clementine after we have witnessed their day together, which culminated in the trip to the frozen lake. Although their behaviour is not unrecognizable between the scenes, with Clementine still displaying a characteristic recklessness and Joel exhibiting an introverted caution, those traits are spun darkly in the scene at the apartment, with neither character possessing the kind of magical innocence we saw earlier in the film. Indeed, we might justifiably conclude that they know too much, or at least profess to know too much. The film invites the contrast by ordering the scenes as chronologically consecutive in the development of the narrative. Again, this allows us to make a comparison in reverse, realizing the nature of the couple's behaviour in the apartment scene in association with the scene on the frozen lake that occurs later in their lives but earlier in the film.

In the apartment scene Clementine and Joel play out adult roles as opposed to childlike ones. Their relationship apparently cannot endure this shift and, indeed, this encounter effectively ends their bond as Clementine leaves the apartment with Joel pleading too late for her to stay. In one sense, the couple thus depart from a convention of the remarriage comedy as Cavell describes it, rejecting the opportunity to 'make room for playfulness within the gravity of adulthood'. As the film progresses, with the dreaming Joel remembering his relationship with Clementine in reverse stages, we appreciate how the playfulness drains from their union. We might see this in a restaurant scene where the couple discuss with painfully forced politeness Joel's leaving hairs on the soap in the mornings or another apartment scene when Joel smears ketchup across his neck and pretends to be dead, only for Clementine to totally ignore him before saying angrily 'I'm fucking crawling out of my skin,' as though it had become obvious that playfulness was no longer part of their relationship.

Hiding

The couple's move from adopted childlikeness to constructed adult roles towards the end of their relationship contrasts sharply with the character's behaviour elsewhere. We have seen moments when they share in the playfulness and invention associated with re-evoking childhood behaviour, but there are also times when they mutually engage in the hardships and discomforts of being a child. This is evident in a scene in which Joel and Clementine lie beneath the covers of their bed, the daylight penetrating through the embroidered patches of the duvet that encases all but their bare feet. The two appear in a series of extreme close-ups shot from underneath the duvet cover and, although in closer proximity to them than the choice of shots in the apartment scene earlier, the intention for the framing here is not to create a similar sense of claustrophobic constraint. Instead, with the delicate cover of the duvet resting on their heads and the yellow light filtering through the material, the two exist comfortably in a protected, private space away from the world around them. As the light shines through the duvet's patchwork surface it creates a thin, rippled, membrane-like shroud around the couple, which becomes like a second skin that surrounds them as they lie together, matching the tone of their skin as it turns golden pink in the sunlight.

And so, whereas in the apartment the series of close-ups brought into focus the stifled, shadowy desolation of a space that reflected the derelict emotional condition of the couple occupying it, here the same choice of shots serve to complete the warmth and intimacy that they share in this cocoon-like sanctuary. We might also note that the same piece of music plays over this scene as played over the scene at the frozen lake from the beginning of the film: a soft strumming of notes on a guitar in a major key that builds into broader orchestral underscoring as the scene progresses. Thus, an audio correlation is created, re-evoking the happiness observed previously between the two and denoting this moment as similarly settled.

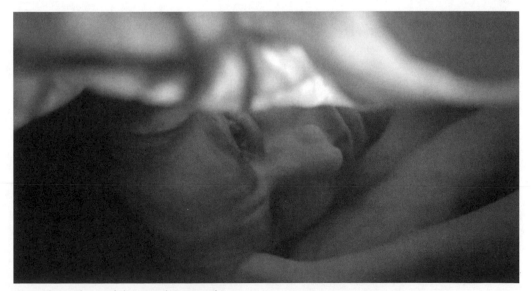

Eternal Sunshine of the Spotless Mind

Eternal Sunshine of the Spotless Mind

Under the covers, Clementine shares an account of suffering from her childhood:

> Joely…Am I ugly? When I was a kid I thought I was. I can't believe I'm crying already. Sometimes I think people don't understand how lonely it is to be a kid…like, you don't matter. So…I'm eight and I have these toys, these dolls. My favourite is this ugly girl doll who I call Clementine. And I keep yelling at her: you can't be ugly. Be pretty. It's weird, like if I could transform her, I would magically change too.

As Clementine relates this memory to Joel her voice breaks slightly with emotion, and he cradles her head with the palm of his hand, lending a small gesture of support and comfort, but also treating her like a fragile object, to be protected and cherished.

As she begins speaking we move from an exterior shot of the bed to a close-up of Joel, then a reverse close-up of Clementine, then back to Joel. In her words '…like you don't matter' the film cuts from his face to a shot of a black and white photograph that slowly comes in focus and is revealed to be a young girl in a cowboy outfit, holding a stuffed toy giraffe. Given that Clementine's voiceover continues over this cut we understand this girl to be her. After she says the word 'toys' we cut to another blurred shot as the camera tracks shakily right, finally settling on an extreme close-up of a doll's face, which we take to be the doll Clementine is now describing. We cut back to close-up shots of Clementine and Joel again before returning to the image of the doll as Clementine says 'like if I could transform her, I would magically change too'. As she says these words the plastic cheek of the doll slowly reforms its shape, as if it had previously been pressed in and deformed.

This delicate moment between the characters begins with Clementine's return to her own childhood, revisiting feelings of pain, insecurity and loneliness. Given the characteristics we have already discussed regarding this pair, it seems wholly appropriate that a point of emphatic emotional kinship should also occur precisely when a return to childhood feelings and experiences is enacted. The looking back to childhood here encapsulates the couple's general return to childlike states, encompassing their need to know and understand each other as children first. In this way, innocence and experience would always be suspended for the couple, and they could always exist between the roles of child and adult. It is like children that these two know each other best, perhaps understand each other the most, because in differing ways they each have clung to their childhood into adult life. The film emphasizes this by having the frozen lake scene towards the beginning of the film, allowing us to appreciate the couple's childlike qualities almost before anything else. Crucially, Clementine's recollections illustrate that revisiting childhood thoughts and attitudes is not only a way of having fun, of always skidding on frozen lakes. Instead, her words evoke the pain and insecurity of childhood; the other side of those formative years that has remained with both characters since then (a fact that crystallizes in relation to Joel later in the film, and in this discussion). Clementine's unstoppable tears reveal the overwhelming impact recalling those emotions has on her and, likewise, Joel's comforting of her, his quiet acceptance of her pain without question or contention expresses his affinity with the thoughts she shares. Her confession provokes an overwhelming emotion within him and he leans across, kissing her over and over, as she says in a half whisper 'Joely, don't ever leave me'. The moment is shattered as the image of Clementine starts to distort and disappear, showing that Lacuna is now erasing this memory. This scene ends with Joel crawling down the bed, clutching at the sheets as though desperately clutching for his memories and pleading 'please let me keep this memory, just this one'. His final words, 'just this one,' exemplify the singular importance of the memory as a moment in which he and Clementine were closest through a shared return to childhood thought and emotion, and – in accordance with the argument I have sketched out thus far – it is apt that he should claim it as special.

Joel's imploring request to keep that one memory marks a turn in his behaviour, whereby he strives to resist Lacuna's erasing process.[14] A potential solution is provided by the imaginary Clementine in his dream. His change in attitude signals a departure in the structure of Joel's imagined world, as he begins to create scenarios rather than simply travel through a series of pre-existent memories, and likewise create a version of Clementine rather than simply remembering a reality of her. Whilst previously Joel was able actively to reflect upon the experiences he re-encountered, commenting upon the moments that were being erased, he now exhibits the ability to shape the path of his thoughts. He thus makes use of the imaginative impulse that we observed in the characters of Wanley and Dorothy in the previous chapter. It is significant and ironic that Joel should realize a sense of active purpose and authority when he is dreaming, whereas his behaviour in real life (as he remembers it) was defined by a passivity and lack of influence, encapsulated by Clementine's complaint at one point: 'I can't hear you. I can never the fuck understand what you're saying'. The assertiveness and resilience he shows takes place only in a dreamworld, when nobody else is around and his only victory would be the rescue of his own memories.

Clementine implies a possible way out of the memory-erase as the couple sit in a remembered scene from his apartment. From here, she suggests that he takes her somewhere else: 'somewhere

where I don't belong and we hide there until morning'. This prompts Joel to conjure a scene from his early childhood, the memory of which is seen to emerge as rain inexplicably starts to fall in the apartment and images of a young Joel splashing in puddles and looking out of a window become intersected with images of the couple sitting together. Further to this, a child's voice is heard on the soundtrack singing 'row, row, row your boat gently down the stream', which Joel and then Clementine repeat. (This rhyme ends with the phrase 'Life is but a dream'; an appropriate sentiment given the film's dramatic structure.) As the sequence progresses, a new space seems suddenly to open up in their apartment and Joel catches sight of a child's bike propped against the wall, which cues another intersected image of the child Joel brushing off rainwater from the saddle of an identical bike. The adult Joel springs from his sofa and dives into the newly emerged space, landing underneath a table that has a corrugated plastic roof, resembling the corrugated roof we then see the child Joel standing underneath as he tastes raindrops with his tongue and catches them with his hand. In a proceeding shot, the adult Joel stretches out his hand in a replicating gesture.

The editing together of images from Joel's childhood and images of him as an adult, along with the audio matching of 'row, row, row your boat...' and the replicated gesture of stretching out the hand that occurs between the adult Joel and child Joel effectively signal a return to early childhood as distinctions between adult and child break down; two temporal states bleeding into one another. Joel relives the sensations of his childhood, allowing them to wash over him and engulf his behaviour. The space that opens up in the apartment, which turns out to be the kitchen from Joel's childhood home, is suggestive of a haven away from Lacuna's probing, and Joel's sliding into that space marks his retreat into an uncharted and therefore safe area of his memory.

The intermingling of adult and child states is given a comic spin when the adult Joel literally inhabits his childhood psyche, hiding under a table in the kitchen, playing with a yoyo and demanding ice-cream. The film marks this shift in tone partly through the sight of Carrey dressed in a pair of children's pyjamas and partly as a slow, poignant piano accompaniment on the film's soundtrack is replaced by a quirky, staccato plucked string arrangement. In this scene, Clementine is recast as Mrs Hamlyn, an adult friend of Joel's mother's but, in keeping with her prevailing attitudes, treats the experience as a child would when dressing up in adult clothes: 'Whoah! Look at this dress man! I wish I could take it with me...' Consequently, Clementine never becomes distanced from Joel despite their apparent adult/child divide in the sequence and eventually she ends up under the table with him, brought down to his level and also, significantly, his size, making them equal again. Despite Joel becoming overwhelmed by the force of his childish need for attention, the hiding strategy appears to work until, in the real world, the director of Lacuna, Dr. Howard Mierzwiak (Tom Wilkinson) is called in to bring him back onto 'the map'. The process of realigning him onto the predetermined path of memory-recall results in Joel and Clementine, who were being bathed in the sink by Joel's mother, falling 'through' the childhood memory in which they sheltered, appearing visually as though they are being flushed down the drain. (Clementine's role as a child with Joel in the sink emphasizes the extent to which she has begun to function as a child with Joel, sharing the moment from his adopted level.) When Joel reappears he is back in an actual memory from his time with Clementine: the sequence where they provide voiceovers for the drive-in movie.

But, as Stan (Mark Ruffalo) the Lacuna technician begins to erase that memory, Joel's world starts to disintegrate once more and he is forced on the run again with Clementine (in the real world Stan is heard to say 'you can run but you can't hide' as though somehow understanding precisely Joel's intentions now).

This running away forces another solution upon the couple, provided once more by (Joel's vision of) Clementine as they walk through the rapidly disappearing interior of the bookshop where she works: 'Hide me somewhere deeper...somewhere really buried. Hide me in your humiliation'. (Joel's repeated imagining of Clementine as the provider of solutions to his problems appears to be a projection of his realizing her pivotal importance to his real survival, and that his wish to erase her, as he struggled to understand her erasing of him, was profoundly misjudged.) Joel's initial response to this is to hide in the memory of him as a teenager in his bedroom being caught masturbating by his mother, but the visceral trauma of the incident distracts him and he and Clementine return again to a scene from his memories with her: the beach in Montauk where they first met (albeit still in the bed from Joel's room). Returning to the disintegrating bookshop, which is now almost totally shrouded in darkness, Clementine implores Joel to hide her 'somewhere *really* buried' at which point the underscore ends abruptly and the sound of children's shouting voices can be heard.

Beginning

We cut to a shot of a fenced yard where a young boy wearing a red cape kneels in front of a little red truck. He has a hammer in his hand and is surrounded by four other boys shouting at him – the voices we heard penetrating through into the previous scene. The children shout 'Hit it! Hit it Joel!' their voices overlapping each other through their enthusiastic aggression. Joel responds weakly 'I can't...I've got to go home' in his adult voice, at odds with his appearance and contrasting with the higher pitches of his peers. Again, we observe the blending together of adult and child identities within Joel's character as he relives moments from his past. This intermingling suggests the extent to which Joel is still troubled by the events of his past, having not yet found the means to overcome childhood trauma and so returning to them whilst retaining elements of his adult self; still suffering from the ordeal even as a grown up. As he pleads 'I'll do it later' we cut to a shot of a little girl sitting in a chair to the left of the group, wearing a blue dress and a pink cowboy hat, holding a pillow. Cutting back to the group of boys in close-up, we see that in the red truck is a dead bird and the boys are bullying Joel to hit it with the hammer. We cut back to the wider shot of the group before returning firstly to a close-up of the bird, and then a close-up of Joel as he raises the hammer. When he brings it down we cut to a medium close-up shot resembling the angle of his viewpoint, looking up at the boys, who have stopped shouting now to be replaced by a slow, reflective sequence of piano chords on the soundtrack. The rapid series of close-ups creates a visual intensity that seems to mirror the anxiety Joel experiences. Likewise, the shot resembling his perspective looking up at the boys emphasizes his diminished position in the scene as they stand over him, taller and intimidating. A shot of a bird taking off from branches overhead marks a break in the scene and, when we return to the group, Joel is now grown-up, still wearing the red cape and holding the hammer. Again, the blurring of adult and child here seems to express the residual emotional torment that Joel still feels, as past and present insecurities merge in the moment.

Eternal Sunshine of the Spotless Mind

A reverse shot from behind and above the group of boys captures Joel breaking into tears just as the girl from the seat walks into frame, except now the girl is Clementine, grown up like Joel. She walks over to Joel and takes him by the hand, leading him away from the group. As we cut to another shot of their exit, the two have changed again into their child personas as the group of boys begin to shout and taunt them.

Yet, when we cut to a different angle as Joel unsuccessfully tries to confront the gang's leader Freddie, they are transformed again into adults.

Eternal Sunshine of the Spotless Mind

The ambiguity of ages here succeeds in encapsulating Joel and Clementine's more general suspension between adult and child states, as observed previously in their real lives remembered by Joel. His reinventing Clementine as an active character within his past allows them to be both adults and children together, as if they had known each other all their lives. When the couple journey to the lake again after their memory-wipes, we might reflect that this is exactly the situation they achieve: children and adults in the same moment together, knowing each other as both. They recreate each other as individuals who know each other as young and older, constructing an imagined history between them that fictitiously predates their meeting in the present.

Joel's placement of Clementine within this private remembrance also addresses his need for her to know his childhood in order that she understand his adult anxieties and insecurities, just as she allowed him access to her childhood in order to communicate the root causes of her anxieties and insecurities when they lay together under the duvet. In that sense, this couple that share a predisposition for childlike play and imagination exhibit a need to know each other properly as children in order to understand each other as adults. Perhaps Joel's failure to communicate underlying reasons for his adult fragility by relating events from his childhood leads to their eventual estrangement, pushing them away from their mutual childlike relationship and towards the adult roles that they prove ill-equipped to perform. Here, in a dreaming space away from the constraints of the world and the weight of adulthood, Joel fulfils a desire to be known by Clementine by allowing her – in his imagination – to understand a defining moment in his life that has shaped his behaviour and attitudes since. And in this dreamspace, Clementine rescues him from the gang, taking him by the hand and leading him home where they play the pretend-suffocating game with the pillow. From the moment she leads him away from the boys, the couple are child versions again, except that their voices are grown up, as though Joel through his imagining were recognizing the intrinsic childlike quality to their behaviour as adults, so that they are not definitely adult or child here but instead gravitate somewhere between the two. The film makes clear again the childlikeness of their behaviour as in their next scene together they play the pillow-suffocation game in exactly the same way, with an identical pillow, so mirroring their playing together as children outside Joel's family home. Crucially, in this second scene the pillow game seems to act as a close precursor to the sexual teasing that adolescents might engage in with each other. Again, the sense is created of Joel and Clementine, despite their status as adults, choosing to linger on the borderline between childhood and adulthood, engaging in games that promote a sense of innocence and fun, but conversely are underscored with sexuality and desire. Those latter qualities are connected with the adulthood that Joel and Clementine seek to escape from together, or at least resist.

This resistance of adulthood is strongly articulated in Joel's final dream-memory: his first meeting with Clementine on the beach in Montauk. The last thing the couple do together that day is visit a vacant beach house. Clementine breaks into the house, against Joel's meekly voiced reservations, and once inside starts mischievously looking for 'candles, matches and the liquor cabinet'. Joel apprehensively crosses the threshold but continues to voice his concerns. Clementine seeks to reassure him, explaining that 'It's our house. Just for tonight. We are...[picking up some unopened mail]...David and Ruth Laskin. Which one do you want to be? I'd prefer to be Ruth but I can be flexible'. By this point in the film, we understand this activity as symptomatic of Clementine's propensity for make-believe and fantasy. In the context of this knowledge, assuming the role of 'Ruth Laskin' represents an extension of a childhood game of pretending to be one's parents or dressing up in adult's clothes and, indeed, Clementine later suggests slipping into 'something more Ruth', thus temporarily adopting the outward accoutrements of an adult society to which she does not belong, just as a child might. The wearing of the clothes, which we do not see, would therefore not necessarily transform Clementine into an adult like 'Ruth Laskin', but might instead stress the incongruity between the two.

Joel, however, is unable to share in the game and instead continues to express his reservations in a series of mumbled responses. We might read this as his level-headed reaction to the misdeed of breaking into someone else's house. However, Joel's anxiety is more deep-rooted than the straightforward fear of criminal activity. As he stands uncomfortably withdrawing himself from Clementine's game, his subdued behaviour expresses an aversion to her reinventing them as the owners of the beach house, as the married couple Mr and Mrs Laskin. This is expressed through his vocal reactions to Clementine, but also visually as he distances himself from her activity by remaining in the hallway, keeping the doorframe barrier between them as she explores the lives of the Laskins in the adjoining room. Clementine treats the beach house as a kind of Wendy-house, using it as a sight of playful invention and seeking out the Laskins' wardrobes as though they were dressing-up boxes. Joel, however, misreads her intentions and instead sees her as being part of the house, thus equating her with the trappings of adulthood that, as we have seen already in the film, he is unable to properly function within. As a result, he takes her reinventing them as a married couple within the beach house too literally and is threatened by it, making him feel insecure within the situation.

Consequently, when Clementine eventually confronts his reluctance with 'So go,' he hears not the tone of a frustrated child but of a reprimanding adult and so runs away, taking flight just as he did when forced to hit the dead bird with the hammer as a child, the same vulnerability recalled now. In the environment of his dream-memories, Joel is able to re-evaluate his response at the beach house, admitting that he 'felt like a scared little kid' and pinpointing Clementine's 'So go' as the moment when he decided to run away. Joel looking over the memories in this way performs a therapeutic function at odds with the design and purpose of Lacuna's mind-wipe technology that is supposed to simply eradicate pain through forgetting, rather than easing it through remembering and understanding. As a result, Mierzwiak's technology is seen for what it really is, brain damage, rather than a cure for hurt and despair.

In his therapeutic dreamspace, Joel addresses the memory by providing, through his imagined Clementine, a solution to the situation: what if he didn't run away? He revisits the scene of humiliation and insecurity and, in doing so, provides himself with the key to finding Clementine again. As they embrace for the last time, his dream of Clementine whispers in his ear 'meet me in Montauk'. That Joel should imagine her saying these words represents not only his understanding of the moment as being compromised by his behaviour, but of Clementine's ability to retain and recreate aspects of those childhood behaviours that he finds comfort in, so realizing the speciality of their union which, in their first meeting, he failed to foresee but which, over time, he learnt to appreciate and then overlook. As he leaves the beach, driven in the car that he originally caught a ride in, images of Clementine from their life together flash up and fade. These memories are destined, as far as he understands, to be forgotten forever. In those moments, his sense of loss is absolute. And when his companions in the car ask who Clementine was, his response 'she was just a girl' affirms that she is apparently, tragically, lost to him now.

Joel wakes the next day wearing pyjamas he doesn't recognize (supplied by Lacuna) with a dent on his car he can't explain (supplied by Clementine) and, for reasons he can't comprehend skips work and heads to Montauk, where he meets a mysterious girl whom he will later lie down on the ice with and gaze at the stars. The morning after Joel and Clementine's visit to the lake, however, they each receive packages from Mary (Kirsten Dunst), a former Lacuna employee, containing the tapes they made before they underwent the memory-erasing process. This results in both of them hearing themselves picking over and pulling apart each other's features and characteristics. These tapes represent their knowledge of each other through time and experience, but also the rejection of that knowledge as they are made at the point where each has resolved to erase the memory of the other.

Two things are interesting. Firstly, the cold, sophisticated, analysing tone and vocabulary of the voices on the tapes (amusingly exemplified in Joel's criticism of Clementine's inability to pronounce 'library' properly) that contrasts with the raw emotional bewilderment each other feels as they listen. The effect, naturally, is of two people listening to thoughts and feelings they cannot understand, that belong to someone else. That Joel and Clementine cannot even begin to recognize themselves in the tapes exemplifies the extent to which they became different people in their relationship: sophisticated, analysing and cold, discovering how to hurt each other as they went along. Innocent and bewildered, they struggle to comprehend how they became those people. Secondly, the voices on the tapes are those of experience and knowledge. As we have seen, the contest of experience and knowledge between these characters resulted in their estrangement from one another, and so those voices on the tapes succinctly encapsulate that bitterness. At the film's conclusion, Joel and Clementine choose each other despite the warnings contained on the tapes, effectively rejecting the advice provided through knowledge. By rejecting knowledge in favour of each other, they rejoin their pursuit of innocence, disowning the adult commodities of wisdom and judgement. Beginning again together takes them back to a childlike state of innocence, allowing them to grow together again from innocence to understanding. And, as we have seen, that relies upon their understanding each other as children first, understanding the childlikeness that defines them as adults, and making room for playfulness as a celebration of their love. As Cavell suggests of the remarriage couple's wish to make room for playfulness within the gravity of adulthood, 'if it could be managed, it would turn the tables on time, making marriage the arena and the discovery of innocence'.[15] As they decide to disown knowledge they stand together in a hallway, laughing like children.

Given the thematic tone of this conclusion, it seems appropriate that the film should end with the repeating image of Joel and Clementine running together on the deserted, snow-laden Montauk beach.

Eternal Sunshine of the Spotless Mind

The repetition of the sequence demands that we attend to precisely what the pair are engaged in. He runs away from her but slows to look back at her, grinning. She pursues him but never speeds up when he slows in order to catch him. In other words, their running has no purpose or product: he never escapes, she never catches him. Ultimately, they simply enjoy the thrill of running together in that moment; they revel in the game they have created together. Bearing in mind the aspects of childlikeness and play that were central to their relationship and tragically drained away, the final frames of the film have reassuring repercussions. Here are two people making room for playfulness beyond the constraints of an adult prison they once constructed for each other and, as the image repeats, continue to do so until the screen fades to white and we see them no more. The sequence does not provide the same conventionally definite ending of *The Woman in the Window*, where Wanley returns to his reality once more, or the *Wizard of Oz* where Dorothy finds herself back in Kansas. Yet those endings were only definite at a surface level, and we were left to speculate upon the characters' lives after the credits rolled, such had been the powerful effect of the dreams we were privy to. The ending of Gondry's film, although unconventional, contains the hope of a new beginning which the earlier films did not. Although the film has certainly made it difficult to ascertain how the lives of its characters might progress, we leave them at the start of a new life together, whereas Dorothy and Wanley return to a life they already knew, the shortcomings of which they had already experienced.

Notes

1. Hereafter *Eternal Sunshine*.
2. This is indicative of the film's resistance to recognized scientific and psychoanalytic processes, preferring instead to present fantasies both of the human mind and of science itself. As I suggested

in the previous chapter, strategic decisions of this kind mark the film out from an example like *Spellbound*, which insists on an account of human psychology at least grounded in actual science.

3. The key work in relation to this critical perspective remains David Bordwell, Janet Staiger and Kristin Thompson's expansive study *The Classical Hollywood Cinema: Film Style & Mode of Production to 1960* (London: Routledge, 1985). Dirk Eitzen explains that 'Thanks in large part to this work, coupled with Bordwell's influential theoretical treatise *Narration in the Fiction Film*, published in the same year, most film scholars have become accustomed to thinking about mainstream American fiction films in a particular way: as driven by protagonists' needs and desires, organized overwhelmingly around the goal of presenting a clear and coherent fictional world, and focusing viewers' attention almost exclusively upon story outcomes...The movie continues as long one problem leads to another; when the protagonists achieve their main goals, the movie quickly concludes'. (Dirk Eitzen 'Comedy and Classicism,' Richard Allen & Murray Smith (eds.) *Film Theory and Philosophy* Oxford: Oxford University Press, 1997, pp. 394-395). Bordwell, Staiger and Thompson's work has indeed profoundly affected the study of Hollywood cinema, providing a firm theoretical foundation that can be used to guide both writing and teaching. But it is also true that *The Classical Hollywood Cinema* has inspired a number of expressive critics to reassess and revisit their own critical investment in Hollywood cinema, resulting in a contesting of the offered truths in Bordwell, Staiger and Thompson's work (Eitzen's argument follows this line, suggesting that comedy films, particularly, provide an exception to the overarching claims of their book). Perhaps the most vehemently argued and persuasively articulated version of this type of response is Andrew Britton's article 'The Philosophy of the Pigeonhole: Wisconsin Formalism and the 'Classical Style,'' *CineAction!*, no. 15, Winter 1988-89, pp. 47–63. In relation to *Eternal Sunshine*, a film obviously produced well after the historical period covered in *Classical Hollywood Cinema*, it is important to note Kristin Thompson's recent attempt to connect the claims of the original book with modern-era films in *Storytelling in the New Hollywood: Understanding Classical Narrative Techniques* (Cambridge, Massachusetts: Harvard University Press, 1999). Thompson maintains a focus upon goal-oriented narratives and, as a statement of intent in the book's preface, proposes that 'In recent years, some historians have claimed that there is something new at work in American cinema – "post-classical" film-making. This claim implies a fundamental shift in Hollywood's basic system of telling stories...I will contend that modern Hollywood narratives are put together in much the same way as they were in the studio era' (x).

4. A further meeting on the ice occurs between Clementine and Patrick (Elijah Wood), the young Lacuna employee who is trying to replace Joel in Clementine's affections by replicating the couple's past experiences. Patrick is able to do this because Lacuna collects the patient's personal possessions that remind them of or describe experiences with the person they wish to erase. Instead of destroying Clementine's and Joel's, Patrick keeps them and, for example, learns their past conversations from diary entries. When he visits the frozen lake with Clementine, we have already seen her original meeting with Joel and therefore see Patrick's mimicry of Joel's earlier words, understanding Clementine's unease as we appreciate the contrivance of her meeting with Patrick compared to her earlier experience with Joel.

5. Many reviewers have commented upon Jim Carrey's restraint in the role of Joel, especially in contrast to earlier roles in films such as *Ace Ventura: Pet Detective* (Tom Shadyac, 1994) and *The Mask* (Chuck Russell, 1994) which launched his screen career and, as a consequence, constructed a hyperactive, infantile and extremely popular screen persona for the actor that persists in more recent

films such as *Bruce Almighty* (Tom Shadyac, 2003) and *Fun with Dick and Jane* (Dean Parisot, 2005), despite moves towards more 'serious' roles in *The Truman Show* (Peter Weir, 1998) and *Man on the Moon* (Milos Forman, 1999). Carrey's restraint in *Eternal Sunshine* is perhaps particularly apparent when we recognize the childlike aspects of Joel's character and consider the risk of Carrey's performance at least partially touching upon the relentless tone and energy of those earlier 'childish adult' roles. That this danger never emerges is testament to Carrey's strong control over the tone of his performance throughout the film.

6. Curiously, Joel's invention, Osidius, sounds somewhat like a mispronunciation of Odysseus (more commonly known as Ulysses). The half-reference to the Greek myth seems to allude to Joel's own 'journey' through his subconscious being comparable to an odyssey (a word derived, of course, from Odysseus' name) in which he attempts a return to Clementine, whereas Odysseus sought reunion with Ithaca and Penelope. Interestingly, in both Joel's and Odysseus' stories, the theme of memory is made paramount: Joel struggles to retain his memory of Clementine against Lacuna's efforts and, likewise, Odysseus is encouraged at various points on his journey to forget his wife and home. The two characters are thus united through their efforts to remember their pasts.

7. Stanley Cavell *Pursuits of Happiness: The Hollywood Comedy of Remarriage* Cambridge MA: Harvard University Press, 1981, reprinted 1997.

8. Ibid., p. 1. The comedies of remarriage are, in the order they appear in Cavell's study: *The Lady Eve* (Preston Sturges, 1941), *It Happened One Night* (Frank Capra, 1934), *Bringing Up Baby* (Howard Hawks, 1938), *The Philadelphia Story* (George Cukor, 1940), *His Girl Friday* (Howard Hawks, 1940), *Adam's Rib* (George Cukor, 1949) and *The Awful Truth* (Leo McCarey, 1937).

9. David Edelstein explicitly suggests the film's relationship to Cavell's Remarriage genre in the opening paragraph of his review of the film for *Slate* (http://www.slate.com/id/2097362 accessed 09/09/2005) and A. O. Scott resurrects this linkage in a later review for the *New York Times* (http://www.nytimes.com/2004/04/04/movies/04SCOT.html?ex=1396414800&en=c68fcaa787ca8b5b&ei=5007&partner=USERLAND accessed 12/09/2005).

10. Cavell has in fact recently considered the possibility of contemporary Remarriage Comedies, providing a list of potentials in conversation with Rex Butler (http://www.sensesofcinema.com/contents/01/13/cavell.html accessed 01/10/05) and further contemplation on the matter in a recent collection of essays (William Rothman (ed.) *Cavell on Film* New York: State University of New York Press, 2005, pp. 342–344).

11. Cavell p. 60.

12. In the accompanying commentary to the DVD version of the film, director Michel Gondry and writer/executive producer Charlie Kaufman speculate on the nature of the pills Lacuna supply Joel with to induce his dream state. Gondry and Kaufman do not conclude decisively whether or not the pills are innocuous sedatives or whether they induce a particular kind of dreaming in the patient. Given the precise reverse structure of Joel's dreamed recollections, it would seem that the latter is true. Were it not for Joel becoming aware of the process he is undergoing, it can be presumed that his dreams would continue to follow this linear reverse path as his memories of Clementine are systematically erased.

13. Ironically, his statement also references Clementine's childlikeness by suggesting that she has a very limited strategy for gaining people's affection, offering a 'fuck' almost as a straight swap.

14. It has not been possible, in a discussion centred upon the relationship of Joel and Clementine, to attend to the stories of the Lacuna employees, beyond mentioning Patrick's pursuit of Clementine.

Mary in fact had a relationship with Dr. Mierzwiak but underwent the memory-wipe to forget him. During Joel's treatment they are drawn to each other again but Mierzwiak's wife discovers them and informs Mary of her past. Shocked at Mierzwiak's behaviour, Mary leaves Lacuna, returning only to collect her belongings and the tapes that all Lacuna's patients made, mailing them out to each of them. Although existing in some ways as a device for Joel and Clementine to discover their actions, Mary is interesting in the sense that she exhibits a desire to grow up – requesting a 'real drink' of Scotch rather than beer and quoting Nietchze and Pope, but also reveals her innate childishness – pulling a face when she drinks the Scotch, learning Nietchze and Pope from a book of quotations but getting Pope's name wrong. Perhaps Mary becomes tragic as she attempts maturity through her attraction to Mierzwiak whilst her colleague, Stan, appreciates the immature aspects of her character that cause her to dance in her underwear, eat junk food and try dope. In this sense, there is a conflict of adultness and childlikeness in her behaviour that links her thematically back to Joel and Clementine.

15. Cavell, p. 60.

PART TWO: POTENTIAL WORDS

5

POTENTIAL WORLDS

'What if you could take all those hours of pain and darkness and replace them with something better?'

Gretchen Ross (*Donnie Darko*)

In the final scene of *Donnie Darko* (Richard Kelly, 2001) two strangers, Gretchen Ross (Jena Malone) and Rose Darko (Mary McDonnell) exchange an enigmatic gaze. Gretchen has pulled up at the Darko residence on her bicycle to find it surrounded by emergency services vehicles and personnel; an articulated truck bearing a huge, damaged aircraft engine passed her as she wheeled towards the house. On the front lawn, among police and government officials, stand the Darko family: a daughter, a father holding his younger daughter in his arms and, to their right, partially separated from the group by the trunk of a large tree, a mother, Rose. Grief and shock register on the faces of the father and his two daughters, their features dark and contorted as they fight hopelessly to control their emotions. Rose also mourns but, just as she is divided spatially from the group, so her demeanour is distinct to theirs. She does not weep as they do and instead carries an expression of resignation and defeat, as though she had accepted a terrible truth with dreadful calm. As she leans on the trunk of the tree, she smokes.

The cause of the family's anguish is the death of their son, which Gretchen discovers as she asks a young boy at the scene what has happened. When he informs her that his neighbour 'got smooshed by a jet engine' she enquires after the neighbour's name. The boy replies 'Donnie. Donnie Darko...I feel bad for his family,' and she agrees 'Yeah'. Throughout this conversation, Gretchen's gaze remains fixed on a specific point in the direction of the Darko's family home, broken only once to look briefly at the boy after he has described how Donnie died. Her responses to him are distant and distracted, as though her mind were focused elsewhere. Initially, we take it that she simply surveys the general scene of awful pain and disruption, especially as the boy to her right stares out in a similar fashion. Yet, once she has delivered the line 'yeah', a medium close-up of Rose looking back across the lawn proposes the older woman

Donnie Darko

to be the subject of Gretchen's gaze, and vice versa. A reverse medium close-up of Gretchen reaffirms the relationship between the characters, confirming that they are held in each other's line of sight (and, consequently, that Rose is not looking at Gretchen's younger companion).

This shot of Gretchen is sustained for ten seconds, in which time the boy asks her if she knew Donnie and she replies simply 'no', her eyes never moving from Rose. As the seconds accumulate in the duration of the shot, so the significance of Gretchen's gaze mounts. Her look becomes unusual for its length and rigid focus, suggesting a depth of connection with Rose that transcends their mutual status as strangers. The meaning of the slight frown that has formed on her features evolves from being an expression of natural sympathy for another's grief to a sign of Gretchen's disquiet at a sensation she struggles to understand. In a reverse shot, Rose tilts her head to one side and is then still, surveying Gretchen as though she too were trying to comprehend the

Donnie Darko

nature of their uncanny connection. Cutting back to the image of Gretchen, we notice her expression develop minimally from perplexity to incorporate an element of sorrowful remorse, as though she actually shared Rose's pain, rather than just appreciating it. As she looks across, her gaze never shifting, she raises her hand in a gesture of greeting. Her fixed stare makes the action look detached and involuntary, as though Gretchen were acting under the force of a mysterious instinct. Back at the tree, Rose reciprocates the gesture, tugging her hand out of her coat pocket and waving back, her gaze also never moving from Gretchen.[1]

The characters do not understand the strength of their bond, but the audience is significantly better placed to speculate upon its meaning. These two have been related with each other through Donnie (Jake Gyllenhaal), but in a different reality, now vanished. Gretchen was Donnie's girlfriend there, while his mother grew increasingly worried by her son's inexplicable behaviour and frustrated in her attempts to reach him. In that parallel world, both characters died: Gretchen run over by a man wearing a home-made giant bunny Halloween costume, and Rose as the plane carrying her and her youngest daughter lost one of its engines and plummeted to earth. In that reality Donnie survived a jet engine crashing through his bedroom because he was sleepwalking on a golf course. However, Donnie has magically reversed time to erase that reality and replace it with a world in which he doesn't survive the falling jet engine and therefore the chain of events leading to the deaths of Gretchen and Rose is never begun. (The jet engine that falls through Donnie's bedroom is the same as the one that fell from Rose's plane in that other reality, having mysteriously travelled through time and space.) One of the consequences of his time-reversal is that he sacrifices himself to save Gretchen and Rose.[2]

As Donnie travels back through time to the point at which the jet engine falls through his bedroom, the film effectively dissolves one potential world, in which he survives, and replaces it with another world, in which he dies.[3] Donnie's existence in the potential world held ramifications which profoundly affected the shape of that reality, such as in the cases of Gretchen and Rose. Thus, as he removes himself from the world, it is bound to form in new, divergent patterns of progression. Gretchen and Rose's exchanged look inscrutably acknowledges the reality now disappeared in a way that neither character understands, but apparently experiences at a primitive level. The film includes an inexplicable echo from the potential world in a way that rejects the laws of time and space, to create a moment of poignancy between the characters. We understand their bond to be centred upon their relationship to Donnie, yet Rose does not have the experience of her son from that potential world anymore and Gretchen, of course, has never known him at all in this reality. As we appreciate the nature of their union, we share in their connection, even though we cannot fully explain it ourselves. The moment between the characters is part of the film's idiosyncratically ambiguous logic, observable elsewhere in the narrative. For example, Gretchen's killer is shot in the eye by Donnie in the other potential world. Once time is reversed, however, we see him alive again on the night of Donnie's death with his newly designed bunny costume. He stares eerily, unblinking, into space and, as the camera pans away from him, reaches up and touches his eye, as though somehow experiencing an echo of his fatal injury he incurred in that other world. These echoes at the end of the film acknowledge that another potential world existed at all, achieving a subtle poignancy as three characters, dead in that other world but alive again now, experience inexplicable phantom-memories based upon their association with a character, Donnie, who was alive there but is now dead.

The existence of a potential world that vanishes to be replaced by another in *Donnie Darko* is reminiscent of a number of other films. Kelly, for example, has cited *Back to the Future* (Robert Zemeckis, 1985) as an inspiration for his film[4] and we can appreciate that a narrative correlation exists between the films, although the outcome of Zemeckis' film is reversed in *Donnie Darko*. Whereas Marty McFly (Michael J. Fox) battles to return to the future but also strives to unite his parents, thus preserving his own existence in that future, Donnie finally returns to the past, guaranteeing his own death in order to save the lives of others. Marty returns to a changed 1985 world in which his parents confidently enjoy a successful and opulent present, whereas when he left them previously to travel back in time, they were only bitter and insignificant. Thus, the world that Marty left has vanished through his actions in 1955 (primarily, giving his father greater self-belief as a teenager) and he returns to a new, more palatable, reality. The conclusion of *Donnie Darko* cannot achieve the same emphatically positive tone, as the survival of certain characters is necessarily dependent upon the death of another. Kelly's final shots of Rose and Gretchen emphasize the fact that Donnie survived in one reality but has died in this one, compromising any relief we might feel at the resurrection of those other characters.

Donnie's final relationship to the other characters essentially defines him as a saviour within the film. A reference to this theme actually occurs when Donnie steps out of a cinema which is showing *The Last Temptation of Christ* (Martin Scorsese, 1988).[5] Kelly states that this shot was included as a 'sight gag' to reference the fact that 'Any time you are dealing with a hero who has to save the world there is going to be a link to Christian mythology'.[6] The relationship to Scorsese's film is worth pursuing further, however. In that earlier film, Jesus' (Willem Dafoe) final temptation takes the form of an offer from a guardian angel of a mortal life in which he is not the Messiah and thus is not crucified and resurrected. The offer is made as he hangs nailed and bound to the cross and seems prompted by his cry to the heavens: 'Father, why have you forsaken me?' The baying crowd is suddenly silenced, a shaft of light breaks from behind the clouds, and suddenly in front of Jesus crouches a little girl (Juliette Caton), who introduces herself as the angel that guards him, sent from God to give this reprieve. Jesus does not realize that his plea has been answered not by God but by Satan, hidden in the form of the guardian angel. The girl takes off his crown of thorns, removes the nails from his hands and feet, and leads him away from the scene. Jesus is no longer the Messiah.

In this alternative existence, he marries Mary Magdalene (Barbara Hershey), who becomes pregnant but dies before their child can be born. As a way of explaining her death, the guardian angel/Satan informs him that God has 'killed' Mary, further distancing Jesus from his Father. Encouraged by the angel's advice that 'there is only one woman in the world' Jesus finds Mary, sister of Lazarus, and they have a large family together. It is also suggested that he forms a sexual relationship with Martha, Mary's sister, acting again under the angel's anti-monogamous guidance. It is only when Jesus lies dying in old age that he realizes the truth of

The Last Temptation of Christ   *The Last Temptation of Christ*

his alternative world. The remaining disciples visit him, sent apparently by God, and Judas (Harvey Keitel) reveals the angel to be Satan, the girl instantaneously becoming a pillar of flame (an iconographic representation of the Devil that occurs throughout the film).

Jesus crawls from his deathbed and, as Jerusalem burns around him, drags himself to his knees to beg forgiveness from God.

The isolated blazes and smoke that surrounds him stand in for the fires of hell, symbolising his descent into temptation and his unwitting allegiance with Satan in this altered world. He raises his face to the heavens and, arms outstretched, pleads: 'I want to be your son. I want to pay the price. I want to be crucified and rise again. I want to be the Messiah'. With these words, he is returned to the cross, the film rejoining the moment before the angel appeared to him. He wears the crown of thorns once more, the blood seeps once again from his wounds. As he surveys the scene, he accepts his place, crying out 'It is accomplished!' in exultant jubilation, contrasting with the wide-eyed desperation of his previous appeal to God in that alternative realm. He murmurs the words once more before closing his eyes for the last time.

Clearly, Donnie's sacrifice echoes the biblical narrative of Jesus' crucifixion. Structurally, however, Scorsese's film also includes a parallel world sequence similar to *Donnie Darko*, whereby Jesus is able to live and experience an existence divergent to the reality that resumes at the film's conclusion. Donnie, like Jesus in *Last Temptation*, will ultimately reject the alternative, thus condemning himself to death. Interestingly, both Donnie and Jesus have a supernatural guide through their alternative realm. Jesus is taken through the potential world by Satan, who prompts his actions and fits him for that other existence. Likewise, in the potential world of *Donnie Darko*, Donnie is visited and guided by a mysterious entity who adopts the name and form of Gretchen's eventual killer: he is called Frank and appears in a giant bunny costume.

In contrast to *Donnie Darko*, it could be said that Jesus' final temptation is in fact a dream sequence: a series of visions he experiences while delirious and near death on the cross. This assertion might be supported by the temporal structure of the potential world that he is led into, whereby chronological shifts take us through choice moments from his whole lifetime up until his old age. However, the notion of a dream or vision does not account for the imperative nature of Jesus' choice, which the film insists upon. It is crucial to the story that Jesus is faced with the real choice of an existence in a world where he is the Messiah or an existence elsewhere, in which he is mortal. His decision to return thus comes after having experienced mortality fully, for a whole lifetime, and rejecting it. This is a different choice than simply waking up or remaining in dreams (and, as we have seen in the earlier part of this study, that choice is rarely made knowingly by characters). Were this a film in which the supernatural had never featured, then the dream argument would carry real weight, as it would be consistent with the logic of the fictional world as presented. However, this is a film in which the supernatural is regularly a facet of scenes, not least when Jesus is seen to cure the blind, raise the dead and tear out his own heart. Thus, it is conceivable within this structure of possibility that Satan would be able to give Jesus a whole mortal lifetime, rather than just a series of key images that fit into the duration of his unconscious period on the cross. The ellipsis that occurs in the film's editing of the potential world sequence can therefore be read simply as a conventional feature of narrative cinema: we never question the fact that we do not see every last detail from a character's life in most films. Scorsese, after all, is the director of the sequence, not Satan.

Both *Donnie Darko* and *Last Temptation* can be read as inversions of the narrative of *It's a Wonderful Life*, a film discussed more fully in the following chapter. An early review of Scorsese's film makes precisely this point, concluding that 'To a filmwise viewer, the cumulative effect of all this resembles nothing so much as an inverted variation on Frank Capra's *It's a Wonderful Life*...Jesus is made to see that it is only by dying that his life will make a difference, that he cannot forsake his Father and future supporters because of his own acknowledged selfishness and unfaithfulness'.[7] Indeed, Jesus' final plea to God to be returned to reality once more echoes the style and tone of George Bailey's desperate request made in the potential world of Pottersville: 'I want to live again. I want to live again. Please, God, let me live again'. Jesus, however, does not ask God for life, but for death and resurrection. Likewise, Donnie does not seek to regain his old life, but rather to forfeit life altogether. It is possible to see Donnie's death in similarly spiritual terms to Jesus', according to the logic that his time-reversal cements the existence of a higher authority. As Anne Frisbie suggests, 'He's sacrificed himself to prove that God exists, that God is indeed sovereign over everything – and if God exists then no one dies alone, it is safe to die, and the world doesn't have to come to an end. His death does change the future, profoundly, but he laughs because he's learned that death isn't the worst thing that can happen to a person, not by half'.[8] Similarly, George Bailey's returning to his life in Bedford Falls affirms the existence of a higher authority, proving that Clarence, his ethereal guide through the potential world, is indeed an angel.

Kelly's, Scorsese's and Capra's films all provide a spiritual explanation for the temporary existence of a potential world, in contrast to *Back to the Future* which instead uses science (fiction) to account for the discrepancy. This tendency persists in yet another inversion of the *It's a Wonderful Life* story, *The Family Man* (Brett Ratner, 2000) in which a wall street banker (Nicholas Cage) is transported to a world in which he didn't leave his fiancée (Téa Leoni) at an airport and instead they married, had a family and found a version of happiness together. In this film, then, the central character comes to realize that his life is not wonderful at all, and that he had missed a vital opportunity for happiness many years previous. Again, as with the films already discussed, the transition to the potential world is facilitated by a spiritual entity (Don Cheadle) who visits him there and provides partial guidance before returning him to his former life. From there, he takes steps to achieve the existence he briefly experienced, tracking down his former fiancée and, in the film's final scene, persuading *her* not to get on a plane.

We can appreciate that, even in narratives that are altered or inverted versions, *It's a Wonderful Life* has provided a structure and tone replicated in a series of films made after its release. Capra's film can thus be regarded as an archetype of a kind of film that presents its central character with a potential world in which their existence, or non-existence, profoundly affects the shape and progression of events. Most significant here is the fact that the characters in such films are presented with a potential world that is as tangible and completely formed as the world they depart from, rather than constituting only a vision or a dream. As Robin Wood maintains in relation to *It's a Wonderful Life*:

> Pottersville – the vision of the town as it would have been if George had never existed, shown him by his guardian angel (Henry Travers) – is just as 'real' (or no more stylized than) Bedford Falls. The iconography of small-town comedy is exchanged, unmistakably for that of film noir, with police sirens, shooting in the streets, darkness, vicious dives, alcoholism, burlesque shows, strip clubs and the glitter and shadows of noir lighting.[9]

Wood's defining the two worlds in generic terms – the film noir of Pottersville against the 'small-town comedy' of Bedford Falls – illustrates in clear terms the gulf between the tonal structures of the potential world George crosses over into and the world he leaves behind. In this sense, we can draw upon a set of pervasive generic distinctions, inherited from the wider context of Hollywood cinema, to understand the places George Bailey encounters in the film. Crucially, as Wood's account makes plain, George experiences the world of Pottersville for real, finally coming to accept that this is a reality that could feasibly replace the world he has rejected (through a structure of revelation I detail in the following chapter). As with Jesus in Scorsese's film, it is integral that George faces the possibility of an actual existence in a potential world, rather than simply dreaming or hallucinating a world in which he was never born. The tangibility of his encounters in Pottersville drives George to vociferously, desperately plead for his life to be restored, having physically engaged with the consequences that an alternative entails.

Groundhog Day, the second film I discuss in detail in this section, is occasionally compared to Capra's film in terms of its narrative structure and its ultimately positive tenor. However, the film also diverges from the archetype by presenting the character with an onslaught of potential worlds through the structure of an ever-recurring day and also by resisting the inclusion of a spiritual entity that might provide some explanation for the emergence of the potential world cycle. Instead, the reasons for the central character's entrapment are left ambiguous and, in Ramis' film, he faces the infinitesimal succession of days alone.

Notes

1. The film weaves a little humour into this poignant exchange as, in a final shot, the boy next to Gretchen raises his hand and waves, apparently believing that Rose was gesturing to him.

2. Peter Matthews suggests that the film does not necessarily invite a straight moral choice between one reality and the other. In the now-vanished world, Donnie inadvertently reveals one character, Jim Cunningham's (Patrick Swayze) child pornography 'dungeon'. With that reality erased, the truth is never uncovered and so, as Matthews reasons, 'the hollowness of the moral interpretation is exposed: it would require us to trade off the lives of Gretchen, Rose, Samantha [Donnie's younger sister], and Frank [Gretchen's killer whom Donnie shoots dead] in exchange for Donnie's – *and* those of Cunningham's victims. The viewer is not meant to choose one over the other, but instead to accept their dual existence as variations on a theme [emphasis in original]'. Peter Matthews 'Spinoza's Stone: *The Logic of Donnie Darko,' Post Script* vol. 25, no. 1, Fall 2005, p. 46.

3. Richard Kelly's term for this parallel is 'The Tangent Universe,' as explained in a fictional work credited to one of the film's characters and included in the accompanying book of the film. Richard Kelly *The Donnie Darko Book* London: Faber & Faber, 2003, p. 108.

4. Ibid. xvi.

5. There seems to be an anomaly here. Scorsese's film was released in the year that *Donnie Darko* is set, 1988. It is strikingly odd that the community of Middlesex, Virginia (Donnie's hometown) should at one stage oppose the teaching of James Joyce because of his allegedly amoral stance, but should allow a film like *The Last Temptation of Christ*, which attracted widespread criticism from the religious right in America, to be screened without comment. Kitty Farmer (Beth Grant), the town's self-appointed moral zealot, would certainly have found controversy in the film's title alone.

6. Kelly, li.

7. 'Cart' 'The Last Temptation of Christ,' *Variety* 10 August 1988, p. 12 quoted in Kenneth Von Gunden *Postmodern Auteurs: Coppola, Lucas, De Palma, Spielberg and Scorsese* Jefferson, North Carolina, and London: McFarland & Company Inc., 1991, p. 160.

8. Anne Frisbie 'Donnie Darko: Darko and the Light,' *Metaphilm* 18 May, 2002 (http://metaphilm.com/philm.php?id=10_0_2_0 accessed 23/06/06) quoted in Matthews p. 38.

9. Robin Wood 'Ideology, Genre, Auteur' in L. Braudy & M. Cohen (eds.) *Film Theory and Criticism: Introductory Readings* Oxford: Oxford University Press, 1999, pp. 673–674.

6

RECLAIMING THE REAL

It's a Wonderful Life (Frank Capra, 1946)

The Stars Look Down

A short title sequence announces the beginning of the film. The credits are written on cards, each one pulled away to reveal the next set of titles on the card underneath and so on. Each of these cards is illustrated with hand-drawn Christmas images and scenes, placing the season in which the film takes place and also recalling the form of the original Christmas card that contained the short story upon which the film was based.[1] The introduction of the Christmas theme may also help to shape early expectations: few films set in the festive period end unhappily.[2] Indeed, the uplifting surge of the accompanying music in this sequence pre-empts the final emphatic upturn of the film's conclusion, as though reassuring us that events will turn out well in the end. But firstly we must wait and see how they almost turned out badly. Although this seasonal story does not end unhappily, quite the reverse, it does sincerely commit itself to the possibility of an unhappy ending. More specifically, it insists that the characters' emphatic joy in the film's final moments should matter precisely because of the pain which has brought them there.

The jubilatory chorus of the titles dissolves into a gentle, more subdued, music-box melody as prayers are spoken quietly in Bedford Falls. The melody we hear is a hymn, O Come All Ye Faithful. Their voices rise up magically in the cold night air so that, even though the speakers of those words are not seen, their prayers are still heard. In truth, we do not necessarily need to see the faces to guess the identities of some of the voices, or at least appreciate their generic importance on first viewing: locations such as the Gower chemist, the garage, George Bailey's old and new family homes are made recognizable either by immediate visual signs in the first two cases, or by associated voices in the second two. A female voice asking 'help my son George tonight' and children's voices saying 'something's the matter with daddy' and 'please bring daddy back' reveal that these homes are inhabited by George's mother in the first instance and his children in the second (making clear that the female voice in that house is their mother and his wife, Mary).[3] These expository features of the film's mise-en-scène and soundtrack combine, acting as signposts for visual and vocal identities just as a signpost first informed us that we were 'now entering

It's a Wonderful Life

Bedford Falls'. The succession of voices from all corners of the town creates the impression of a community sharing one central focus: George Bailey. Yet this union is not made in celebration, but rather in desperation. The film finds its low note very quickly. The quiet hesitancy of the music and the hushed reverence of the pleading voices – some almost cracking with emotion – combine to create a sombre mood. The strength of the pleas seems so heartfelt, so anxious, that their emotional force fills the air, carrying the voices out of the houses, through the people-less streets and into the darkness.

It is in the darkness that those prayers are heard and answered. The camera slowly pulls back from above the Bailey home, rising ever higher. The ascending motion of the camera begins a journey that will take us into an entirely new space high above the human world. A dissolve marks the transition from one space to another. The camera travels forward as it enters this new environment, continuing – from a reverse perspective – the movement of the upward journey made in the previous shot. The dissolve between shots replaces snowflakes with stars, their sharp brightness, distinct against the dark nothingness of space, rhyming with the earlier contrast of the white snow falling in the ink-black night. The complementary movements of the camera across the two scenes, the dissolve that marks their change, and the visual matching of snowflakes and stars combine to create a smooth transition from Bedford Falls to the skies above, attaching a feeling of naturalness to an extraordinary passage. In the new starry expanse, two wispy clouds of galaxies are briefly seen before a large planet sweeps past gracefully on its trajectory and disappears out of the frame. If any doubt remained as to where we were, the assertive appearance of the planet reassures us that we have entered outer space. As we journey from Bedford Falls to the outer reaches of the universe, the praying voices linger, faintly heard, as though – still propelled by sheer force of emotion – the words travel through the cosmos. After the planet has disappeared beyond the frame, the camera continues forward for a moment before resting on the two galaxy clouds glimpsed earlier, now positioned centrally within the frame.

The camera settles into stillness. The two clusters begin flashing and talking to one another. Judging from this behaviour, they were never galaxies at all, but something else entirely. Likewise, these inexplicable events occurring after such a dramatic shift of location might suggest that this isn't the kind of film we might first have taken it to be. The boundaries of its fictional world have expanded somewhat significantly beyond the small town of Bedford Falls.

Two galaxies become two angels. One is Joseph and the other is more senior, unnamed except for Joseph's calling him 'sir'. This chief of angels might be God.[4] Earlier, as we crossed intergalactic borders, a musical chorus of seraphic voices and strings mingled with the praying voices from Bedford Falls. That chorus becomes stronger as, having reached their destination, the human voices fade. The ethereal nature of the chorus, more prominent now, reaffirms our ascension into a celestial realm. In visual terms, the film has faced the universal dilemma of how to depict heaven. It is notable that many films resist portraying an image of heaven at all, and instead opt to depict angels visiting earth (cf. *Meet Joe Black* (Martin Brest, 1998), *Ghost* (Jerry Zucker, 1990), *Wings of Desire* (Wim Wenders, 1987), *The Bishop's Wife* (Henry Koster, 1947) etc.) thus staying literally and figuratively on firmer ground. The film resolves the issue of representation by providing an ambiguous portrayal of the divine kingdom in which the night sky is the dwelling place of angels which themselves are the stars above, or are at least able to take the form of stars. Spirituality and science fuse to form a scenario that hardly conforms to common perceptions of the solar system or heaven offered by scientists or believers. Crucially, by merging aspects of natural science and Christian religion, the film creates a world in which stars and angels are one in the same and any 'facts' about such things are wholly dependent upon the fantasy the fictional world proposes.

With this sort of freedom, Capra can decide where angels might be found, or how stars might speak to one another. By creating an ambiguous depiction of heaven, the film avoids taking its religious references too literally. In turn, we are perhaps discouraged from making any literal readings of our own. After all, the film's central interest is emphatically George Bailey, a focus shared by the praying townspeople of Bedford Falls and the collection of angels as they discuss him exclusively in the heavens. In fact, as the story devotes itself to George, the intervention of spirits from beyond the human realm becomes a *deus ex machina* of sorts, although not perhaps in the Classical sense of the term. Rather than solving the problems of the plot at a stroke[5] by descending into the world, Clarence merely provides George with the means to face and resolve certain problems for himself, if not *by* himself. Precisely what he faces will become a key concern in the following discussion.

In a film whose alternative vision of Bedford Falls is often described as dream-like or, particularly, nightmarish, this celestial framing also serves to discount the notion that George Bailey's vision is merely a dream.[6] Rather than hesitating over the possibility that the visions might be the product of George's imagination, the film introduces at a very early stage a divine force capable of shaping and reshaping the world. (Therefore, Clarence emphatically does not exist only in George's subconscious: he exists firmly beyond the consciousness of any living thing. In this way, his appearance has implications distinct from the conjuring up of an imaginary figure.) The concept of the world's events being 'shaped and reshaped' is in fact raised as the angels, having called Clarence, freeze an image of George Bailey during the showing of what would appear to be the edited highlights of his life thus far. This moment is often taken as Capra's manipulation of the film's story to evoke, expose or refer to the act of film projection itself. Just as significant, however, is the fact that the act of film projection seems to have been evoked, exposed or referred to for storytelling purposes: namely to demonstrate the extent of the powers available to those unearthly beings. They may stop the world at will. Clarence's later ability to make George experience a world in which he was never born therefore makes sense within a coherent pattern. Rather than constituting a break in continuity, as any break in temporality might, the freeze-frame complements exactly the kind of fantasy the film proposes. The margins of fictional possibility have been set especially wide almost from the start. The world of the film obeys a set of physical rules particular to itself, whereby prayers are sent through space to stars that are angels and flash when they talk and who review people's pasts as though they were films and stop these projections at will. Therefore, reinventing the world in order to make George Bailey an unknown entity in his own town does not overstretch plausible expectation. A certain kind of magic is occurring here that belongs entirely to the world of the film.

An Everyday Magic

It might be argued that magic of a less dramatic, or celestial, kind infuses the whole narrative of It's a Wonderful Life. Particularly, the motif of wishing, which itself displays a belief or half-belief in a kind of invisible magic, recurs throughout the film. Acts of wishing are made significant in the film as, in its very first moments, wishes made in the form of prayers are heard and acted upon. It seems appropriate, therefore, that we should linger upon these acts of wishing, principally because we have been shown the potential for wishes to form or reform destinies.

Our investment in the act of wishing is guided by the film's divulgence of certain information from the outset; namely that some words said into nothingness are unexpectedly heard and taken seriously (although wishes might just as easily be made without speech, and in some cases might benefit from remaining unsaid). But our certainty of this can hardly be shared by the film's characters. Where we have knowledge, they have only faith: the blind faith held by anyone who makes a wish. It is curious that, without any evidence of its effectiveness, people should continue to make wishes at all. It leads us to consider what exactly might be taking place when someone wishes for anything. The making of a wish is undoubtedly an expression of one's desires but, more than that, the act discloses one's knowledge, acknowledgement, of those desires. To wish is to state that one knows oneself truly enough to be able to crystallize desire into a few words or sentences. A wish made into nothingness, as some wishes are, is a hopeful request to something unseen but also a reminder to ourselves of certain hopes and dreams that we harbour.

The angels' vision of the world centres on the story of George Bailey, which they recount to Clarence. Within that story, they often watch him make wishes. However, of the wishes he makes in his life, only two of George's are ever granted: the wish that he had never been born and his final wish to live again.[7] (These wishes are also made when Clarence has adopted a more active role, no a longer passive observer). The two wishes bookend the film's Pottersville sequence, and the wish to live cancels out the wish to have never lived. The granting of George's second wish eradicates the existence of the first: meaning that, ultimately, he only has one wish granted: the wish to live again. George's wish of unbirth thus joins a whole series that are never realized. The film asks us to accept that angels are ever aware of mortal desires, and are ever able to intervene and grant certain desires. That the angels never enter George's life to grant any of his other wishes should therefore be a point of interest for us.

In considering this, let us stay for a while with George's wish: 'Please, God, let me live again!' Leland A. Poague begins his analysis of the film at this moment, interpreting the wish, 'uttered in close-up, George's elbows bearing his weight against the bridge rail with his fists pressed into his eyes' as a 'recognition that he had been living, living *at all*; asking to 'live again' acknowledges his life to date as his own, as a *life* [emphasis in original]'.[8] In Poague's terms, George's wish thus becomes synonymous with revelation, acceptance and (re)vision. This final theme is given particular importance in Poague's argument when he suggests that:

It's a Wonderful Life

> I imagine this recognition to be accompanied by some kind of inner vision, figured by George's rubbing of his eyes with his fists, in which George sees his life as his...I take it he is seeing the same film we are seeing, have just seen, are reseeing in memory.[9]

Interesting in this interpretation is the event of George's gaining sight, or rather insight, through the covering of his eyes. Not just covering but, through sheer emotional desperation, pressing his fists into them.

The anxious force of the action brings to mind George's attempt to wipe away the images of the world Clarence has shown him whilst simultaneously straining to hold on to the visions of his former life, trying to make its events tangible once more, reclaiming his life again.[10] And, if George sees his life properly now in the terms that Poague suggests, he implicitly did not see it accurately beforehand. Moreover, the film's handling of this moment means that the act of seeing is inextricably linked to his act of wishing. Of wishing he could live his life again. Following on from this, I would suggest that moments occur in the film in which George's wishes are similarly linked with his *inability* to see events as they really are; his *failure* to see his life as it really is. Within this pattern, there exist a series of false wishes before the final defining wish is made (which I take to be George's wish to live again, as it replaces his earlier wish to have never lived at all). Furthermore, these instances represent George's failure to realize or articulate his own worth and, instead, involve him espousing a series of aspirations that are expressions of certain desires throughout his life, but which involve a rejection of his present life, rather than incorporating facets of the society he knows, experiences and makes a difference to.

Moreover, I would propose that George's repeated inability to see his life properly is countered by Mary's constant ability to appreciate the value of his life for what it is, not what it might have been. As George's acts of wishing illustrate his clouded view, so Mary's counterpart acts, which are also sometimes wishes, encapsulate her clarity of vision. In this sense, divine intervention might never have been required precisely because Mary's presence had preserved George's life: she had always been aware of and willing to reveal the value of George's real life. Finally, I will suggest that the possibility of George's absence in Mary's life and Mary's in his, as revealed to George in the Pottersville sequence, finally drives him back to beg for his life to be restored. Implicitly, in a departure from Poague's argument, I take George's wish to be an acceptance of *their* life, rather than merely his own. A final acknowledgement of their wonderful life together. By presenting George with a dark fantasy of the world, the angels succeed in reacquainting him with the truth about his life with Mary.

Telling Wishes

A boy of about twelve bursts through the doors of a chemist's soda parlour, closes his eyes, holds the crossed fingers of one hand in the air and places his other hand on a counter-mounted cigar-lighter. Eyes closed, fingers crossed, he says aloud: 'I wish I had a million dollars' and flicks the lighter chamber forward to produce a flame.

For the boy, the sight of the flame is apparently a sign that the wish has been registered and, on seeing it, he calls out 'Hot Dog!' in satisfaction. George Bailey's (Bobbie Anderson) first wish of the film is made out loud and with the flimsiest guarantee of success. A million dollars might mean any number of things to George Bailey at this point. Certainly, it represents an imaginable amount of money, a tangible figure that any boy of twelve might pluck out of the air, such is the pervasiveness of the millionaire dream, and somewhat takes the place of any deeply felt desire. (In another film, with a different set of circumstances, the dramatic emphasis might have been placed upon George's effort to achieve this sum of money. This might propose the choice of demonstrating the greedy thrill of capitalism or, indeed, its ultimate limitations, bringing us somewhere close to the defining tone of Orson Welles' *Citizen Kane*, released six years earlier, which is the archetypal portrait of a man whose accumulation of mass wealth runs contrary to his happiness.) The tilt-and-flick of the lighter raises notions of the wish being quickly deposited or discarded, the cry of 'hot dog' signals it being cast aside, put from mind as soon as it is made. Both motifs dispel any sense that this wish is lingered over or that it represents the climax of long-held desire. The wish itself spurts from George's mouth with a speed and ease that would indicate a well-versed routine: made and forgotten until the same time tomorrow.

However, two children are in that soda parlour when George makes his wish. We do not see whether Mary Hatch (Jean Gale) made a wish in the same way when she entered but her proceeding actions in this scene would suggest that she did not. After a brief interjection from Violet Bick (Jeanine Anne Roose) and a lecture on the origin of coconuts, George bends down below the soda counter to scoop ice cream for Mary's chocolate sundae. Mary perches up on her stool and leans over the counter; her rising movement seemingly triggered automatically by George's disappearance under the counter, as though she were used to stealing secret moments of intimacy with him. A shot from behind Mary captures her lean over the counter and her asking, in a hushed voice: 'Is this the ear you can't hear on?' Then, her face newly framed in extreme close-up, Mary whispers into George's ear: 'George Bailey, I'll love you till the day I die'. The move to extreme close-up – the closest shot of the film so far – heightens the impact of Mary's words, enclosing her from the world as a sole focus of attention.

In synthesis with the change of shot, the performance skills of Jean Gale as a young Mary carry the significance of those words. As the camera moves from behind the actress to the extreme close-up in front of her, Gale slides her elbows further forward on the counter. The move

It's a Wonderful Life   *It's a Wonderful Life*

complements the camera's change of perspective and also gives the impression of Mary getting as close as she can to George without touching, of making her confession most intimately without being discovered. The hushed delivery of Mary's admission of love creates degrees of solemnity and reverence. Indeed, Gale's bowed head and low whisper are suggestive of a religious confession, an occasion where one is allowed the rare freedom to express seriously the otherwise unrepeatable secrets of the self without reproach. Gale shakes her head slightly and slowly as she speaks: her gentle movement punctuating the soft rhythm of her words and disclosing the emotion Mary experiences in saying them. The choice of shots and Gale's performance technique combine to convey the importance of Mary's words.

And Mary says these words to herself. No other character hears her confession of love: she makes sure of George's deafness to them before she speaks, Violet has left the shop and Mr Gower (H.B. Warner) does not appear from the back until George starts whistling again. In every sense Mary expresses them for herself, reaffirming her love for George in secret. The secrecy of the declaration is reminiscent of the act of wishing, of one's desire spoken to oneself. It follows, therefore, that comparisons might be drawn between its delivery and George's wish delivered moments earlier. George's wishing for a million dollars represented the fact that he had little that was definite to wish for: the out-loud declaration and lighter-trick affirmation exposed both the inherent lack of sincerity in his words and his lack of real faith in them coming true through this act. In this context, a million dollars is as good a thing as any to wish for and, as has been suggested, would constitute a commonly held desire among boys of George's age. Here was desire as a passing thought, however, quickly expelled and easily forgotten.

Instead of wishing for an event to happen to her, Mary expresses the fact of her undying love for George Bailey. The solemn secrecy of Mary's words evokes the ritual of wishing, yet her stated affirmation only follows the conventions of an actual wish. The replacement of a wish with a confession of sorts reveals that Mary does not need to wish, such is her uncanny sureness of her love at this early stage of her life. Whereas George's words represented a lack of tangible desire, Mary's words acknowledge the deep-felt resolution of her love for him. Where George appeals for an outside force to shape his destiny for him, Mary accepts her own potential to shape destiny for herself. We might reflect that sureness of this kind is extraordinary for a girl of Mary's years and could be easily dismissed as charming but childish dreaming. Yet, all the way into her adult life, Mary lives by those words spoken softly over the soda parlour counter. Her expression of everlasting love represents not only knowledge of her own thoughts and desires, but also knowledge of George strong enough to guarantee her love forever. Mary's first appearance therefore discloses the considerable extent to which she knows herself and knows George.

George, unaware of Mary's delicate expression, continues to speak of his longing to 'go out exploring someday' and have 'a couple of harems and maybe three or four wives'. This is the first mention of George's desire to travel and, coming immediately after his wish for a million dollars, might be similarly questioned on grounds of wisdom and sincerity. Again, we could merely dismiss George's wishes as 'charming but childish dreams'. Yet, like Mary, George stays true to one part of these desires, constantly returning to the dream of travel and exploration. Indeed, when we first encounter George as an adult, he is attempting to buy a case large enough for his voyages. Mr Gower has already supplied a suitable case and, when stopping by the drugstore to shake hands with his former employer, George (James Stewart) catches sight of the old cigar-lighter, puts his case down, places his hand on the lighter and repeats a wish from his youth: 'I wish I had a million dollars'. Dreams of travel thus become synonymous once more with dreams of fortune in George's life. Both wishes are repetitions from George's childhood and their re-enactment calls into question the extent to which he has progressed, grown up.

Certainly, the million-dollar wish hasn't changed at all: the same words delivered in the same way in precisely the same place. But the travel wish has also failed to develop over the years: indistinct talk of harems and multiple wives are replaced (during a conversation later that day with his father) by plans to 'build things...design new buildings...plan modern cities...all that stuff'. George's architectural ambitions in fact remain with him throughout his life, culminating in his building of Bailey Park and brought to the fore again when, in a moment of rage and despair after Uncle Billy has lost the eight thousand dollars, he smashes his model designs set up on his architect's table. George's desire to build seems to imply his desire for people to recognize his worth and abilities in the large, emphatic statement that a building or 'modern city' provides. It is also indicative of a desire to change a landscape, to reinvent surroundings and, presumably invent a place unlike his home of Bedford Falls, hence 'modern' cities.[11] Although Bailey Park is in many ways a 'new' way of living for the town's residents, it is significant that its buildings are modest, functional and none extend beyond two floors. Thus, they do not provide the kind of statement that George intended to make with his original designs. In a somewhat crueller extension of this theme, the model buildings on the tables in the Bailey house represent a miniaturized version of grand-scale designs.[12]

The coupled wishes for travel and fortune become linked in the two scenes discussed and their combination exposes George's habit of wishing for those things distanced and removed from his present existence. More specifically, they expound his inability to see the value in what lies immediately before him: the life he already has. Contrastingly, Mary's earlier expression of her love for George is an emphatic appreciation of what she sees before her. Rather than chasing distant, invisible horizons, Mary devotes herself to one tangible feature in her life: George Bailey. Unlike George, she is able to discover the value in her immediate everyday world, rather than dreaming of a world elsewhere. From an early stage, the film makes these key distinctions between the characters that will endure throughout the narrative.

Rescuing the Ordinary

These various references to wishing in the drugstore sequence prefigure a later scene in which George and Mary (Donna Reed) both make wishes while throwing stones at the old Granville house. This sequence again contrasts the characters' differing views of the world around them. After an eventful Charleston competition that concluded in the high school swimming pool, the pair stand in costumes raided from the locker room: him in a mismatched football uniform, her in an oversized bathrobe. At one point, in an attempt to stop Mary in her tracks as she walks away from him, George suggests throwing a rock at the Granville house. His subterfuge works, as she returns at a pace to discourage him: 'I love that old house'. George explains the ritual of throwing a stone at the house, breaking some glass and making a wish but Mary, still unconvinced, says that the old house is 'full of romance' and that she'd like to live there one day. Her reaction is curious as the view we gain of the house, rundown and slightly foreboding, doesn't match her sense of romance. Due to a visual representation of the Granville house that fails to justify the sentiments she expresses, we are asked to accept that Mary is seeing something else, something more than ordinary perception can offer. Certainly more than George, who 'wouldn't live in it as a ghost'.

George throws the first rock, picking out his window and smashing it with a satisfying tinkle, the throw depicted in a long shot from behind the couple. According to his particular brand of folklore, with the glass broken the wish can be made. However, when Mary asks George what he wished for, he responds:

> Well, not just one wish. A whole hatful, Mary. I know what I'm going to do tomorrow and the next day and the next year and the year after that. I'm shaking the dust of this crummy little town off my feet and I'm going to see the world. Italy, Greece, the Parthenon, the Coliseum. Then I'm going to college and see what they know...and then I'm going to *build* things. I'm gonna build airfields. I'm gonna build skyscrapers a hundred stories high. I'm gonna build bridges a mile long...

George's tour through the fantasy plan of his life reveals but one truth: he didn't wish for one thing at all. (In straightforward terms, there simply wasn't time to wish for all of those desires to take shape.) Instead, his plans are filled with a whole cacophony of details, with no singular desire emerging. As he expands upon the theme of his grandiose designs, Mary takes *her* turn to stop George in his tracks. Looking slowly across at the house, she picks up her own rock and tests its weight in her hand. George, distracted by her action, trails off. Why should Mary lose interest and try to break his flow? Why not stand and listen? It would appear that, having known and loved George for a great deal of her life, she recognizes that this fanciful portrait of a life spent elsewhere in a dreamland of travel and adventure contains precious few details of George's life now and the visionary impulse, which itself attracts Mary to him, threatens to take him away from her and away from his life in Bedford Falls. This troubles her not only because of her devotion to him but because she recognizes the importance of his vision and ambition to the town. Perhaps Mary glimpses, for the first time, the tragic fact that George does not know the value of his own life, and stops him.

Mary doesn't simply distract George. She throws her own rock, making one wish that binds them both together within the Granville house itself (her wish, it later emerges, is to live there with him). George's throwing of the rock is associated with his rejection of the town and everything in it – his action destroying a part of a house that, for him, might itself represent the dreary dustiness of this 'crummy little town'. But Mary's throw represents a reconnection with the house and with the town again. For both of them. It reverses the sentiments of George's speech: the rhymed percussive smash of her wish seeming to cancel out his and with it the possibility that any part of his might come true. Mary even adds that if the wish is told it might not come true, so hers is made and kept in silence (with neither George hearing nor, crucially, ourselves. This contrasts with the 'wish' made as a child, which she spoke out loud, and the wish she makes now, which really is a wish and thus remains unspoken). Coming after George's whole hatful of wishes, blurted out for the world to hear, her silent message becomes the more intriguing and meaningful. We are on familiar ground here, of course, with George making loud declarations that don't amount to anything real and Mary making unheard confessions that mean everything to her. Their first scene together, as children, followed this very pattern. Mary didn't exactly make a wish in the soda parlour, but she is willing to accept George's rules of wishing here, adding one of her own, to realize her dreams of a life with him.

More than that, she wishes that he could have a life of his own, not the dream of one found in the two-dimensional images of his postcards and National Geographic magazines. George's desire to escape Bedford Falls into a world of dreams is a desire to escape himself, to reject all that he has become up to that point. This fact becomes more and more pronounced in the film. But Mary sees this desire as ill-judged. She recognizes that George is lost to – what is in her eyes – the magnificence of his own existence. Loving him, having always loved him, she sees his life as the best anyone could have, to the extent that she is desperate to share any part of it with him.

If Mary's interrupting George is a rescue attempt of sorts, then she performs similar rescues at other points during the film. For example, Peter Bailey (Samuel S. Hinds) dies that evening, which leaves George running the building and loan (his hand effectively forced after a run-in with Potter). When younger brother Harry (Todd Karns) is offered a lucrative research position in his new father-in-law's business, George's dreams of adventure finally end. (Shortly before this realization, we are again given clues as to the nature of these dreams as George lists to Uncle Billy (Thomas Mitchell) the three most exciting sounds: anchor chains, plane motors and train whistles; the implication being that George likes the *sound* of travel, using it to fire his natural inclination to imagine. The tragedy of the film is that these sounds will always have to be a substitute for real

It's a Wonderful Life

travel, as George's potential to take flight is finally dismantled on his brother's return.) Having left a party celebrating Harry's return, George finds himself at Mary's house. And then he leaves. And then he returns for his hat. And then he reluctantly returns to speak on the telephone to an old school-friend, Sam Wainwright (Frank Albertson), to whom Mary is dubiously betrothed.[13] Tightly framed in close-up, they share the telephone as Sam speaks, their faces agonisingly close to one another without touching, in a tender composition of hesitancy, intimacy and private longing.

On Sam's offer of a job in plastics, George drops the phone and, grabbing Mary by the shoulders, says:

> Now you listen to me! I don't want any plastics! I don't want any ground floors, and I don't want to get married – ever – to anyone! You understand that? I want to do what I want to do. And you're...and...you're...

He never finishes. Instead, he breaks down, pulling Mary close to him, desperately crying out her name and smothering her face with kisses. The tears on his cheeks touch and mingle with those already on hers as she breathlessly repeats his name back to him. The fierce passion in George's words is unveiled as intense desire for Mary. His words, expressing a refusal of any kind of marriage, are betrayed by their delivery, loaded with emotional longing, and the couple's proximity to one another as they are physically 'married' within the tight frame. As he presses his face close against hers, George connects and reconnects with the realness of her features. Finally, after a life thus far spent dreaming of places in pictures, a figure of previously unknown desire is made wonderfully tangible to him. It is interesting to consider whether, without this discovery, without Mary coming back into his life, George would have recovered from the death of his dreams. It is doubtful that he would have been able to return to and reaccept his existence so quickly and so emphatically, given that the fear of being trapped in Bedford Falls had revealed itself to him so cruelly that day. Mary makes the reality of his life more bearable to him by making herself part of it, by becoming the centre of George's world in that moment and thus giving his life a steadier trajectory. In rediscovering Mary that night, George is essentially able to rediscover himself: to realize his special capacity for love and tenderness through his overwhelming desire for her. In claiming her so passionately, he reclaims his own life in the moment, an act he will repeat more emphatically at the film's conclusion.

Mary's ability to bring security and contentment to George highlights the fragility of his self-perceptions and sense of identity. This fragility scores through the entire film as an undercurrent that threatens to engulf him entirely (as it does before Clarence makes his visit) but Mary seems consistently to understand it, accept it. Even anticipate it. Later in the film, having vigorously rejected Mr Potter's (Lionel Barrymore) lucrative offer of a job, George returns home and enters his bedroom, where Mary is apparently sleeping. He walks slowly through the doorway, his shoulders slumped and his head bowed. His gaze settles and lingers upon his sleeping wife. He quietly closes the door before crossing over to the dressing table, removing his hat and jacket and looking into the dressing mirror. Potter's earlier offers of the nicest house in town, fine clothes for Mary, trips to New York and Europe, stay with him in his thoughts and become mingled with his own words from the past. First the multi-faceted wish made at the Granville house and then a later promise to lasso the moon for Mary. This memory occurs as he catches sight of Mary's embroidered depiction of George lassoing the moon. The humbleness of the picture's form becomes a succinct metaphor for the meek state George feels his life to be in when compared to the lifestyle Potter could offer. In a better state of mind, he might regard the embroidery as a symbol of Mary's enduring devotion to him and to his visions. However, memories of former dreams and promises only highlight George's overwhelming sense of failure and he tortures himself with them.

The potential for Mary's embroidered image of George lassoing the moon to convey different, even conflicting, meanings throughout the film resonates with a series of 'contradictory connotations' Robin Wood identifies in the cartoon's form. Wood states that 'From Mary's point of view, the picture is at once affectionate (acknowledging the hero's aspirations), mocking (reducing them to caricature), and possessive (reducing George to an image she creates and holds within her hands)'.[14] The ambiguity that Wood identifies in the cartoon represents an interchangeable set of meanings that, within the film, depend not only upon Mary's perspective but also, particularly in this scene, upon George's state of mind. Thus, in another moment, the embroidery could also possess a positive meaning for him; a fact that alludes to George's particularly volatile emotional condition throughout the film. More broadly, Wood's account of the cartoon emphasizes the extent to which even small, apparently incidental, elements within a film can represent a series of compound meanings, and how such objects can come to convey sometimes disparate meanings within a narrative structure.

George's thoughts, his recollections of Potter's words and his own, were overlaid on the film's soundtrack. They were not actual sounds in the film world, existing only in George's mind. It is the introduction of a real sound that draws him out of this reverie: Mary begins to sing 'Buffalo Gals', a song that became synonymous with their romantic youth in scenes outside the Granville house and at Mary's home.[15] Those scenes also became synonymous with relationships of realness and fantasy and, more specifically, the realness that Mary could offer in place of George's fantasies. It is appropriate, then, that Mary should choose that song now when interrupting George's imagined sounds with a sound from reality. Her interjection seems to remind him that she was also there when he made those wishes and promises, and she is still there now, as real as ever, even though those dreams never materialized.

Yet, Mary cannot hear the words that George hears. What then are we to make of her knowing interjection? Only someone with a special, verging on supernatural, knowledge of George could sense his mood simply from the way he walks into a room, without even looking at him. And yet, we know that Mary has known and loved George for a great deal of time. Particularly, she has always cherished George's real life over his fantasies of a life elsewhere: always cherished the fact of who he is rather than who he might be. She thus draws him out of his gloomy reverie by re-evoking the reality of their life together. And later in the scene, when he begins to question why she ever married him, she stops him in his tracks once more by revealing the fact of their real child that is growing inside her. She lays to rest George's fear of failure by showing the definiteness of his achievements: a wife and burgeoning family. It is not hard to imagine that George's insecurities might have led him back into making wishes. It's likely that the tone of those wishes would have fallen somewhere between earlier dreams of escape through travel and the later request to have never been born at all. Yet Mary seems profoundly sensitive to George's wishing once more, making sure that no bitter wish is offered in haste again. She replaces his wish for escape with the fact of his child: one wish he never thought to make.

Walking Among Shadows

When the film's events are taken in this way, we can view Clarence's intervention in George's life as being necessitated by Mary's temporary inability to save her husband. Mary has become saviour in the ways I have suggested: in more direct ways such as her remembrance of two thousand dollars in her handbag during the run on the Building and Loan, and more mysterious ways such as her reintroduction into his life on the very night when his father dies. George's fragility always seemed to have been known, accepted, even anticipated by Mary as an imperfection that cannot ever be completely subdued, that she would never try to completely subdue, as it forms a part of the whole man she loves so dearly. Thus, to her, it is no imperfection at all, but a facet of the perfection she recognizes in George. In understanding him better than anyone (and there is no other character who seems to replicate her special closeness to George)[16], she recognizes where happiness could lie for him, but also sees that he might sometimes overlook the possibility of happiness in moments of self-doubt, frustration or despondence. With the benefit of immortality and hindsight, the company of angels also recognize the value of George Bailey's life. Yet, Mary's recognition is the more remarkable because it is instinctive: formed without supernatural certainty or foreknowledge. Her influence and achievement is such that, when she becomes momentarily estranged from the workings of George's mind, it actually requires a divine intervention to straighten matters out. It is as though a power beyond the realms of the mortal world is needed to provide the help that Mary has throughout George's life.

Let us return to George then, somewhere near the end, standing on a bridge and pleading with all he has for the chance to live again. What has brought him here? What has the potential world of Pottersville revealed that has made him so dramatically reverse his earlier death wish? Donald C. Willis suggests that 'what finally moves [George] to plead to be restored to life is a sense of not belonging anywhere, to anyone; an exaggerated, absolute sense of what one can feel in life, an extension of feelings of alienation, loneliness, and rootlessness'.[17] Willis' assertion relates to Pottersville in general, and the phenomenon of George being unknown to everyone found there. Before, in the reality of Bedford Falls, he was profoundly familiar to almost everyone in the town. This much is concluded in Willis' succinct assessment that 'He's life to them, and they're life to him'.[18] It is hardly contestable that the overall impact of Pottersville weighs upon George in some of the ways Willis suggests. Yet, this broader interpretation does not account for the manner in which the Pottersville sequence builds structurally to a definite climactic event that finally sends George running back to beg for his life. Let us make that proposed climax our concern here.

George's desperate plea to reverse his wish of un-birth brings to mind (and has brought to the minds of many critics) the fervent appeal made by Ebenezer Scrooge to the Ghost of Christmas Yet To Come: 'Assure me that I yet may change these shadows you have shown me, by an altered life!'[19] Scrooge's words are said at a gravestone, his own: the bitter facts of his life revealed to him in the passionless event of his death. The vision of his own death is to be Scrooge's last before waking; his final desire is to 'sponge away the writing on this stone' through comprehensive reform. The night time revelation reaches its climax at the graveside. George too visits a grave in Pottersville: his brother Harry's who, in this version of events, was never saved as a child by George and so perished. But George, unlike Scrooge, has one more vision to come, one more trauma to endure. Kneeling, having brushed the snow from Harry's grave, George turns to Clarence (Henry Travers) and, his tone now quiet, brittle, defeated, asks simply 'Where's Mary?' Clarence is at first evasive but George leaps to him, grabbing him by the collar, pleading 'I don't know how you know these things, but tell me – where is she?' As Clarence stalls further, George becomes more desperate: 'If you know where she is, tell me where my wife is'. On Clarence's statement that he's 'not supposed to tell', the camera moves to close-up, framing the pair together, enhancing an appreciation of both Clarence's entrapment and George's rising ferocity. Finally Clarence surrenders the fact that Mary's 'an old maid. She never married'. This revelation only feeds the growing violence of George's emotion. Grip ever tighter on Clarence, face contorted into a grimace of tortured passion, he visibly shakes as he begs relentlessly 'Where's Mary...Where is she...Where is she?' On learning that she's just about to close the library, he releases his hold on Clarence and flees. The old man falls to the ground, revealing the force with which he was being held.

George's claim to not know how Clarence 'knows these things' represents a lingering denial of the conditions proposed to him. The sentiment is somewhat lessened in comparison to his rejection of Harry's death seconds earlier but, nevertheless, he remains confused. His thoughts turn to Mary, as though the sight of her will prove things one way or another: if she is changed then the world is changed. A hierarchy of revelation is thus established as George progresses through Pottersville, beginning with details such as miraculously restored hearing, dry clothes and mended trees; then the altered Martini's – now Nick's – and Mr Gower; on through the strangeness of Pottersville with no Building and Loan, Violet Bick-turned-streetwalker, Bert and Ernie-turned-dark cynics; then visits to the Granville house, now in disrepair,[20] and his 'mother', now hard and bitter; before finally arriving at Harry's grave. Each step of the journey places more and more at stake for George as increasingly important facets of his life are made strange to him. And yet, despite this series of jolts, he still remains detached from the truth of his experiences. It becomes clear that the road through Pottersville is not ended – George cannot accept the truth of what he sees – until Mary is found. According to the established hierarchy, she is most important to George; the mere knowledge of her existence in Pottersville is not enough: he must see her with his own eyes. Again, if she is changed, the world is changed.

It's a Wonderful Life

George finds Mary as she leaves the library. She is dressed in a drab hat and coat, thick-framed glasses perch on her nose. She clutches a dowdy handbag, crossing both arms close across her body, giving her a look of timidity and diminishment as she looks meekly about her. She looks in excess of her years, 'flat and dried up'.[21] As George calls her name, she stops, but merely looks him up and down quiet and impassive, with no flicker of recognition. She passes by. George - framed in close-up, eyes wide in terror, beads of sweat forming on his face - calls after her and begins to pursue. But this only causes Mary to hurry away from him; the effort of holding her bag at pace unbalancing her step, causing her to move in an awkward, bent-over fashion. Her crooked stance emphasizes the change in Mary: she is become the old maid that Clarence described. Unable to accept this, George catches up to her and, turning her body towards his, holds her close. We cut to a tight close-up of them facing one another that recalls their earlier closeness during their shared phone conversation.

The correlation between the images only serves to emphasize the gulf between the two worlds, however, as this composition is a cruel distortion of that moment: Mary uses her hands to push and beat George away from her, horror forming across her features as she desperately tries to free herself. Finally she succeeds, fleeing into a nearby bar, but George follows her. Inside, swathes of people form a barrier between them - people whom George once knew, but who now look on him with blank indifference as he calls their names. He points through them towards Mary, crying out: 'that's my wife'. At this, Mary faints and collapses, as though George's declaration had finally, physically, overwhelmed her. We cut back to George in close-up as he first tries to reach Mary, calling out her name once more, but then falls into quiet despair. The sound of a police siren revives him and he turns away from the scene, eyes bulging in mad anguish. He calls out Clarence's name, as though recognizing a potential escape from this trauma-filled world, and makes for the exit. Outside Bert the cop accosts him, but George knocks him to the ground and runs off into the night, limbs flailing in crazed desperation. Bert's errant gunshots fail to halt him and, when we next see George, he has reached the bridge, ready to make his wish for restored life.

Just as Scrooge's final vision is his own gravestone, so George is finally confronted with a vision of Mary. And, as Scrooge's vision proves to be life changing, likewise George's final encounter drives him back to the bridge to wish desperately for his life again. Mary had always known George - knowing him was to love him - but now does not even recognize him, has never known him at all. Has never loved him. George's experiences are thus crucially different to Scrooge's. Whereas Scrooge observes the unhappy progression of his life invisibly, George is made to bear the trauma of being visible in the world, but not being recognized. The most painful consequence of this occurs as he meets Mary whose blank confusion turns quickly to terror. In this moment, George realizes that not being recognized by Mary is the same as having never existed at all. Her special knowledge of his existence was existence itself. To be *seen* by her was to *be*. This profound fusion consequently means that the eradication of his life is also the evaporation of *their* life. To deny his own life would be tantamount to stealing the life from Mary. And, as she appears in the Pottersville sequence, Mary has indeed had the life stolen from her. When George and Mary meet as strangers, they meet as two people who had never lived because they had never lived together. In Pottersville, George lives an imitation of life, having no identity in the world and so as near to death as one human can be. Mary, robbed of all joy and vigour, also leads only a colourless, distorted imitation of her former effervescent life, the effect of which is itself a death. Scrooge is moved to change when faced with the event of his own death. So fundamentally entwined are the lives of George and Mary that having never known one another would be synonymous with death itself. When Mary looks on George's features and sees nothing, when no glimmer of recognition emerges in her own expression, George effectively suffers his own death. And, when George cries out in the bar that she is his wife, Mary faints and collapses in a gesture that mimics the act of dying, re-evoking notions of George's wish to end his own wonderful life ending Mary's wonderful life as well. On returning to the bridge, begging for his life to be restored, George doesn't merely claim his life as his own: he acknowledges that his life was shared by Mary, and her life was shared by him. The life he wishes for is not his own, is not her own, but the life they led together. To experience a world in which he had never existed, was never recognized, distressed George profoundly, but Mary's strangeness to him, and crucially his strangeness to her, almost destroys him.

In their eagerness to emphasize that George reaccepts Bedford Falls, may critics overlook the fact that his wish is to be taken back to his wife and family. Just as the shocks in Pottersville formed a hierarchy that led to Mary, so when George opens his eyes again in Bedford Falls, he travels through a similar hierarchy of restored features (Bert the cop, Zuzu's petals restored to his pocket once more, his wrecked-again car, the Bedford falls sign, some townsfolk, the movie-house, the emporium, the building and loan, Mr Potter, his home, the bank examiners, the faulty banister-knob, his children) that lead finally to Mary as she enters their family home.[22] He pulls her close to him, smothering her face with kisses, holding onto her hair and face saying: 'Let me touch you! Are you real?' Once more, George connects with the realness of Mary's features, just as he did many years earlier. But now he acknowledges that realness, and in acknowledging understands Mary to be the crucial part of his life. In understanding Mary he accepts the fact – and, implicitly, the wonderfulness – of his own life. The words he spoke before his wish on the bridge, 'I don't care what happens to me', fulfil their true importance now: no event could threaten the joy of his life with Mary. Shame, imprisonment and poverty cannot diminish them.

In keeping with her special abilities throughout the film, Mary has provided a remedy for current difficulties by rounding up the townsfolk to shower George with money that will replace the missing eight thousand dollars. Through the fact that Potter is never punished for stealing that money, the film resists a conventional narrative resolution based upon the emphatic punishment of crime. Perhaps similar events might occur in the future: life will sometimes be difficult again.

Indeed, given *It's a Wonderful Life*'s ability and readiness to confront certain darker realities in the lives of its characters, Robin Wood has suggested that:

> The film recognizes explicitly that behind every Bedford Falls lurks a Pottersville, and implicitly that within every George Bailey lurks an Ethan Edwards of *The Searchers*. Potter, tempting George, is given the devil's insights into his suppressed desires. His remark, 'You once called me a warped, frustrated old man – now you're a warped, frustrated *young* man,' is amply supported by the evidence the film supplies [emphasis in original]. What is finally striking about the film's affirmation is the extreme precariousness of its basis; and Potter survives without remorse, his crime unexposed and unpunished.[23]

Wood's account succinctly captures the film's refusal to conveniently smooth out the underlying complexities and hardships that have affected – and may continue to affect – the lives of George Bailey and the wider community of Bedford Falls, Mary included. Wood's achievement here is to see Pottersville not only as an alternative to Bedford Falls, but as a *product* of some of the underlying tensions that exist there, embodied in the characters of George Bailey and Potter. Thus, the two worlds are not necessarily dichotomously opposed as societal perfection against imperfection, but rather Pottersville becomes a fantastic expression of some hardships and constraints that enter the lives of the residents of Bedford Falls and will continue to do so.

It is appropriate, therefore, that there is no easy balancing of justice through the discovery and punishment of Potter's crime against the Bailey's. Rather than seeing this ending as morally unsatisfactory, we might consider that George, in rediscovering his special union with Mary, embraces the fragile volatility of life that can deal out extreme joy or despair. George's brittle emotionality has always left him particularly susceptible to both, but as he rediscovers the life shared with Mary, he rediscovers the means to overcome darker days. Part of the film's achievement (and we must acknowledge that *It's a Wonderful Life* represents a number of different but significant achievements of which only some can be mentioned here) lies in its utilization of fantasy to reacquaint its central character with the facts of his own reality. This reacquainting is perfectly encapsulated in George's grabbing the loose banister knob, a potent symbol of humdrum everydayness, and kissing it gleefully when he returns home having magically visited the potential world of Pottersville. All of George's fantasies remain unrealized until his wish of unbirth is granted. Given the chance to live that dreadful fantasy as a reality, George eventually learns the value of his own real life and begs for the real world to be restored to him. His recognition of this stems finally from his not being recognized by Mary in Pottersville. By showing us the nature and history of those tensions as they arose (and were temporarily allayed by Mary) in reality, the film justifies the need for its fantastic interruption and integrates elements of fantasy and reality within a coherent pattern of events that lead, eventually, to George's rescue and resurrection.

Notes

1. Having the narrative take place at Christmas perhaps also begins the series of often-noted characteristics that the film shares with Charles Dickens' *A Christmas Carol*.

2. As Mark Glancy observes, this was particularly true in the war and post-war years in America. Glancy cites a number of films made in that period in which characters' 'lives are found to be lacking and dominated by selfish ambitions and cold materialism. Christmas then serves as the occasion and the solution for these ills, as humanism overcomes materialism, disunity gives way to unity and nearly miraculous reunions are granted to separated families or lovers' (H. Mark Glancy 'Dreaming of Christmas: Hollywood and the Second World War' in Mark Connelly (ed.) *Christmas at the Movies: Images of Christmas in American, British and European Cinema* London; New York: I.B Taurus, 2000, p. 60). The themes of reunion and return to stability clearly address an historical social need in America, and *It's a Wonderful Life*, released a year after the war, can be seen as belonging to this tradition. The key thematic deviation from Glancy's description, however, is that George Bailey does not have to overcome 'selfish ambition or cold materialism', but instead the weight of rejecting those qualities, embodied instead in the character of Potter.

3. The careful listener might also recognize the voice in one house as Bert's and the voice in the garage as Ernie's. Different versions of this opening sequence must exist as Robert B. Ray refers to Martini's voice being heard and matched by a shot of building complete with a flashing 'Martini's' sign. Ray even includes a frame of this image to illustrate his point, proving its existence in some versions of the film. Robert B. Ray *A Certain Tendency of the Hollywood Cinema 1930–1980* Princeton, N.J.: Princeton University Press, 1985, pp. 180–181.

4. Ray takes him unequivocally to be God (ibid. p. 182).

5. '*Deus ex machina*, the "god from the machine" who was lowered on to the stage by mechanical contrivance in some ancient Greek plays (notably those of Euripides) to solve the problems of the plot at a stroke'. Chris Baldick *Oxford Concise Dictionary of Literary Terms* New York: Oxford University Press, 2001, p. 64.

6. Ray Carney's comprehensive discussion of the film makes reference to the 'Dreamland' of Pottersville, a term that, I think, evokes the strong connection made structurally between the world George is introduced to and dreams or, indeed, nightmares (Ray Carney *American Vision: The Films of Frank Capra* Hannover: Wesleyan University Press; University Press of New England, 1996 pp. 377–435). It might lead us to say that the potential world shown to George is like a dream that he cannot wake from, although the crucial term here is 'like': in fact it is of paramount significant that the world in which George finds himself *is* a world, and that he is made to realise its tangibility, especially in relation to the characters he encounters and, particularly in relation to Mary. If Pottersville were a dream or nightmare that George could wake from and account for rationally, the effect would be somewhat different.

7. Clarence does suggest at one stage that his appearance is an answer to George's plea to God, made in Martini's bar, to be shown the way. But we have already seen that the angels' interest in George stemmed from the prayers of many others.

8. Leland A. Poague *Another Frank Capra* Cambridge: Cambridge University Press, 1995, p. 186.

9. Ibid.

10. George's reclamation of his own life, having seen it properly, contrasts starkly with another film made two years later. In *A Letter From an Unknown Woman* (Max Ophüls, 1948), Stefan is made to see the events of his life from the point of view of Lisa, his former lover and mother of his child, as detailed in a letter she sent to him. She is unknown to him up to that point and, in rediscovering Lisa through her letter, Stefan discovers unbearable truths about himself: Lisa was cruelly mistreated by him. A montage of moments from their brief life together reflects his realization. 'His response to finishing

the reading of the letter', as Stanley Cavell elucidates, 'is to stare out past it, as if calling up the film's images; and his response to the assault of the ensuing repeated images is to cover his eyes with the outspread fingers of both hands in a melodramatic gesture of horror and exhaustion'. (Stanley Cavell *Contesting Tears: The Hollywood Melodrama of the Unknown Woman* London: The University of Chicago Press, 1996 p. 81) Two characters, both covering their eyes having seen their lives properly for the first time; yet one balls his hands into fists, desperately trying to *reclaim* that life as his own while the other spreads his fingers to form a screen before his eyes, trying desperately to *reject* a life too painful to bear.

11. Just as a different turn in the narrative might have seen George pursuing his early dream of riches, thus aligning the character's story somewhat with Charles Foster Kane's amassing of riches and power, an equivalent turn could result in George chasing his desire to build magnificent 'modern' structures. This might bring him closer to Howard Roark, the central protagonist in King Vidor's *The Fountainhead*, released two years after *It's a Wonderful Life* and adapted by Ayn Rand from her 1943 novel. Roark, played by Gary Cooper, insists that the individualism of his designs remains intact, a stance he justifies in a famous climactic courtroom speech. The entwining of architecture, as an expression of personal ambition, with wide-ranging duplicity and eroticism creates a fictional world dramatically distinct from Capra's, providing one speculative portrait of what George's pursuit of his particular dream 'to build things' might entail.

12. A real way for George to move towards realizing his dream of building is to attend college, something the film makes clear he is capable of. But, of course, Harry's marriage and employment end that possibility.

13. Sam is shown on the other end of the phone in his office, reclining on his chair with a girl leaning over his shoulder, playing with his hand and blowing in his ear. When Sam asks George 'What are you trying to do – steal my girl?' he looks back at the girl behind him, inadvertently highlighting the insincerity of his concerns. In its brief portrait of Sam, the film constructs an image of success and wealth that is out of step with the wholesome values of Bedford Falls, rendering them unattractive alternatives. The path to the 'wide world' beyond Bedford Falls, which George himself professes a desire to follow, is thus shown to have certain undesirable consequences: foremost that George might turn into something like Sam Wainwright.

14. Robin Wood 'Ideology, Genre, Auteur' in L. Braudy & M. Cohen (eds.) *Film Theory and Criticism: Introductory Readings* Oxford: Oxford University Press, 1999, p. 673.

15. George and Mary sang 'Buffalo Gals' as they strolled after the eventful high school dance. Mary, in an apparent attempt to recapture the mood of that evening, played it once more on her gramophone when George visited her house. In this scene, she also presented George with the embroidery that captured his words from their earlier night together, again suggesting her attempt to recapture the tender romance of that evening.

16. In fact, certain members of George's family actually seem to operate antagonistically in his life: Uncle Billy loses the eight thousand dollars, which raises the threat of bankruptcy and jail; Harry announces his life elsewhere, leaving George to run the Buildings and Loan; his father's last wish is for George to abandon his dreams and stay in Bedford Falls to run the family business.

17. Donald C. Willis *The Films of Frank Capra* Metuchen, N.J: Scarecrow Press, 1974, p. 71.

18. Ibid. p. 72.

19. Charles Dickens *The Christmas Books* London: Penguin Books Ltd., 1994, p. 70.

20. This is markedly different to the romanticised disrepair of the Granville house earlier in the film when it became the location of George and Mary's honeymoon. In the Pottersville sequence, Capra physically darkens the house to a far greater extent than before, with Ernie's cab-spotlight throwing oppressive, gothic shadows when it is shone upon the building's façade.
21. This description is supplied in the film's screenplay. Frank Capra, Frances Goodrich & Albert Hackett *It's a Wonderful Life* California: O.S.P Publishing Inc., reprinted 1994.
22. A similar hierarchy exists much earlier in the film, one that also leads finally to Mary and the family she has made with George. When the praying voices are heard in those first few moments, we hear the thoughts of a range of different characters (Mr Gower, Mrs Bailey, Bert, Ernie) before finally reaching Mary's pleas and then her children's, as though these final prayers will provide the ultimate impetus that propels all of the prayers skywards.
23. Wood, 'Ideology, Genre, Auteur,' p. 674.

7

THE SEARCH FOR TOMORROW

Groundhog Day (Harold Ramis, 1993)

Establishing Motifs

The film begins by fading up from blackness to a single shot of thin white clouds formed across a blue sky. This settled image is complemented by the gentle rhythm of a polka played out on light wind instruments: flutes and oboes with trumpets and trombones accompanying quietly, almost tentatively. The tranquil tone of both image and sound is not maintained, however, as the picture proceeds to cross-fade again and again into shots of clouds racing across different blue skies, speeded up to emphasize their gliding movement and their ever-rising, ever-falling forms. The visual change of tempo is echoed in the soundtrack as the band rises suddenly to a crescendo, picking up pace to begin a particularly tumultuous section of the music that contrasts sharply with the calmer preceding segment. Percussion instruments strike up and the deeper, more dynamic tones of the trumpets, tubas and trombones impose themselves with greater force upon the melody. That these alterations of style and pace in the images and music should combine and synthesize with one another raises notions of an intentioned change, of the shift in tone and pattern being crafted to create a wild ballet of dancing clouds and frantic music.

The nature of this short introductory sequence presents at least two themes that are expanded upon within *Groundhog Day*'s wider story. Most prominently, the accelerated motion of the image relates to the phenomenon of disrupted temporality that is fundamental to the film's narrative structure, whereby a string of potential worlds are rendered within the cycle of one day repeating: 2nd February, Groundhog Day. In this sense, we might view the title sequence as a thematic precursor to the film's broader concerns. Additionally, however, it is worth noting the fact that no force is shown to control this abnormal occurrence. As will be detailed in this discussion, there is an inclination later, during the film's cycle of recurring days, to suggest that Phil Connors (Bill Murray) is being tested, that some force deliberately reinvents the world in order for him to reinvent himself. Indeed, it could be argued that there is a strong sense of this in certain features of the narrative such as the mysterious blizzard that appears contrary to meteorological opinion and traps Phil in Punxsutawney. Yet, crucially, this remains just a sense as no such presence is referred

Groundhog Day

to explicitly, as it was emphatically in *It's a Wonderful Life*.[1] As the camera points towards the rolling skies we are not taken beyond the clouds, as we effectively are early on in Capra's film. Likewise, in this short introductory sequence, we observe the unusual shift in temporality without fully understanding it, beyond a familiar conventional use of speeded-up images in films. We might discount the sequence as simply a functional pre-emption of the film's main interests yet, read in the context of those main interests, the supernatural alteration in the opening titles also possesses an enigmatic quality that anticipates the tone of the ensuing narrative. An omniscient force never takes shape in *Groundhog Day*, as the film presents a world without clear natural reason, where inexplicable events can simply occur without necessarily being clearly motivated. In showing the accelerated flight of the clouds in this sequence, without revealing what force affects their behaviour, the film places the weight of relevance on the altered state itself (the hastened motion of the clouds) preferring to withhold the exact reasons for the temporal corruption. It therefore pre-echoes the film's overall storytelling strategy of resisting any reference to an 'embodied supernatural agency',[2] placing emphasis more upon the effects of the disrupted world than the force which causes disruption.[3]

Having introduced the possibility of a world in which the physical laws of time can be altered, the film introduces the character around which this distortion will centre. The blueness of the sky cross-fades slowly to another flatter blueness that fills the screen. The music also fades and an even-toned male voice is heard: '...someone said to me today "Phil, if you could be anywhere in the world, where would you like to be?" And I said to them: "Probably right about here..."' At this moment a hand appears from the right of the frame and gestures to a point on what is now revealed to be a blue-screen background. The camera slowly zooms out and pans right to reveal a TV weatherman delivering his report.

The weatherman, Phil Connors, is the film's central character and, as with most televised weather reports, Phil is standing in front of a blue background whilst the actual places he refers to are superimposed onto the television screen for the audience at home. Thus, when he pointed to the blue screen he was in fact referring on the TV screen to Nevada which, he informs us, will be 'the nation's high at seventy-nine today'. During the report, we cut to images on the TV monitor demonstrating the special effect the viewing public at home would see: Phil standing in front of a map of America. These shots draw attention to our initial view of Phil in front of the blue screen, which we return to again during the sequence.

It is perfectly conceivable that the whole sequence could have been shot in the more interesting way it would appear on the television screen, with the textured graphics of the map and weather symbols. Yet in resisting that singular perspective, the film encourages a consideration of Phil's appearance against the blue screen. The blankness of the screen constructs the space he occupies as a featureless, dislocated place. These issues of space and place are made potent later in the film as Phil's final transformation from cold cynic to warm optimist becomes synonymous with his acceptance of Punxsutawney as a home, rather than a trap. With that journey yet to be started, evidence of Phil's cynicism begins to emerge in the jaded smugness and ironic detachment with which his weather report is delivered. Murray's performance skills and style of delivery are crucial to this hollow portrayal. His doughy, saggy, worn-out face displays a kind of emotional neutrality that lacks any authentic expression; his lips do not curve far enough one way to form a convincing smile or far enough the other way to communicate genuine displeasure. His droopy eyes and slumped posture communicate a mood of perpetual apathy meaning that, even when he is making jokes or miming to blow away clouds during the report, he maintains a pronounced detachment to the activity. Murray has a control of his vocal register that allows him to deliver his lines in a low-key, almost monotonous style, coating Phil's every utterance with understated sarcasm. And, throughout the opening scenes, the actor maintains this style of vocal delivery: his unemphatic monotone allowing him to draw out words and the gaps between words as though it pains his character to even address fellow human beings. Even the lids of Murray's eyes seem too heavy, as though they could shut and stay shut at any time, so disenchanted is his character with the world around him.

Any suggestions of Phil's interior emotional self are effectively shrouded in this downbeat performance, which itself discloses a shallow, worn-out brand of human behaviour. This, certainly, forms part of Phil's humorous appeal now and throughout much of the film (drawing upon Murray's particular aptitude for droll humour built up over time in previous film roles such as Dr Peter Venkman in *Ghostbusters* (Ivan Reitman, 1984) and Frank Cross in *Scrooged* (Richard Donner, 1988)), but there is also an early sense of Phil's resistance to enthusiasm, as he selects a cynicism that withstands empathic interaction of any kind and successfully maintains distance between himself and his world. As has been suggested, Phil's eventual emotional awakening becomes fundamentally associated with his discovery of a place for himself within the world. Taken this way, it seems wholly appropriate that Phil's 'nowhere' self should be placed against the blank hue of a 'nowhere' space. The shots of Phil stood against the nowhere background provides a visual representation of a man who has cut adrift and isolated himself in his world. The simple placement of Phil against the empty blue screen conveys his character's situation without overstatement. Isolated against the stark blue of the screen background, he is just a man pointing to thin air and pretending it is the world. Crucially, the screen is a false image: one thing pretending to be something else, which correlates with Phil's performance as he fakes enthusiasm for his task of reading the weather in a way that barely conceals his sense of despondency. Phil's estrangement from the world is therefore evoked immediately in the film through the character's composition within, and interaction with, elements of the film's *mise en scène* in this opening scene.

The film resists an entirely bleak portrait of Phil, however, as the scene concludes with a brief glimpse of his unanticipated, impulsive attraction to another person and, therefore, hints at his potential for change. As he leaves the studio having delivered waspish responses to the studio anchorwoman (whom he nicknames 'hairdo', a term that alleges intellectual vacuity beneath her polished façade) a colleague draws his attention to Rita (Andie MacDowell) who will be his producer on the trip to Punxsutawney. Phil looks across to where his associate gestures, and his gaze remains there, as though he were involuntarily transfixed, despite the conversation continuing beside him. Murray opens his eyes slightly wider as he gazes across, providing a marked contrast to Phil's half-lid glances of derisory contempt which have previously defined his interactions with individuals. Likewise, he lets his expression relax from the taught, pained look of feigned discomfort he had adopted in conversations thus far. These slight changes in appearance constitute a reflex, unguarded response as Phil is momentarily drawn to the figure beyond the frame, subtly depicting the extent to which he is stopped in his tracks by Rita's presence. A reverse shot of Rita standing by the blue screen resembles his point of view. She holds her hands up and flexes her fingers, checking the effect of her movement on the monitor as though enchanted by the effect of the technology. A cut to the TV monitor replicates her view in close-up, showing her image on the screen, the blue of her jacket disappearing against the blue background, making it seem as though her hands and face were floating in the air as she plays with the visual effect she has created.

The film cuts back to a close-up of Phil's face as he stares at her, lingering on his moment of stillness as he is stopped in his tracks, moving closer to him in order to emphasize Rita's powerful effect on him. Murray performs the stillness to perfection: his eyes flicking up and down with the slightest movement like a child trying to comprehend the vision that has captivated him; the corner of his mouth forming into the faintest hint of a smile, as though he is absent-mindedly charmed by Rita's actions, the safeguards of sarcasm and scorn having deserted him.

At an extreme level of subtlety, Murray's deft changes of expression indicate Phil's potential for emotional affinity with another human, and the camera's lingering on his face emphasizes this effect. The few seconds of him gazing at Rita represent a fleeting transformation in his behaviour as he is momentarily silenced and stalled in his admiration for another. The film minimalistically suggests another dimension to Phil's character, unseen by those around him (as it remains hidden from others in this scene, with no other character appreciating his delicate change in behaviour) and apparently repressed by him in his life. Indeed, he jolts out of his reverie with the sarcastic quip 'Mmm mmm! She's fun...but not my kind of fun'. The depiction of Phil in this brief moment intimates that an affecting sensitivity exists behind the veneer he allows the world

Groundhog Day

to see. Indeed, it exposes his behaviour elsewhere as an act, suggesting it to be a defence which restricts others glimpsing the unchecked vulnerability he displays in that brief moment gazing at Rita. These seconds prove crucial in establishing the character's underlying enchantment with Rita, explaining the truth of his pursuit of her in the cycle of days, and also transitorily uncovering his propensity for sensitive engagement with his world. This means that his eventual transfiguration into town hero and devoted lover, each involving a heightened sensitivity and level of engagement, do not constitute a total reversal of his characteristics, but rather the expansion of an interior characteristic that he previously keeps concealed from the world. Rita's behaviour in front of the screen is also crucial as she transforms the nature of the space he previously inhabited, converting it from a dull, disingenuous location to a site of enjoyment and playful experimentation. As he looks on, Phil perhaps appreciates this woman's ability to change the conditions of the world by finding positive potential where he only saw tiresome routine. This establishes a pattern that will be repeated later in the film, and discussed more fully later in this chapter, when Rita suggests to Phil that his entrapment within the unending cycle of days may in fact represent a wonderful opportunity rather than a curse. This item of advice will be seen to transform Phil's perspective on his predicament and thus profoundly change his behaviour within the string of potential worlds, eventually culminating in his escape. Likewise, Rita's visual depiction in the studio corresponds with a later assertion of Phil's, made on the same day as she offers her advice, that when she stands in the snow 'she looks like an angel'. His words lend a supernatural quality to Rita that aligns with her pivotal saviour-like words to Phil which, apparently, lead to his eventual release. In a film bereft of unearthly intervention, Rita is the nearest equivalent to an angel in the world, and this is referenced early on as she is seen ghostlike and ethereal on the TV monitor, near-transparent against the superimposed graphic images of the weather map. Again, in a film that resists depictions of a divine force, this strange image suggests an everyday visual depiction of a magical entity. And, indeed, Phil sees her behaviour as magical in this moment through her ability to change the terms of his environment in the small studio space. This magic will overtake him as he engages and re-engages with her in the seemingly endless succession of days.

The Death of Death

Phil's manifest lack of sincere expression or meaningful connection is such that he perhaps requires the limitless repetition of re-engagement with human society that the potential worlds provide to enable his final reawakening. This point is made plain as, having realized that the recurring days carry no lasting repercussion, Phil begins almost immediately to abuse this new freedom for his own hedonistic or perverse pleasure.[4] For example, he crashes a car, delivers a full kiss to his bewildered landlady, punches an annoying ex-classmate who has turned up in Punxsutawney selling life insurance, orders every dessert in a diner, smokes incessantly, robs a bank, gains information about a woman one day to seduce her the next, and then attempts to perfect this same trick in a series of unsuccessful efforts to seduce Rita. Finally, having reached his limit with the tedium of the world he finds himself in, he resolves that the only way to stop the endlessly repeating day is to kidnap and kill the groundhog (another Phil). His reasoning behind this action is that part of the Groundhog Day festival involves Phil the groundhog coming out of his burrow and predicting whether winter will pass or last according to whether he can 'see' his shadow. As Groundhog Day repeats, so groundhog Phil continues to predict that winter will continue (his 'words' translated by one of the town elders). In a show of twisted reasoning, Phil apparently interprets this as a prediction that *his* personal winter – the eternal, snowy day in Punxsutawney – will continue. According to this logic he declares, during his routine piece to camera at the beginning of the Groundhog ceremony, that 'There is no way this winter is ever going to end...as long as this groundhog keeps seeing his shadow. I don't see any other way out. He's gotta be stopped. And I have to stop him'. Walking away from the festivities, he appears later, telling Rita 'I've come to the end of me'; he proceeds to steal a truck containing the groundhog and speeds off. As he drives, pursued by the police, two town elders, and Rita and Larry, he puts the groundhog behind the wheel, maniacally advising him to check his mirrors and providing cautionary advice such as 'don't drive angry'. They end up in a quarry and, having apparently decided to end their lives, Phil drives them over a cliff.

Although possessing a manic humour and pace, this last act of Phil's is clearly distinct from the earlier hedonistic pursuits. Instead, it marks the climax of his growing despair at the tortuous predictability of his predicament. Phil takes himself to the edge of his world and throws himself off, forfeiting the chance to test its limits any further. Driving off the cliff thus represents a genuine attempt at suicide, as Phil believes he is capable of ending his life. But the attempt fails: Phil cannot die in this repeating world and 'next' morning he wakes up again in bed. Undeterred, he creatively tries out other ways of ending his life: dropping a toaster into his bathwater; stepping out in front of traffic.[5] Finally, we witness Phil throwing himself from a building on the town's main street. The camera tilts up to reveal him standing on a ledge, his coat and hair flapping in the breeze. We cut to a close-up of his face, his eyes narrowed into an expression of hopeless, bleak determination. A quick shot looking down at the empty street below precedes a cut back to a medium-shot of Phil on the ledge. Arms outstretched, he gently tilts his frame forward and we cut to a wider-shot capturing his descent in slow motion.

As he falls, his body turns slowly over in the air, all sense of control being lost. Arms outstretched, Phil seems to embrace this loss, relinquishing his time on earth and hoping for the grim release of death. This sequence is underscored by a lilting elegiac string arrangement that, along with the use of slow motion to prolong and intensify the fall, heightens the scene's poignancy and its quiet impact.

As we linger on the moment of falling, we linger on Phil's moment of desperation. None of his other suicides is afforded such a considered emotive treatment. Indeed, each of them is short and characterized by elements of ironic humour. Although the truck's fall is captured in slow-motion, the moment is undermined by Larry saying, with the vehicle lying in the ravine, 'he might be okay', at which point the truck bursts into a ball of flame leaving Larry to conclude

Groundhog Day

'well no, probably not now'; the moment the toaster is dropped into the bath is marked by the lights in the dining room briefly fading and the absent-minded landlady gasping in sudden realization ('so *that's* what he wanted it for'); and when Phil is knocked down by a lorry, he steps out quickly in front of it, opening and closing his mouth and hands stupidly like a flashing pelican beacon. The music in each of these preceding suicides does not match the mournful tone of the underscore during the leap from the building. Phil's final act of jumping from the tower is made poignant as it completes a sequence of suicides, whereas the others merely constituted parts of that chain. There is a finality that marks it as almost a real end to life.[6] Despite the variance in their portrayals, all of the examples share the visual motif of falling: the car falling through the air, the toaster falling into the bath, the camera movement producing the effect of Phil falling under the car and, finally, his fall from the building. This recurring theme helps to define the suicide attempts as gestures of resignation and attempted release from the world as Phil accepts that the conditions of his entrapment lie beyond his control. For a man whose profession it was to make predictions, life has lost its predictability. Even death, the one universal guarantee, has lost its bitter promise. As he realizes this properly, Phil falls into despair: without the certainty of death, life loses all meaning.[7]

This film finds potential, however, even in despair. In suggesting earlier that Phil had become emotionally estranged from the world, we might also reasonably suppose that his own feelings had become lost to him. Certainly, the tonal neutrality and cynical sarcasm that we noted in the opening scenes would suggest a failure of sincere human sentiment. Indeed, Phil's sarcasm surely acts as way of maintaining distance in situations, rather than engaging with them. Taken in this context, his misery during the suicide sequences constitutes a keenly felt emotional reaction to his condition in the world. Up to this point, he has been playing with the possibilities presented in the ever-repeating day, and playing different roles within them. But the pleasures of this play evaporate as the eternal day evolves into relentless purgatory and so, as he reaches into the seemingly hollow depths of despair, Phil experiences a crucial emotional response. The self-discovery is painful, but this pain reshapes Phil's perspective as, for the first time in the film, he touches something real.

Truth for Truth's Sake

Phil's 'trueness' manifests itself almost immediately as he shares with Rita the reality of his predicament. He chooses his moment in the diner, first announcing his half-belief that he must be a God ('not *the* God') and then treating Rita to a virtuoso tour of the lives of the customers in the diner, singling them out one by one and relaying information about them that he could not possibly know outside of the potential world cycle. If we persist with the theme of Phil's emotional reconnection with the world, this sequence eloquently illustrates his emphatic bond with those around him. As well as providing details about their family members and their backgrounds, Phil discloses revelations about these stranger's thoughts and dreams: Doris wants to see Paris before she dies, Debbie has doubts about her marriage, Gus wishes he'd stayed in the Navy. Phil, although oblivious to the fact, has systematically engaged, through listening, with a group of people for whom he previously held only cold disdain. In the recurring structure of days he is forgotten to everyone with each repeating dawn, but he remembers everything about them. Consequently, the ever-renewing day forces Phil to forge certain alliances with the world that he would not otherwise have attempted (and certainly not in Punxsutawney). He recounts their life stories as though he had lived in the town all of his life; as though it were his hometown. His knowledge of these people marks his unwitting entwinement with their community and, by definition, their town. Phil becomes inextricably involved with Punxsutawney, the small town whose values he used to loath and its inhabitants he used to despise. This can be read as him, unwittingly, beginning to find some kind of place within the world, a feature ostensibly missing in his first appearance against the blue 'nowhere' space at the beginning of the film. The repeating day has thus allowed Phil to connect with the town to the extent that he now behaves as if he had always lived there and, although facilitated through his inability to escape, as if he belonged there.

By exposing his uncanny relationship with the townspeople of Punxsutawney, Phil is also forging a new alliance with Rita, allowing her to share in his situation and consequently allowing himself to be seen properly for the first time by anyone in the film. The extent to which this bond is forming between the characters becomes clear as Rita asks what Phil knows about *her*. Exhibiting a new and unexpected emotional honesty, he replies at a slow, even pace:

> ...You like boats but not the ocean. You go to a lake in the summer with your family up in the mountains. There's a long wooden dock and a boathouse with boards missing from the roof, and a place you used to crawl underneath to be alone. You're a sucker for French poetry and rhinestones. You're very generous. You're kind to strangers and children. And when you stand in the snow, you look like an angel.

Words of this kind have not been spoken before in the film, certainly not by Phil, and Murray delivers the lines with a tenderness that his character has never before achieved. Indeed, the final line of the speech particularly displays a poetic flourish, using a simile to create an image of Rita that transcends everyday notions and conveys Phil's deep fondness of her. The words are instinctive, indexing directly Phil's deep affection for Rita in a way that is distinct from his ordinary, often self-consciously droll, expressions. The film devotes time and attention to this moment by settling in medium close-up to frame Phil as he speaks, switching only once to a reverse shot of Rita, appropriately capturing her amazement at words that short-circuit any perception of Phil she may have held. A gentle underscored string melody complements the poignancy of his words. Having allowed Rita to understand him a little better, Phil now shows his understanding of her. In recounting objects and places she has affection for, and describing her own affection for others, Phil consequently lays bare his affection for Rita. As the scene draws to an end, he uses language again to introduce vitality to the matter of their staying together that day, saying that 'In ten seconds Larry's going to come through that door and take you away from me but you can't let him. Please believe me. You've got to believe me'. Although delivered in a soft, delicate style, these words imbue the matter of Rita's staying with a melodramatic urgency, creating a narrative of her being taken away from him, rather than simply choosing to leave. The plea reveals Phil's need for someone to share his existential burden, but also makes clear his desire for Rita to stay close and understand, even though this closeness and understanding will come to nothing when the day repeats again and her knowledge of this moment evaporates. Phil strives only for the memory of a tangible connection with Rita. Convinced of his abilities to know unknowable truths and perhaps persuaded by the honesty and warmth of his confessions, she elects to stay with him.

Phil shares two truths with Rita that day. The first has been detailed: the nature of his temporal entrapment. The second truth, however, is told as the day draws to an end. Having spent the day together, the two lie on Phil's bed, vainly attempting to fend off sleep by reading poetry: Phil reads and Rita listens. This replaces an earlier scene in the film when Phil recited French poetry in an attempt to act as Rita's 'perfect man' (she studied French poetry at College). The nature of his reading in that instance, of reciting a poem he couldn't value in a language he didn't understand, exposed the hollowness of his act. That disingenuousness resounded in all of his behaviour during those scenes, as Phil attempted an empty construction of a persona he thought Rita would conveniently fall for. The film exposed this calculating insincerity through its depiction of Phil endlessly refining his behaviour based upon Rita's reactions to him over many days. Indeed, Harold Ramis comments upon one scene in the sequence in which Rita and Phil lie in the snow, and Phil desperately attempts to re-position himself exactly as he was the night before, hopelessly stage-managing the moment and killing any spontaneity it may have once held.[8]

Murray affects a stylized, almost theatrical, mode of performance during these sequences, making plain the manipulative superficiality of Phil's actions and words. Phil attempts to build a mental shopping list of Rita's likes and dislikes (commenting after one unsuccessful date 'no white chocolate, no fudge', crossing off two things to be avoided in the future based upon Rita's professed aversion to them) and, inevitably, his actions carry all of the profundity of someone running through such an itinerary. Rita often speaks of an uneasy sensation during these scenes, of things being not quite right and, indeed, she is spending time with a man trying relentlessly

Groundhog Day

to act like somebody else by acting on an extraordinary knowledge of her that she cannot begin to explain. Phil's one-dimensional portrayal is rewarded in those scenes only with a series of blows to the face, as Rita rejects his advances over and over again.

Compare, then, the comfortable image of the two now: lying on the bed, her face resting against his chest, his face pressed gently into the curls of her hair, her arm resting over his as he holds the book; both at the very edge of slumber.

Rita succumbs to sleep but Phil lies for a while, eyes open, before softly lifting Rita over on the bed, reaching across and pulling the blanket around her. With this careful – and caring – action completed, he reclines again on the bed, close to sleep. But before surrendering, he says a few words:

> What I wanted to say was…I think you're the kindest, sweetest, prettiest person…I've ever met in my life…I've never *seen* anyone that's nicer to people than you are…[he leans over and kisses her lightly on the cheek]…The first time I saw you…something happened to me. I never told you…but…I knew that I wanted to hold you as hard as I could…I don't deserve someone like you…but if I ever could…I swear I would love you… for the rest of my life.[9]

Phil's voice is calm and tender as he lingers between waking and sleeping. His own semi-consciousness highlights the emotional sincerity of his words: they are said without calculation or pretence. The pauses between phrases denote thoughtful deliberation as he searches to find words that might express what he feels, rather than those that he thinks Rita might want to hear.

These hesitations also suggest vulnerability, as if Phil's vocal eloquence of earlier scenes had deserted him once he begins to speak with tentative sincerity about himself. Importantly, he tells Rita of his love for her while she sleeps, when the articulation of that love cannot be reciprocated and he cannot benefit from his words. (We understand that Rita has not heard him when she stirs at the end of his speech and murmurs, 'Did you say something?').[10] This is a reversal of Phil's earlier attempts to seduce Rita, when his intentions were entirely selfish. He speaks the truth now, without agenda, without goal. These words are not said for himself, or even for Rita, they are said because they tell the truth about his feelings for her. It is enough for him that they are said. As Phil speaks, the underscored music incorporates an oboe, then a flute. It is apt that these wind instruments traditionally associated with the human voice should emerge in the moments when Phil himself finds his own voice. Phil describes an inexplicable feeling he had when he first saw Rita – of wanting to hold her – but now that feeling has become explicable to him: the repeating days have taught him to love Rita and thus embrace the emotion he once felt briefly, but never quite understood. As she sleeps, Rita misses his declaration of love. When she wakes, she will never know this scene took place at all.

Of Views and Viewing

The tender union evaporates as Phil wakes to the sound of Sonny and Cher on the radio alarm clock, looks over to where Rita was lying and, seeing she is no longer there, realizes the day has repeated again. He throws back the covers, rises from his bed and looks out of the window. This view yields further proof that it is 2nd February once again, but instead of registering disappointment, Phil turns around, looks about him, takes a deep breath and, fists clenched, walks purposefully out of the frame to the right. These actions mark a continuation of Phil's waking actions throughout the film, but also establish a change to that pattern. On the first Groundhog Day morning, he gets up, walks right to the small bathroom and splashes water on his face, before looking out of the window. On the second day, he repeats these actions, slightly disconcerted by the repeating music and dialogue on his radio alarm clock, the look out of the window telling him that 'yesterday' is today. Later, when Phil has resolved to take full self-indulgent advantage of the recurring structure, he repeats the pattern of behaviour, looking out of the window to check that he has another chance to do it all again, shouting out jubilantly 'Yes!' However, when he slips into the period of despair that leads to his repeated suicides, he is unable to face the reality that lies beyond the windowpane, instead lying motionless, wordlessly repeating the disc jockeys' banter before smashing the radio alarm clock in various ways in an effort to block out the fact that it is Groundhog Day again (a futile action that proves particularly fruitless in one instance as the smashed alarm clock continues to play through its broken speaker, as though mocking his desolation).

Looking out of the window becomes important in this waking pattern: firstly to register Phil's disdain for Punxsutawney, then his shock that the day has repeated, then to convey his glee that the opportunity for hedonistic pursuits has presented itself once again, and finally disillusionment when he cannot even look out of the window to check whether the day has reset once more. The pattern of looking, or not looking, out of the window becomes an index of Phil's emotional reactions to the repeating days. Therefore, his purposefulness in the scene after his night with Rita signifies an immediate and energetic change in his attitude and outlook.

Phil sees something in the world outside that he never saw before. Occurring directly after many sequences where he was unwilling to even get out of bed, this new behaviour registers as a dramatic adjustment to his emotional perspective.

It is perhaps appropriate to relate this new vigour to Rita's advice from the night before: 'I dunno Phil, maybe this isn't a curse, it just depends on how you look at it'. The comment is apparently innocuous, but Phil follows her counsel resolutely now by taking a different view of his situation and surroundings: his looking around and breathing deeply contribute to the impression of him 'taking in' the world in a way that is both new and refreshing to him. Without realizing, without ever knowing, Rita has presented the means by which Phil will eventually escape his recapitulating nightmare. Crucially, Phil is unaware that acting on her advice will affect him in this way, but is willing to trust that his life will be improved for it. Ultimately however, in terms of the film's wider narrative, the 'angel in the snow', as Phil called Rita, rescues the condemned man. George Bailey had Clarence, a real angel, to point him towards recovery. In a world without a heaven, or at least where heaven remains off-screen, the film finds its version of divine intervention within the human realm: someone who possesses the potential to be seen as an angel rescuing someone who possesses the potential to be seen as a hero.

A sequence thus begins in which Phil seizes the opportunities that life presents. Importantly, this sequence starts and ends with an old man on the street whom Phil has passed before but always managed to avoid (by sidestepping, pretending to search for his wallet and walking on, or saying 'I'll catch you tomorrow', a cruel joke that only Phil could truly understand). However, when confronted again on this occasion Phil pauses and takes out a bundle of money, begins to sort out a few notes but then hands over the entire amount to the amazed old man. We do not see the man for a while as the film focuses upon other elements of Phil's self-improvement: he learns to play the piano and ice sculpt, treats Larry and Rita with kindness and consideration, embraces a fellow-resident and more passionately (thus most amusingly) his annoying insurance-selling ex-classmate, Ned Ryerson (Stephen Tobolowsky), who had bothered him at the same time on each repeating day. But we return to the old man as Phil passes him near-to-collapse in an alleyway. Phil walks over to him and supports him, calling him 'Father', a surprising term that nonetheless evokes 'respect, love, and reverence'.[11] Phil takes him to hospital only to be informed later that the he has died, of old age.[12] He refuses to accept that this can happen ('not today') and a following scene shows Phil sitting with the old man in the diner, treating him to several courses of a nutritious meal. But this does not work, and we cut again to an image of the old man collapsed in another dark alleyway, with Phil kneeling over him, desperately urging him to breath. We move to a closer shot as Phil administers mouth-to-mouth resuscitation, but to no avail: the old man dies quietly, his last breath lingering as vapour in the cold night air. Phil leans forward and listens closely for any signs of life before resting back onto knees and looking up towards the black night sky.

Daughton reads this moment as Phil's realization that 'he is not a god: there are limits to what he can do...He cannot control other people; he can only work on himself'.[13] I might expand this by adding that Phil, having cheated the rules of life and death so many times, is suddenly faced with the real impact of death and made to suffer its consequences. Whereas his earlier

Groundhog Day

transcendence of life's rules made him powerful, he now feels the helplessness of one faced with true loss. His look up to the sky, beyond himself, acknowledges that helplessness and consequently relinquishes of any sense of power he might have once felt, perhaps even experiencing guilt for the endless times he took his own life as he kneels next to a man who had no choice over his life being taken. Just as the absence of death paralysed life's meaning, so this death forces Phil to contemplate life's realities: even if he should escapes this endless cycle of days, the old man will always be dead.[14]

And yet, Phil's gaze up to the skies, his acknowledgement that 'he is not a god' is a reaction to received and traditional notions of where god should be: in heaven above. If we read this in Phil's behaviour, it surely is an assumption that the character makes rather than an idea that the film proposes. After all, as asserted earlier, there is apparently no god-like presence in *Groundhog Day*. Phil is alone. It is certainly true that, by existing outside of ordinary temporality, Phil enjoys a greater awareness than those individuals around him who remain oblivious to the looping of time. This might breed a feeling of omniscience within him and, indeed, he even referred to himself (in jest) as being 'a god'. Yet, here Phil's sense of his own omniscience has become painful to him, just as the impossibility of death coincided earlier with his despair. By helplessly watching the old man dying over and over again, he has seen too much, more than any person should have to endure. The ruthlessness of destiny is felt too strongly; its force overwhelming him. As Phil kneels by the old man, he is brought to his knees, humbled by his experiences and defeated. To live beyond the boundaries of human existence causes him to face the unrelenting truths of ordinary life. We can only imagine that now, worn out and beaten, Phil wishes to break the cycle and rejoin the real world again. As he gazes out at the night sky, therefore, it is as though he gazes beyond the barrier of his world, searching fruitlessly for a place beyond the cycle of potential worlds that he finds himself belonging to. In this moment, we might see Phil pondering the nature and potentialities of his world as he acknowledges that, even under the spell of an enigmatic brand of magic, this world still carries some of the inevitable traumas found in the real world he has become divorced from.

Today is Tomorrow

The final Groundhog Day begins with Chekhov recited in the snow and ends with beauty captured in ice. The reading of Chekhov occurs in Phil's sentimental, but genuinely felt, eulogy to the people of Punxsutawney at the Groundhog Festival, a speech that showcases his re-discovered vocal eloquence, applied for entirely different purposes than those acerbic sideswipes of his past. Rita is clearly impressed by his display (while the rest of the assembled crowd is overwhelmed) and is drawn to him, but Phil is unable to stay with her, instead rushing off to perform a series of 'errands'. These errands are rather extraordinary: he catches a kid who falls from a tree, he changes a flat tyre on a group of old ladies' car and performs the Heimlich manoeuvre to save a choking man, pausing on his way out to light a lighterless-lady's cigarette. Listed like this, these activities form a catalogue of emphatic physical connections that Phil makes with the inhabitants of the world around him: catching the kid, jacking the old ladies' car, squeezing the man's gut, touching the end of the lady's cigarette with his lighter. (These actions bring to mind a similar sequence in It's a Wonderful Life where part of George's celebration at being part of the world once more involves him hugging his children, smothering Mary with kisses and, of course, kissing a loose banister-knob as it comes away in his hands.) Such connections make these people physically part of Phil's world but also situate him as an active part of theirs. He is made to live their lives with them.

This fact is expounded when later, as Phil dances with Rita at the Groundhog Ball, these people approach him and enthusiastically voice their thanks, reaffirming their bond with Phil. During this sequence, it also emerges that Phil has carried out deeds that day which we did not see: fixing a gentleman's back and counselling a jittery bride into marrying her groom. We might reasonably assume that more 'errands' have been performed for people who, like the boy in the tree, do not thank Phil at this occasion. Once again, the notion of Phil being part of a world is expressed visually. As different people approach and embrace him, he is also surrounded by the residents of Punxsutawney and, as the camera stays with his movement, is consistently positioned as the centre of their community. If there was a sense earlier of Punxsutawney becoming like Phil's hometown, then this feeling is re-evoked ever more emphatically here. Whereas before, in the diner, he was only able to expose his knowledge of the townsfolk, in one day he has ensured that he is as familiar to them through his deeds and words as they are to him. Rather than making inexplicable connections with the townspeople that left them puzzled and confused, Phil has allowed them to form authentic unions with him on their own terms. And, rather than passively absorbing their life stories, he has actively involved himself in the story of their lives. As they visit him one by one, they demonstrate their acceptance of him into their society. His central positioning is important within this sequence as it reinforces Phil's having found his place somewhere, at the heart of the community.

Groundhog Day

In accepting the everlasting cycle of Groundhog Days, Phil has accepted Punxsutawney and embraced the town and its people. And in turn he is accepted and embraced (literally expressed as the people who approach him at the ball each hug him enthusiastically). When comparing this scene of Phil surrounded by human warmth and affection with our first image of him isolated against the stark, featureless blue screen delivering his hollow routine to camera, the redemptive nature of his journey becomes clear.

There is a sense of a final culmination in this sequence, of the film reaching its climax (perhaps due to the assembly of familiar faces around Phil at the Ball that mirrors the congregated mass of townsfolk around George Bailey in *It's a Wonderful Life*'s final scene) yet, of course, Phil cannot share in this feeling. To him, this may be just another day in the cycle of repeats and tomorrow he may wake only to relive it all again. An appreciation of this forcefully reminds us of Phil's altruism: this string of deeds is performed without an ultimate personal reward. They might all have been enacted countless times before and may well be countless times again. And still he persists in rewarding and assisting those around him, even attending to small details such as allowing his piano teacher to take credit for his playing (he gives a soulful performance at the Ball) and providing the newlyweds with 'Wrestlemania' tickets. It is within the repetition of these events that Phil has found emotional satisfaction and, as this sequence makes emphatically clear, he becomes defined by his selfless actions.

To her bewilderment, Rita becomes caught up in events as she dances with Phil. Her only contact with him that day had been to witness his Chekov-inspired speech at the Groundhog Festival before he left to run 'errands' and now she sees him at the centre of the community, with townspeople thanking him and addressing him confusingly as 'Doctor' Connors and 'that nice

Groundhog Day

young man from the motor club'. Later, led by a force of emotion she hardly understands, she bids a winning amount of three hundred and thirty-nine dollars and eighty-eight cents for him at the evening's Bachelor Auction. Initially, the bidding is between two other women, and Rita is not seen to be part of the contest, so there is a particularly dramatic impact to her calling out her bid, glimpsed between the massed audience, holding aloft her purse to suggest that she had actually been counting out the amount whilst the other bidding war was taking place. Her declaration, coming unexpectedly, is thus made emphatic. That the amount of money should be so random leads us to reflect upon what it actually represents: all that Rita has in her purse, and what it symbolizes: Phil is worth all that she has. She walks forward, holds out her hand to him and claims him as hers.

In precise terms, although Rita could never understand this, her reaching up towards Phil also performs a symbolic function, beginning a process of her leading him back to the real world, ending his entrapment. This is his final recurring day and, at the film's conclusion, she seems crucial to the perpetual cycle being ended. As she takes Phil's hand in this moment, the film acknowledges her role as unwitting guide in his eventual return.

Later, the couple find themselves out in the snow, Phil chipping away at a block of ice and Rita seated, as though posing for a portrait. She is not a patient subject, however, making faux-complaints about the cold and teasing Phil about the sculpture's completion. Eventually it is finished and, the camera moving to a close-up to amplify the effect, Phil slowly turns the block around to present a face captured in ice: Rita looks upon an engraved image of herself. Crucially, this is not a mirror. It is only an impression of her features, the smoothness of the ice enhancing the delicacy of her beauty. What Rita sees is an emulation of her features, created by someone who knows that beauty profoundly ('I know your face so well, I could have done it with my eyes closed'.). He took an indefinable length of time, but Phil has learnt to devote himself totally to another person. By showing Rita his version of her, Phil expresses his love for her without words. It is possible that this moment seals a journey for both of them. Certainly, Phil's final gesture, having touched so many people, is to reach out to the one he truly loves. But what of Rita's journey? Earlier in the film, when Phil asked who her perfect guy might be she reeled off a list:

> First of all, he's too humble to know he's perfect... he's intelligent, supportive, funny...he's romantic and courageous...he's got a good body but doesn't have to look in the mirror every two minutes...he's kind, sensitive, gentle and he's not afraid to cry in front of me... he likes animals, children and he'll change poopy diapers...oh and he plays an instrument and he loves his mother.

The 'old' Phil interjected with snide comments about each of the virtues and, to a certain degree, we might take his point. The qualities she listed were an impossible A to Z of hollow clichés that pointed not towards perfection but towards one defining truth: Rita had no idea what her perfect man might be. In this sense, there is the suggestion that her life might have been unfulfilled in a similar way too, although perhaps not to the same extent as Phil's, and as they reach this point together, she is also completing a journey of her own. As Phil turns the ice-sculpture around he displays none of the attributes Rita required earlier[15] but its creation reveals the depth of his love for her. As he reveals his capability for genuine, selfless love, he reveals himself to be worthy of love. Earlier, the townspeople suggested to Rita that Phil might be worthy of *their* love as they approached again and again to reaffirm their bond with him. And now this wordless act of devotion seals Rita's conviction that Phil is worthy of *her* love. She chooses happiness with a man whilst her criteria for selection were temporarily forgotten. Phil is doubly discovered, by the people of Punxsutawney and by Rita. Unknown to the world no longer, he is reclaimed. In this moment, the perpetual chain is finally broken.

And tomorrow comes. Phil awakes, expecting Groundhog Day again, but instead Rita reaches across and shuts off the alarm, the two DJs having already launched into a patter that didn't exist yesterday (wonderfully, they play Sonny and Cher again, making us believe for a moment that it is still Groundhog Day). Phil lies, amazed, and traces the shape of Rita's arm, checking to see if it's really there. That established, he continues an earlier pattern by leaping to the window and checking outside. The snowscape outside confirms his belief and he turns around saying 'They're gone, they're all gone!' evoking Ebenezer Scrooge's 'It's Christmas Day! I haven't missed it!' and George Bailey's 'Zuzu's petals!' all at once. He jumps back onto the bed and says to Rita 'Do you know what today is? Today is tomorrow. It happened, you're here,' thus binding together her presence now and his happy escape. Conversation ensues before we leave the couple to themselves, a smooth pan across the room taking in the clock as it reads 6:01 before resting at the frosted windowpane.

Cross-fade to a shot of the guesthouse white-topped in a snow-blanketed landscape. The shot transition that moves us from interior to exterior also seems to move us in time, as though more than a few hours had passed since waking. The final scene is thus bracketed off as though it were an epilogue.[16] A cut moves us closer as Phil and Rita emerge through the front door, him saying: 'it's so beautiful'. They walk down the steps in silence as the camera slowly pans in, the two movements combining to bring characters and audience closer to one another. The couple stop at the foot of the steps and he says to her 'let's live here'. Phil chooses Punxsutawney as his hometown, acknowledging his profound affinity with it. His cycle of enlightenment has given him a lifetime's knowledge of the town to the extent that he can rejoin the world again as though he had always lived there. He can feel that he always belonged there. Again, we might compare Phil's emphatic sense of belonging with his visual positioning at the start of the film as he stood isolated in the middle of a blue 'nowhere'. Phil has found his *place* in the world at last. Rita accepts his suggestion with a lingering kiss before another thought comes to Phil's mind: as the kiss fades, he adds: 'we'll rent to start'. By introducing the clause, Phil shows primarily that he has not lost his sense of humour. In addition, however, these uncertain final words might represent the completion of Phil's journey, beyond his freedom from 2nd February. He cannot be certain of their future, whether their surroundings might one day change, but he is certain that their future will be spent together. His life was once founded upon professional prediction but, having endured predictability beyond human comprehension and having created perfection there, he now embraces the unknowable future with the woman whose love he cherishes. According to the film's redemptive logic, he has proved himself worthy of a tomorrow.

We cut to an image of them walking out into the white snowy landscape. The covering of snow allows features such as houses, trees, fences and cars to remain discernible, recognizable to any who knew the street. And yet, the newly settled snow has partially transformed the scene, making it distinct and different from yesterday. The snowscape symbolizes two aspects of Phil's position: it transforms the town to the extent that it is significantly different from his endless cycle of days spent there, encapsulating his release, and yet retains features that re-emphasize his sense of familiarity and belonging in Punxsutawney. The scene reinforces Phil's connection with his surroundings through his repeated engagement with them in the past and simultaneously reaffirms his release from the cycle of days as he embraces his future. Themes of settlement and change, familiarity and newness are balanced here. Phil and Rita face these possibilities together and, as they walk away from us, they walk together. This is the first time any character has walked away from a stationary camera position in the whole film. The inactivity of the camera represents a settlement, and encourages a feeling of settlement in the viewer: we should be satisfied with events now. V.F. Perkins has attended to such moments by suggesting that 'The apparent distance between the spectator and the characters on the screen is steadily increased, and the physical withdrawal detaches us psychologically, or helps us to detach ourselves, from the illusion'.[17] Such an effect occurs here, as we are encouraged to detach ourselves from the story of Rita and Phil, withdrawing our interest in their lives. A cross-fade to a shot of clouds now settled into normal motion completes our satisfaction with events: the world is once more as it should be. The fusion between character and narrative is most apparent now: an unexpected reinvention of the world having caused an unexpected reinvention of Phil's life.

Notes

1. Andrew Culbertson makes a similar point, suggesting that: '...what may be *Groundhog Day*'s most ingenious aspect, is that whatever is responsible for Phil's plight is never identified. Introducing the entity...would certainly have complicated what is essentially a minimalist plot. More significantly, it would have had the deleterious effect of cheapening Phil's transformation'. Andrew Culbertson, '*Revisiting Groundhog Day*,' Film Journal 2003: 1(5) http://www.thefilmjournal.com/issue5/groundhogday.html accessed 28/10/03.

2. Kristin Thompson *Storytelling in the New Hollywood: Understanding Classical Narrative Technique* London: Harvard University Press, 1999, p. 132.

3. It was, in fact, a problem for the studio that no explanation was offered in the script as to why Phil's world should re-shape in the way that it does. Eventually, the writer Danny Rubin was obliged to write a 'gypsy curse' scene that was actually filmed by Ramis to satisfy the studio executives. This scene was later cut from the final treatment, an agreement that had been reached by Ramis and Rubin before the section was even committed to film (Danny Rubin, telephone interview with author, 21 November 2003).

4. Suzanne M. Daughton situates hedonism as the third of the 'seven steps of Connor's transformation' that he must pass through, likening them to 'the seven gates through which Inanna, the upperworld goddess, must pass in her journey to surrender to the netherworld goddess, Ereshkigal'. The precise significance of this parallel is not attended to fully in Daughton's article, but her notion of 'seven steps' within *Groundhog Day* is a workable strategy with which to view Phil's journey. They are as follows: Cynicism, Alarm, Hedonism, Depression and Anger, Denial and Avoidance, Resignation, Acceptance and Growth. Suzanne M. Daughton 'The Spiritual Power of Redemptive Form: Steps Towards Transcendence in *Groundhog Day*' Critical Studies in Mass Communication No. 13, 1996, pp. 145–151.

5. There would appear to be other ways in which Phil attempts to kill himself: he later tells Rita that he has been 'stabbed, shot, poisoned, frozen, hung, electrocuted and burned'. We have, of course, witnessed only one of these events described (electrocution) in the succession of suicides shown in the film. We only become aware of a further catalogue of desperate attempts to escape this perpetual nightmare through Phil's words.

6. Even the irony of Larry's brief speech at the morgue ('He was a really, really great guy...I really, really liked him...a lot') cannot pierce the sombre tone of the event.

7. Matthew Coniam's existential reading of the film is useful here, particularly as he asserts that 'However unsatisfying life may seem to one in the throes of existential despair, the prospect of death's oblivion usually makes it seem more palatable'. Coniam's point is clearly made here: death can make life worth living. It follows, then, that once Phil's life contains no possibility of death, it loses any meaning. Matthew Coniam 'Rodents to Freedom,' *Philosophy Now*, June/July 2001, Vol. 32, p. 11.

8. Harold Ramis quoted in 'The Weight of Time' documentary, featured on the *Groundhog Day* Collector's Edition DVD, Columbia TriStar Home Entertainment, 2001.

9. A number of people, including the screenwriters Danny Rubin and Harold Ramis, wrote versions of this speech. Eventually, however, it was Bill Murray's own version that was used in the film. These words had particular poignancy for Murray, relating somewhat to aspects of his own life. It is interesting to reflect upon the ways in which the actor's emotional authenticity produces the authentic tone in the character's speech (Danny Rubin, 2003).

10. Daughton also reads Rita's response as an indication that Phil 'is finally sincere, because Rita is dozing off and hasn't really heard him' (Daughton, p. 149). Daughton's use of the word 'sincere' is central to an understanding of Phil's position at this point in the film, inviting an appreciation of his words being honest and genuine expressions of what he truly feels, and what he truly has become.

11. Daughton, p. 149. This assertion is given weight as Phil later refers to the man as 'pop' and 'dad,' establishing the term 'father' as part of a definite pattern.

12. As an example of the film's meticulous continuity, in the background of the hospital reception sits a young boy in a wheelchair, his leg in plaster. Eventually, Phil will save this boy from falling out of a tree, thus preventing the injury that causes him to be at the hospital.

13. Daughton pp. 149–150.

14. It is interesting to note the extent to which Phil's reaction to the old man's deaths resembles Kubler-Ross's five stages of death and dying: Denial, Anger, Bargaining, Depression, Acceptance (Kubler-Ross quoted in Daughton, p. 151). At first Phil refuses to accept that the man has died, and is angry that it should happen on that particular day. He then enters into a kind of bargain: if he feeds and looks after the man perhaps he won't die at all. When the old man dies anyway, his depression is marked by his hopeless attempts to keep him alive. His acceptance comes as leans back, looks towards the skies, and stops trying to prevent the inevitable.

15. Jude Davies 'Gender ethnicity and cultural crisis in *Falling Down* and *Groundhog Day*,' Screen 36:3, Autumn 1995, p. 228.

16. Kristin Thompson also sees the scene as an epilogue, timing it at one minute in length. (Thompson p. 131).

17. V.F. Perkins *Film as Film*, New York: Da Capo Press, Inc., 1993, p. 134

PART THREE: OTHER WORLDS

8

OTHER WORLDS

'What if all this is just a matter of semantics...Let's, let's just readjust our definitions. Let's redefine ourselves as the real world and *them* as the world of illusion and shadow...'

Henry, a 'fictional' character
(*The Purple Rose of Cairo*)

The final category of alternative world, Other worlds, represents perhaps the strongest manifestation of the dramatic device I have discussed thus far. Whereas the imagined worlds and potential worlds in films retain certain tangible connections to reality (in the first instance, the imagining character always remains in their real world, and in the second an altered version of the real world is presented, the significance of which emanates from its key dissimilarities to the reality the character previously knew) other worlds in films are divorced from reality to a greater extent, providing an ontological zone discontinuous to the real world that is left behind. In these films, an access point is provided into a realm dramatically distinct from the ordinary (fictional) world of the film. In this sense, characters travel literally into another world.

The evocation of other worlds in film narratives can be understood as part of a widespread investment in the subject, occurring across nationalities and cultures. The suggested existence of other worlds can be readily found in religion, folklore, myth and legend throughout history, often occurring in stories of the afterlife and represented in places such as Heaven, Hell, Naraka, Hades, Olympus, Valhalla etc. These stories propose the existence of unplottable realms beyond the spatio-temporal dimensions of our world and, of course, in certain cultures such stories have been taken as literal truths. Taken as fact, the proposition of a world beyond this one carries with it the promise of a life beyond and, thus, the comforting assertion that death is not an end. The convenience and security of this notion has subsequently been troubled in art and literature across the ages, from Greek mythology, where characters such as Orpheus, Theseus and Heracles cross over into the world of the dead, to the famous ghost visitations in fictional narratives such as *Hamlet* or *A Christmas Carol*, where inhabitants of the netherworld temporarily re-enter the realm of the living. The crossings over of the living and the dead between their respective dominions in these stories serve to disrupt the stable dividing line between the two worlds, constructing passage between them as a two-way process.

Therefore, just as it was unsurprising that dreams should have rapidly become a dramatic focus in cinema given that, as Ian Christie pointed out, they 'had long served artists as an excuse for fantasy and a means of exploring the forbidden and the impossible', so it is understandable that the world of the dead should constitute a central concern in certain film narratives, given the abundance of the theme elsewhere in literature and art. Naturally, the multitude of films depicting ghosts and angels inhabiting earth allude to a world elsewhere, from *Topper* (Norman Z. McLeod, 1937) to *The Sixth Sense* (M. Night Shyamalan, 1999) and beyond, but other films have devoted themselves more specifically to the task of representing the world of the living alongside the world of the dead within the same narrative framework. The nature of those representations is a point of interest here.

For example, Fritz Lang's *Liliom* (1934) and Michael Powell/Emeric Pressburger's *A Matter of Life and Death* (1946) both interpret the afterlife as a society concerned primarily with the preservation of natural law and order, with each film making their crucial dramatic focus an individual's violation of governing universal protocols. In Lang's film, the central character, Liliom (Charles Boyer), has committed suicide and, after death, finds himself taken up through the clouds and into the solar system by two strange entities who describe themselves as 'God's policemen'. As they journey through the stardust, arrangements of cherubs and angels are glimpsed, much to Liliom's surprise and delight. The trio's magical ascent takes them to a particular star and, travelling 'through' this image, they arrive at a building entitled simply *commissariat*. Liliom is amused to find that this establishment operates under a similar regime as police stations he knew well in the living world, with a desk clerk insisting upon silence and a sign instructing visitors that spitting is not permitted. In this world, however, signs are written in an array of glittering lights and the desk clerk has two dainty angelic wings sprouting from his back as he sits reading his *Paradis-midi* newspaper.

The 'police station' turns out to be a bureaucratic holding area for those who have committed suicide and here Liliom is presented with the choice of revisiting the living world for one day or being condemned to Purgatory. Unable to think of any matters he would need to settle on earth (despite the fact that he had mistreated his wife there before leaving her alone and heartbroken) he is sentenced to sixteen years in Purgatory before he is permitted to visit his (as yet unborn) child for one day only after he enquires after them. In this rendition of the heavenly world, Purgatory simply exists behind a side-door in the commissioner's office, unseen expect for a blast of light that emits when the door is opened. Little fuss is made of Liliom's entry into the room, as though he were merely being transferred to an adjoining cell of the kind found in police stations on earth. Indeed, the ordinariness of the place is exemplified as, when he reappears after sixteen years, Liliom has apparently aged by that very time span, his hair now grey, his youthful exuberance diminished, as if he were still subject to some of the everyday affects of the mortal world.

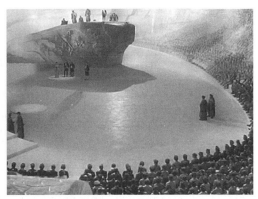

Liliom   *A Matter of Life and Death*

Similar to the tone of the afterlife world presented in *Liliom*, a key scene in *A Matter of Life and Death* involves a vast celestial courtroom in which the fate of Squadron Leader Peter Carter (David Niven) is decided.

The court abides by the same procedures and rules in the living world, with a judge, jury, council for the defence and council for the prosecution. In the gallery sits a colossal population of the deceased from all ages and nationalities; the film's vision of heaven being a kind of utopia in which diverse individuals of all backgrounds converse and communicate without conflict, a particularly potent notion given the film's post-war historical context. The question of unlawfulness which the court debates surrounds Peter's unwitting evasion of death due to an angel having failed to find him amidst a thick fog as his plane was shot down during the Second World War. A complication occurs when Peter meets and falls in love with an American radio operator whom he'd spoken to in what were to be his final moments on earth: he subsequently refuses to be taken from her. The court seeks to redress the balance of natural law in the same way one might seek to rectify a faulty balance sheet. Indeed, the heaven of *A Matter of Life and Death* involves a bureaucratic drive similar to the equivalent depiction in *Liliom* whereby human entities must be recorded and accounted for.

In keeping with this system of efficient book-keeping, the gates of heaven in Powell/Pressburger's film resemble a rather sterile-looking reception area in which new incumbents must register themselves in an official book before receiving their wings, neatly packed in transparent casing. In our first glimpse of this world, an angel-secretary shows a new arrival (Peter's now-deceased wingman, in fact) a vast records section beneath the check-in area. As they peer down at the endless shelves of documents she explains: 'Everyone on earth has a file. Russian, Chinese; black or white; rich or poor; Republican or Democrat'. The film thus unites the nationalities, classes and political sensibilities within the neat bureaucracy of its other world heaven, making all equal in a gargantuan system of filing and processing. The stiff lines of the angels' costumes and the smooth contours of the heaven sets contribute to this atmosphere of accuracy and efficiency, complemented by the decision to film the heaven sequences in black and white, and the earth sequences in colour, which gives the afterlife an appearance of sterility and rigid organization.

Like *Liliom*, *A Matter of Life and Death* physically places the world of the dead somewhere within the solar system. Both films share this representational strategy with *It's a Wonderful Life*, discussed earlier in this study. However, unlike Capra's film, these other examples proceed to provide a more solid depiction of the other world, each presenting a realm in which the customs and orders of the living world have become transposed in the pursuit of celestial law-keeping and universal balance. In Lang's film the idea of a divine police force is used and the joke is made regarding its similarity to the constabulary on earth; in Powell/Pressburger's film a celestial courtroom and records library are run like earthly equivalents. Each film provides the security of a benevolent community of the dead watching over the affairs of the living and intervening to provide justice and lawfulness. A further reassurance exists in the familiarity of these spaces, due to the repetition of familiar customs and orders, and the extent to which the next life will, in many ways, operate in a similar fashion to this one, without strangeness or threat. In this sense, both films could be seen to provide comforting versions of a potentially disconcerting concept.[1] Indeed, *A Matter of Life and Death* would seem to go further to suggest that the other world is very much like this one, only better.

These kinds of convenient reassurances do not run through all cinematic depictions of the afterlife as another world, however. The plot of *Flatliners* (Joel Schumacher, 1990), for example, involves a group of medical students who are coaxed into experimenting with the experiential effects of death by one of their peers, Nelson (Keifer Sutherland). This process involves one of their number being induced into a state of death for an agreed length of time and then brought back to life to share their insights. Nelson is the first to undergo this process and, as his electrocardiogram machine begins to flat-line, the film cuts to a mobile shot hurtling rapidly forward across an expanse of fields before the camera cranes up and over a large tree, as though Nelson's viewpoint were suddenly liberated from the ontological constraints of ordinary human perspective and movement. The change in visual perception signals that he has travelled across to the world of the dead. This sequence is underscored with exhilarating, rapidly paced music that complements the thrilling burst of accelerated, unfettered motion. The combination of sound and image imbues the space of the afterlife with a freedom and vitality distinct from the dark, grimy, near-gothic space of the makeshift operating theatre that Nelson leaves behind.[2]

The camera swoops over the tree and down to pick out three figures running through the high crops, their movement complementing the pace and rhythm of the film's compositional style in this sequence. A cut makes this group more distinct and we recognize them as three boys, captured in an image of playful exuberance, the sunlight filtering through and catching the golden hues of their hair and the tall flowers they run through, lending a warmth and light-hearted innocence to the composition.

A close-up reveals that one of the children closely resembles the adult Nelson, thus placing the character within the group as a younger version of himself. Suddenly, however, the light seems to drain from the environment and the music incorporates a discordant minor tone as the scene darkens spontaneously to night. With this transition, the landscape shifts from the warmth and comfort of childhood nostalgia to become strange and foreboding.

Flatliners

The new tension inherent in this environment is reciprocated in a series of inter-cut shots from the world of the living that depict Nelson's peers' increasingly frantic attempts to bring him back from the dead. Nelson's afterlife experience culminates in his coming face to face with another child, not seen previously, in a dark, claustrophobic alleyway before life is returned to him once more.

The shift in tone from light to dark in Nelson's other world experience defines the nature of his interaction with the world of the dead (and the interactions of his peers as, in turn, they undertake the same procedure). Rather than being a place of comfort and reassurance where benevolent spirits carefully watch over the mortal world, the afterlife in *Flatliners* is eventually revealed to be a malevolent environment centred upon retribution and repentance. Thus, the young boy that Nelson encounters at the end of his journey in the other world is revealed to

Flatliners

be a childhood acquaintance, Billy Mahoney (Joshua Rudoy), whom he bullied and chased. Nelson was the inadvertent cause of Billy's death as he threw rocks at him whilst Billy cowered in a tree: as Nelson's stone struck him, Billy fell. The film rewards Nelson's invasion of the other world by having Billy visit *his* world, brutally beating him over and over again in retribution for his childhood cruelty. At the film's climax, Nelson's only way to end these visitations is to return to the world of the dead and experience for himself the pain and fear of Billy's fall. Once this is done, the dead boy appears to forgive him and Nelson returns to the living world, finally brought back to life by the other students.

Flatliners presents the concept of traffic between the worlds of the dead and the worlds of the living in an extension of traditional stories of ghost visitations. In this sense, as well clearly belonging to a different culture and period, the film is generically distinct from both *Liliom* and *A Matter of Life and Death* as it shares traits more common in horror cinema. The narrative of a later film which might also be regarded as a horror story, *The Others* (Alejandro Amenábar, 2001), involves these two worlds being fused together, with the living and the dead (at first unwittingly) coexisting alongside one another, sharing the same space but in different dimensions. The outstanding strategic decision in this later film is the telling of the story from the perspective of the deceased, centring predominantly upon Grace (Nicole Kidman) and her two children (played by Alakina Mann and James Bentley), without disclosing the twin facts that they are dead and the 'ghosts' that inhabit their house are actually the living. This twist on the conventional haunted house story results in our regarding Grace and her children as living entities for the most part and encourages us to accept their complex emotional perspectives as if they were real people within the film's broader fictional world. Thus, a sympathetic bond is created between the audience and characters that would not necessarily be common in conventional ghost stories more usually concerned with the effects of the supernatural upon the living.[3]

One of the consequences of this overlaying of two worlds in the film is that actions in one world occasionally take effect in the other, so that when the living inhabitants take down all the curtains, for example, the curtains are removed in Grace's world and, try as she might, she cannot find them. (The issue of the curtains is made important as, when they were alive, her children suffered from an allergy to sunlight and, not yet knowing they are dead, Grace believes it will still harm them.) Except for when a psychic old woman (Renée Asherton), whom the new inhabitants have apparently hired to communicate with the dead, inhabits the body of her daughter, Grace doesn't see the living properly until the end of the film. This finally occurs when she discovers the living family engaged in a séance, the events of which reveal to her the horrifying truth that she committed suicide after she had smothered her children. We too do not see the living members clearly until this point and so Grace and her family appear real to us, their supernatural-ness concealed as the film stays within the world of the dead. And, indeed, within their own realm they are real. The film eventually crosses over into the world of the living during the séance scene when Grace shakes the table the group sit at and tears apart the sheets of paper the psychic old woman has been writing upon. Temporarily cutting to the world of the living, the film shows the table rocking with an invisible force and the paper ripping itself in midair to the shock of the assembled group. If any doubt lingered in our minds as to whether Grace was a ghost or not, this scene dispels it emphatically.

The Others

A similar visual crossover between the two worlds occurs at the film's conclusion when, unable to identify in conventional religious terms the world they now inhabit, Grace and her two children resolve to remain in their house: their one firm response to their predicament. In a final scene, we see the trio approach a window at the front of the house and look out. A shot from outside captures them, framed behind the glass pane barrier.

The Others

As the camera tracks back from the window, the image of the mother and her children slowly fades, as though the film were marking its return to the world of the living again, finally leaving Grace and her family in their world, visible no more.

As the three fade from view, they are replaced by an image of the world outside reflected on the glass and, sweeping down from the window, the camera finds the living inhabitants of that world as they prepare to leave the house for good. Only their young son, Victor (Alexander Vince), recognizes the presence of Grace and her family, looking up at the window with an expression of recognition. Indeed, throughout the film, it appeared that he alone possessed the ability to see and interact with the spirits, striking up a friendship with Grace's daughter, thus possessing an uncanny ability to see and interact with aspects of that other world, breaking the dimensional barrier that separates other characters from it.

The Others presents the world of the dead as being physically entwined with the world of the living and, further to this, suggests that this dimension can be accessed to a degree by individuals in possession of a special sight, as in the cases of Victor and the psychic old woman. The notion of hidden, unplottable realms within the world we know and experience is not uncommon, however, and is not particular to ghost stories. Popular works such as J.M. Barrie's Peter Pan or C.S.Lewis' The Lion, the Witch and the Wardrobe are examples of fictions in which passage to another world is found within this one. Barrie's characters fly to the magical realm of Neverland by sprinkling themselves with fairy dust and flying there; in Lewis' book a wardrobe functions as a magical portal to Narnia, a world dimensionally separate from our own. The structure and tone of this type of fiction has transferred into films, either through being directly adapted for the screen (both Peter Pan and The Lion, the Witch and the Wardrobe have had recent cinematic releases) or through influencing the narratives of children's films such as Labyrinth (Jim Henson, 1986) or Hook (Steven Spielberg, 1991).

References to other worlds of this sort are not necessarily restricted to tales of childhood adventure, however. Indeed, J.M. Barrie provides a somewhat darker incarnation of a neverland in a later play, Mary Rose. The story revolves around the character of Mary Rose who as a child disappears on the 'Island That Likes To Be Visited' in the middle of Loch Voshimid in the Outer Hebrides for thirty days, returning with no memory of any time having passed. The same happens to her on a later visit, three years after her marriage, but this time she is gone for eighteen years. When she returns Mary is unchanged, not knowing such a passage of time has elapsed, only to find that her husband and family have grown old in her absence. In the play, she haunts her family home until a chance meeting with her son frees her to return to the island. Barrie's play represents a sophisticated consideration of the consequences associated with the appearance of an alternative realm in the world. For the characters of Mary Rose, the occurrence does not represent a wonderful adventure but rather a dreadful, irreconcilable tragedy.[4]

Woody Allen explores similar consequences in his film The Purple Rose of Cairo (1985). Here Tom Baxter (Jeff Daniels), a character in a film also entitled 'The Purple Rose of Cairo,' is compelled to step out of the screen to meet a cinephilic audience member, Cecilia (Mia Farrow), to whom he is drawn and very quickly falls in love with.[5] This, naturally, causes a degree of anxiety in the world, not least that expressed by the actor who played Tom Baxter in the film, Gil Shepherd, who can see his burgeoning career being thrown onto the rocks by this outrageous turn of events. Gil travels to the small town where the incident took place and by chance meets with Cecilia, who at this stage has become strongly attracted to Tom ('I just met a wonderful new man. He's fictional, but you can't have everything'). Gil begins to pursue her as well and, finally, she is forced to choose between the reality that he offers and the fictionality that Tom represents. She eventually opts for Gil and returns home to pack her bags, with Tom resigned to a life lived on the other side of the screen. Returning to the theatre to meet Gil, however, Cecilia is told that he has fled back to Hollywood and she is made to realize that his words were insincere and self-serving. In tears, she enters the movie theatre as she always used to do and sits down to watch Fred Astaire and Ginger Rogers in *Top Hat*. As she sits in the darkness watching their swirling bodies on the screen, an enigmatic smile begins to form on Cecilia's face.

A fundamental attribute of Allen's film is the extent to which the world of the film that Tom leaves is represented *as a world*, replete with its own logic and order. The film is often related to Buster Keaton's *Sherlock Jr.* (discussed in Part One of this study) due to the shared vision of a character stepping in and out of a cinema screen, despite Allen's clear declaration that the earlier film was 'in no remote way an inspiration' for him.[6] It is worth emphasizing the distinctions between the films as *The Purple Rose of Cairo* belongs to the category of 'other worlds' rather than 'imagined worlds' precisely because it proposes the alternative world of the film-within-a-film to actually exist within the fictional world, whereas Buster only dreamed a world in *Sherlock Jr.* Thus, Tom's transgression from one world to another is seen to not only affect the inhabitants of Cecilia's 'real' world, but also chaotically disrupts the inhabitants of the 'film' world: the characters that exist within the world of 'The Purple Rose of Cairo'. They sit around, unable to continue with the plot of the film, venting their frustration, occasionally commenting upon and conversing with the people who watch them from the other side of the screen. Thus, these characters are defined as real people within their screen-world (and within the 'real' world, were they to step out of the screen also), capable of independent thought and idiosyncratic behaviour. Previous to Tom's departure, they apparently have merely been following a script as actors in the theatre might and, as real people, have possessed awareness that they were doing so. As a consequence, when a *maitre d'* in 'The Purple Rose of Cairo' realizes that he is no longer obliged to follow the pattern of the plot anymore, he turns to the band, shouts 'Hit it boys!' and improvises an elaborate, impressive, tap-dance routine rather than continuing to wait on his customers. Thus, the characters possess a consciousness beyond their role within the confines of the film's plot, making them complex beings within the narrative. In addition, the occupants of 'The Purple Rose of Cairo' world possess a spectrum of knowledge and experience particular only to their world, so Tom has no understanding of the concept of God, for example, because no such notion is contained within or referred to in his world. Instead, he only has an awareness of his film's writers, Irving Sachs and R.H. Levine, who are like Gods to him as they created everything he has ever known.

The film offers Cecilia a literal escape from her depression-era world, in which she is tied in an unhappy marriage to her abusive husband, Monk (Danny Aiello). At the film's conclusion, her world is proved to be more dreadful than she first thought, as the one person she thought she knew and trusted there, Gil, deserts her in an instant. (His surname is made bleakly ironic here as he turns out to be a poor kind of Shepherd.) Potentially, her life is made bleaker due to this revelation. In one sense, the film provides a binary opposition to this gloom in the world of 'The Purple Rose of Cairo', which provides the brand of escapist pleasure films of the depression era are often described as doing. Cecilia experiences these pleasures for herself when Tom takes her into his world and treats her to a night on the town, depicted in a montage of images reminiscent of a representational style common in films of the thirties and forties. Yet, this account of the two worlds is troubled by suggestions that the world beyond the screen is not the site of matchless happiness Cecilia might take it to be. These hints run from small details such as champagne being replaced with ginger ale to the abiding sense of a monotonous obedience to the routine of the film's script which the characters must endure there. Indeed, Tom's very action of stepping off the screen signals his own sense of dissatisfaction with his own world, proposing quite clearly that the apparent utopia of the world beyond the screen is not without its faults. For Tom, it contains nothing like Cecilia. The comparison between two worlds that Allen's film invites is therefore not only based upon a contrast of good and bad, but rather incorporates a sense of a character's inability to belong in their own worlds, however good or bad, and seeking an existence elsewhere. Ultimately, in *The Purple Rose of Cairo* the coalescence of two worlds is shown to be problematic for those inhabiting both sides of the screen. Therefore, Cecilia's final return to her position as passive observer of the screen world at the film's conclusion marks her return to a condition in which her visits to that other realm will only ever occur in her imagination. Indeed, if we are to believe the words of the producer of 'The Purple Rose of Cairo' the prints of his film have all been destroyed by now and Tom Baxter is literally no more.

The two films discussed in the following chapters, *Brigadoon* and *Pleasantville*, both present a real world and another world in ways similar to the films referred to here. Each depicts characters travelling to a world that is divorced from the reality they leave behind, rather than existing as a figment of their imagination or, indeed, as a potential version of their world as they know it. Both films go beyond the construction of dual worlds to draw significant comparisons between those worlds, finding strong resonance in the differences between events and attitudes from one realm to the next. Ultimately, the characters in each film are made to choose between the two worlds offered to them, although their choices are not identical as one chooses a life in the alternative world and another chooses a return to his reality. The nature of their individual choices will necessarily become a matter for consideration in the following chapters.

Notes

1. In the case of *A Matter of Life or Death*, there is also potentially a nationalistic endorsement for the contemporaneous post-war English audience as, although heaven in the film welcomes all nationalities, it is without exception ruled by the English.
2. The film draws a further contrast between the two spaces by depicting much of the action back in the living world through the lens of a video that another character, Joe (William Baldwin) uses to film events. The image through the lens is grainy and monochrome, distinguishing it from the vibrant palette of the other world Nelson has travelled to.

3. Complementary to this, the film refrains from depicting in any real detail the living occupants of the house, choosing to remain in the world of the dead until the final moments when the two worlds merge into each other and Grace can see the living. Further to this, the individual who makes contact with the dead is a rather frightening-looking old woman who might well be mistaken for a ghoulish apparition, thus tricking the audience into further accepting Grace as a living character.

4. No filmed version of *Mary Rose* exists, although it was a project Alfred Hitchcock wished to pursue on a number of occasions but, despite having gone some way towards preparing a screenplay and casting the central character (Tippi Hedren was apparently chosen) his attempts never bore fruition. Indeed, Universal permitted Hitchcock to make any film he desired under $3 million as long as it wasn't Barrie's play. Bill Krohn *Hitchcock at Work* London: Phaidon Press Ltd., 2000, pp. 272–278.

5. I use *The Purple Rose of Cairo* to mean Woody Allen's film and 'The Purple Rose of Cairo' to mean the film that is featured within his film.

6. Stig Bjorkman *Woody Allen on Woody Allen* London: Faber & Faber, 1993, p. 148.

9

LIFE BEYOND REASON

Brigadoon (Vincente Minnelli, 1954)

Voices Off

The world of the film emerges gently. After a robustly scored title sequence, the music dwindles and the image dissolves to become the scene of a mist-covered valley: loch and hills stretching out into the background; spindly, wild trees and ferns skewering out at unkempt angles in the foreground. Only the rolling mists provide movement, lightly caressing the landscape as they blow gradually across the scene. The setting is calm, a calmness replicated in the accompanying sounds. An orchestra plays a light arrangement, a flute sounds a two-note trill before male voices chime in softly 'Once in the Highlands, The Highlands of Scotland...'

The union of sound and image in these brief initial moments reveals certain ambitions that the film possesses regarding the world it wishes to construct. Whilst all fictional films present a storyworld, *Brigadoon* seems to assert the 'story' traits of its world with particular transparency as those opening words evoke the conventional style in which a tale or fable is recounted by the teller. The voices that perform the telling here are off-screen, not located in the world they describe, speaking out from a position beyond the diegetic boundaries of the image. This is a spatial consideration, yet the word 'once' in the voiceover also places the storyworld *temporally* somewhere in the past, positioning the narration in the present and further distinguishing the voices from the image. The storytelling voices are thus placed between the scenario they describe and the audience they describe it to as they relate the events of the past to the listeners of the present. Although we can establish that the voices do not emanate from any aspect of the visible world represented in the image, we cannot so easily place their location or origin. The voices are mysterious, floating sounds that defy definition according to ordinary logic. They are ethereal, existing nowhere and tethered to nothing.

And the voices are music. As the unseen chorus expel their first lines, the film makes clear that a world is being presented in which words and thoughts can be sung. With this distinction in place, we must expect that the world presented in this film will behave differently to the world we know and experience ourselves. The voices convey their words with serene rhythm and harmony, further distinguishing the sounds from the ordinary patterns of everyday speech. A single voice narrating in plain speech would signal a particular storyteller, and the idiosyncratic inflections of their speech – their tone, pace and style of delivery – would evoke a particular personality. No such single entity can be defined here. In addition, a single spoken voice might introduce a sense of realism, implying that the voice, although unidentified, belonged to a person of the world, who knew the story, who had experienced parts of it, had perhaps heard it as a local myth or even made it up entirely. A retelling of this kind would constitute a normal ritual of everyday storytelling. The openings of two films, *The Magnificent Ambersons* (Orson Welles, 1942) and *The Reckless Moment* both include unseen, and fairly ambiguous, narrators whose exact relationship to the story remains unclear. Yet, their narration takes the conventional form of a story being recounted from one person to another, even if we don't know how they came about knowing it, even if we don't know which parts, if any, are true. Being visible to us is not a condition to this. We can at least identify the voices as belonging to residents of the world and imagine them existing somewhere in it.[1] The voices we hear in *Brigadoon's* opening moments remain unidentifiable as such, and the chorus is instead rendered uncanny, mysterious and magical. Their hushed, elegiac sound haunts the scene, more spirit than human. Having already suggested that they exist beyond the boundaries of the natural world we see on screen, and given their unearthly nature and tone, it seems reasonable to now define these voices as supernatural; a celestial choir unconstrained by time and space. Their invisible presence in these opening moments establishes the film as fantasy.

The fantastic nature of the sounds in this moment is continued in aspects of the film's visual composition. There is a similarly unreal quality to the landscape we view. The trees and hills, valley and loch, give an illusion of depth, yet are imbued with a picture-book quality (in keeping with the once upon a time-ness of the accompanying lyrics) that challenges our acceptance of the scene as real. Rather than present a natural environment, the film represents one, constructing a portrait of nature rather than searching nature for the portrait. Exquisitely composed as the scene might be, we are unlikely to mistake it for a real view of the Scottish Highlands.[2] Indeed, within the generic conventions of the Hollywood musical, it is quite acceptable to us that a scene of this sort should not strive for absolute realism (an equivalent being the studio representations of Paris in Minnelli's musical *An American in Paris*, released three years earlier). So the image is a fantasy landscape, just as the narration is sung by fantasy voices. The mysticism inherent in those voices is echoed in the rolling mists that soften the edges of the rugged earth, shrouding details and lending the scene a mythical, enigmatic quality. Sound and image fuse here to produce an idea of a place that resembles reality but could never be mistaken for it.

I dwell on the film's opening seconds for two reasons. Firstly, there has been consistent attention across this study of alternative worlds to the ways that films establish the early boundaries of their worlds in preparation for the phenomenon of an alternative world being introduced. Hence, opening sequences have frequently been offered for consideration. In the case of *Brigadoon*, the fantasy of the discontinuous alternative world – a village called Brigadoon that materializes once every hundred years – is continuous with the fantasy of a world the film creates from the outset. The mythical landscape and mystical voices provide an environment in which such magic can credibly take place. Indeed, when eventually Mr Lundie (Barry Jones) delivers the revelation of Brigadoon's miracle without urgency within a hushed, still environment, this undramatic peacefulness seems to complement the absence of shock or surprise in our own reaction as we discover the secret of the village. Perhaps our response is symptomatic of the film having constructed a world of fantasy from the start, so broadening our boundaries of expectation.

Secondly, there is a point to be addressed regarding the nature of the somewhat negative criticism that Brigadoon has attracted over the years. The question of authenticity lies at the heart of much criticism because, unattended to so far in my account, those ethereal voices on the film's soundtrack also describe a location: the Highlands of Scotland. In his extensive study of the film's wider contexts of production and consumption, Colin McArthur details the extent to which 'the Scots intelligentsia' have, with growing force, found the film's depiction of the Scottish Highlands overly romanticized, inaccurate, even offensive. McArthur relates a number of critical reactions, including John Caughie's response as he emerged from his first viewing of the film in 1982: 'Now I know what it feels like to be a woman'.[3] We are not able to discern the precise tone of Caughie's words, but the same cannot be said of Donald Dewar's, the late First Minister of Scotland, when he asserted that: '[T]he Brigadoon image has done Scotland no favours. It has encouraged a whimsical, romantic vision of a land full of peat smoke and Harry Lauder which is awful to behold'.[4] The vehement disdain Dewar feels towards the world of Brigadoon is scarcely concealed here and represents a view that is, McArthur demonstrates, abundant among a good deal of Scots commentators.

Yet, criticisms are not only restricted to those declaring objections on the grounds of their own national identity allegedly being misrepresented on screen. Stephen Harvey takes issue with the film's set design in the following way:

> ...the painted scrim Scotland erected on Metro's Stage 15 was too literal for wistful fancies, and less vivid than any one-reel travelogue. Once confined indoors, Minnelli ought to have indulged his bent for unrestrained artifice, and transformed his Brigadoon from a cramped approximation of the Highland retreat to a refuge as intangible as dew, and seductive because it resembles no place on earth. Instead, George Gibson's diorama looks like the world's biggest nature morte: distant lochs glint like silver cardboard, unseen clouds cast static shadows on a flat sea of heather.[5]

Harvey's mention of Minnelli's confinement 'indoors' references the fact that originally the film's producer, Arthur Freed, and star, Gene Kelly, travelled to Scotland scouting locations, but due to bad weather discounted the idea of shooting there. On returning to the United States, they found some highlands above Monterey that could have stood in for Scotland, but a 'studio economy wave' put paid to that notion and finally the film was to be shot on a soundstage.[6] Harvey's bruising assessment of the film's set rests upon his conviction that it does not go far enough in its representation of the fantasy world, his assumption apparently being that the ideal fantasy should resemble nothing found in life. The position of the Scots intelligentsia, articulated most vociferously by Dewar, forms a counterpoint to this in asserting that the film fails because it does not represent Scottish National Heritage with appropriate realism. Both perspectives fail to come to terms with the film's blend of reality and fantasy, insisting that a binary choice be made between the two. Within this criterion, combination becomes unacceptable.

We find flaws in Harvey's argument when we begin to pursue some of its recommendations. In advising that Minnelli should have 'indulged his bent for artifice' and created 'a refuge as intangible as dew, and seductive because it resembles no place on earth', he overlooks the simple fact that the film *should* resemble a place on earth: the Scottish Highlands. At a fundamental level, the story demands that some recognition of geographical fact should be made. Likewise, the fantasy village of Brigadoon should *resemble* a community of 1754, and so historical reality must be at least observed. (It might also be noted that criticism as strong as Harvey's could be accompanied by more particular and practical advice than that provided in his brief, somewhat indeterminate recommendations.) *Brigadoon* presents a fictional environment existing beyond natural laws, but to overplay the fantasy to the extent Harvey suggests would risk undermining the basis of its story, threatening the plausibility of its world as a world at all.

The Scots intelligentsia pull inevitably in the opposite direction as invariably they struggle to comprehend that, although a particular location and people are used, the film constructs a fantasy world from the outset, compositionally in some of the ways I detail above. It is difficult to ascertain how a viewer witnessing the first few seconds of the film could credibly expect the ensuing narrative to encapsulate a historically accurate account of Scottish life circa 1754 or, indeed, 1954. And yet, McArthur provides examples of reviews from the time of *Brigadoon's* release that actively criticize the film's perceived inability to recreate reality effectively. Forsyth Hardy, writing for the *Scotsman* newspaper, complains that the director 'has gone out of his way to make the film as inauthentic as possible', whilst Donald Bruce, writing in the *Daily Record*, describes the backdrops as 'an elementary blunder the French or the Italians, those impressive sticklers for film reality, would never have made'.[7] The latter reviewer expresses a traditional attitude in British critical culture, still observable today, that holds film 'realism' in higher esteem than film 'fantasy' and, perhaps on similar grounds, champions European cinema whilst deriding Hollywood. Yet, both critics also misread this film's ambitions, and fail to acknowledge the blend of fantasy and reality that renders their demands for total authenticity to historical document inappropriate. Perhaps in the cases of Hardy, Bruce and later Dewar, the issue of national identity, albeit important, has clouded both judgement and clarity regarding what actually appears on the screen.

I have suggested that the criteria of authenticity proposed by the Scots critics and alluded to in Harvey's call for a more fanciful depiction is unsuitable in an evaluation of the film's achievements. However, the film *is* bound by the dramatic limits it sets itself and in that sense events must remain authentic to the world as created. The world in the film must adhere to its own logic if it is to be accepted as a credible world by the audience. Crucially, this does not depend upon the exact recreation of the world we know and experience. V.F. Perkins sets out guidance when approaching the issues of credibility and authenticity in the following two statements:

...credibility...depends upon the inner consistency of the created world. So long as this is maintained, the premises are beyond question...But the created world must obey its own logic. There is no pretext, whether it be Significance, Effect or the Happy Ending, sufficient to justify a betrayal of the given order. In a fictional world where anything at all can happen, nothing at all can mean or matter...

...it is important that we avoid confusing credibility with authenticity. The question of authenticity simply does not arise when we enter a fictional world. There is no actuality against which we can check images derived from One Million Years B.C. or 2001. But the image must be credibly derived from the created world in order to maintain its reality.[8]

In the first statement, Perkins lays out some conditions for credibility in film, and in the second draws attention to the common confusion of credibility with authenticity, whereby attempts are made to compare the film against realities that are themselves often notions rather than facts. Crucial to Perkins' assertions is the demand that fictional worlds in films maintain their *inner* consistency so that, although they patently are not our worlds, they are coherent as worlds nonetheless. In dismissing authenticity as an evaluative measure, the terms of these criteria are far more sensitive to the actual nature of fictional worlds in film. Returning to *Brigadoon*, we realize that a world is presented from an early stage whose nature diverges from our own: magical voices sing out across time and space, the land is half-real, half-unreal. *Brigadoon* is merely a more extreme manifestation of the storyworlds that all fiction films engage us with. An attempt is made to establish a fantasy world and, according to Perkins' reasoning, it is the internal logic of that world which must be maintained in order for the film to succeed as a fictional work. In this way, meaning and significance emanates from the world of the film as it is, rather than as it should be.

Awakenings
Just as the film's world emerged gently and slowly from the opening titles, so the village of Brigadoon gradually awakens. From the opening shot described earlier, the camera tracks back and down, sweeping across patches of thistle, heather and bracken. The image dissolves to be replaced by another landscape of green-crested cliff faces washed in the golden light of dawn. The camera continues its free roam of the environment as it glides down to reveal two men picking their way through the undergrowth. The unseen narrating voices have already introduced these characters as 'two weary hunters who lost their way'. The matching of visual detail to vocal description again evokes notions of a story being spun out for us in a game of show and tell. The unrestricted camera movement rhymes with the uninhibited invisible voices, further evoking a greater narrating presence moving through this world with fluency and freedom, introducing us to a location and picking out characters for the story. The dissolve between scenes emphasizes the choosing of images for purposeful display, like pictures changing in a slide show presentation, but also instils a gradual, even pace, creating a deliberate and whimsical storytelling tone. The convention of the dissolve between scenes recurs without exception throughout the film, maintaining the tranquil narrating tone. The repetition of the dissolve draws attention to its use, calling to mind its resonance with the story

of a village that appears and evaporates every one hundred years, complementing the elusive transience of that narrative event.[9]

A strong baritone voice rises up as the chorus begins a wordless, seraphic accompaniment: 'And this is what happened, the strange thing that happened, to two weary hunters who lost their way'. This is the last mention of the travellers for now as the image of them fades to be replaced by a view of a clearing in a wood and a stone bridge, distinct through the haze. The unseen singing chorus announces the location 'Brigadoon' smoothly, richly, drawing out each syllable with neither urgency nor haste. The measured pace of the word complements the still and serene image, where only the gentle flutter of bird wings provides motion. The fullness of the choir's tone, replete with all the company's voices now, creates depth but also warmth, matching the warmth of the first dawn rays that spill across the foot of the bridge. Likewise, the elongation of the word 'Brigadoon' rhymes with the gradualness of dawn, the vision of a world slowly awakening.

The golden light of the dawn carries on breaking, extending across the scene as it strikes the brickwork of the bridge and the gently flowing stream below. We cut to the other side of the bridge as the light carries on, sweeping past two oxen, one of which springs to its feet as the beam passes across it, as though impelled into action by its touch. After this swift movement, the ox looks in puzzlement around and behind itself, as though it has been touched by something it hardly understands, finally gazing curiously beyond the frame to where the light seems to be travelling still.

The behaviour of the animal is a wonderful moment, perhaps unintended by Minnelli, which refers exactly to the uncanniness of the dawn that breaks across the scene with unnatural speed. As this takes place, the invisible choir continue over the action in a hymn of celebration devoted to Brigadoon. The travelling light, the ox's startled reaction and the ghostly voices convince us that we are witnessing more than the dawning of another day. We are being shown an event of magnitude, made of magic. We cut again. The dawn light behaves yet more supernaturally as it races through thickets of web-like branches and twigs, the mobile camera tracking its progress. The curious beam takes the form of a searchlight here, travelling with force and purpose. The camera settles as the beam disappears into the mists and then, slowly, the vapour lifts to reveal houses and a village square.[10]

This revelation underlines that a search has indeed been underway, that the mysterious light has in fact sought out the location that the magical voices described. The narrative force of sound and light has propelled us to this spot to witness a community conjured from the shadows. Again, as we watch and listen, we might be struck by the storytelling conventions inherent in this extended play of show and tell. (A play on the themes of lost and found would also appear to be in motion, with the two weary hunters lost in the hills whilst the mystical beam and voices find Brigadoon. This anticipates the event of those two characters, Jeff and Tommy, finding the village later, it appearing to them from beneath the mists just as it emerges here, only to lose it when they return to their own world.)

Brigadoon

The journey of discovery continues, as we are taken closer to one of the houses by means of a cut. From here, the camera tracks from left to right, complementing the movement of the light as it sweeps across the white brickwork and straw roof of the dwelling. Another cut takes us inside this building, where a young woman sleeps in a chair by an open fire, a copper kettle hanging over the glowing coals. My sparse description here fails to communicate Minnelli's accomplished balancing of light and shadow in this interior. At first, only the small fire and a thin shard of sunlight illuminate the scene. In the half-light, small details are picked out such as the paleness of the woman's face and hand, the patchwork of her modest blanket, the golden copper of the kettle, the grey tin of a little pot, the vibrant orange radiance of the burning coals, the wooden frames of furniture and the dull, dry lines of the brickwork. The humble sources of light subdue the colours of the scene, complementing the calm restfulness of the image in which only the tiny spirals of rising smoke move.

The composition and inherent stillness of the image resonates with Minnelli's assertion that, on this film, 'interiors were lighted to suggest Flemish paintings'.[11] Indeed, painting appears to have provided

Brigadoon

Woman Holding A Balance

inspiration, and McArthur continues that Minnelli 'seems to have had in mind for the interiors Dutch painting and for the exteriors English Romantic painting'.[12] Taking this into account, we might be struck by the similarities between this interior and the work of an artist such as Jan Vermeer. A painting like *Woman Holding A Balance* (Vermeer, c.1664) for example, provides comparison in the ways that light and shade are balanced to define textures and surfaces.

In the Vermeer painting, details such as the pale smoothness of the woman's face and neck, the delicacy of her linen veil, the downy fur of her jacket and the glinting amber of the metal balance she holds, are picked out by light stealing obliquely around the edges of nearly closed shutters in the upper left-hand corner of the composition.[13]

Yet, Minnelli does not only enjoy referencing the form of another medium. Instead, he proceeds to exemplify the differences between painting and film. As light pours into the scene, the woman stirs, yawns, then bolts upright, throwing down her shawl to reveal a cream nightgown, its brightness accentuated in the now-sunbathed interior. The sudden burst of movement immediately shatters the scene's allusions to painting, demonstrating the vitality of the moving image in comparison to static composition. Thus, Minnelli's initial evocation of the tranquillity of a still-life composition heightens the impact of the woman's brisk movement. Her rapid reaction also rhymes with the impulsive start of the ox earlier and again we are given cause to reflect upon the nature of this light that sweeps across the land and seems to give immediate vitality to all it touches. It continues to rouse various other members of the village in three short proceeding scenes: a young man throws open the shutters on his cabinet bed as a beam touches its surface; a young woman stirs in bed and picks up a heather from underneath her pillow as her room is magically flooded with sudden brightness; a dog and then a young boy rise from their straw beds as isolated patches of light fall across them. The isolation of the beams that touch dog then boy reveal the process that is enacted throughout the montage of awakenings: the light rouses each resident of the village in turn, a shining ray beckoning each member individually from their sleep. This phenomenon corresponds with the mysteriously travelling column of light that searched for the village earlier. In this sequence, light is not so much an element as a force, displaying choice and purpose. Understandably, this unusual dawn enhances the magical quality of the sequence and convinces us that we are watching something more than just the everyday awakening of a village. The members of this village are being awoken. The film began in the conventional style of a fairytale – 'once in the Highlands' – and here a fairytale logic is at work once again. Anyone familiar with the tale of Sleeping Beauty will recognize the scene of a spell being broken, an enchantment lifted, and a kingdom awakening.

Glimpsing Nowhere

The young boy in the straw is awoken by light, but also by sound, as a resounding voice sings out: 'Come out to the square...' This marks a change in the pace of events, as others make their way to the square (and musically this change is signalled as the voice brings in a new key signature). The boy runs out to see a group passing by, laden with baskets of goods and trailing a horse-drawn cart. We cut to images of other villagers making the same journey, burdened with a cacophony of game, furs, fish, bundles of wood, baskets of wool, herds of sheep, flagons of ale. Travelling from all angles and directions, each group joins the song, as the pace and volume steadily grows. Finally all the groups converge on the market square, flooding in and swarming the frame with crosscutting streams of activity, traipsing carts of goods and wares across the scene in a seemingly unending procession. The mobile camera moves fluently through the crowds, accentuating their bustling activity, and the quantity of voices build until everyone in the market is involved in a song of celebration (the number *Down on MacConnachy Square*).

The rapid build of activity reinforces the notion of a community coming to life. Minnelli communicates this idea with striking impact, as this community is imbued with a special liveliness as they go about their business with joy and vigour, their voices breaking into song and their actions eventually erupting into dance. Very soon, the scene is alive with movement and music. The incredible velocity of action overwhelms and delights, exploding from the peacefulness as the world awoke. The soaring vivacity of Alan Jay Lerner's lyrics and Frederick Loewe's music is matched in the breathless whirling, lifting, darting, springing, skipping and jigging of the crowds. Minnelli packs the frame with activity and colour to present a community united in celebration of the everyday, rejoicing the fact of their existence. Clearly, this world is full of song and dance, but it also possesses an infectious exuberance. (More generally, the film makes clear that the occupants of this world experience waking from a night's sleep, rather than a hundred year sleep, emphasizing that their life continues as usual, irrespective of their special enchantment.) The song invites all to come to the market square and, surrounded and enchanted by the spectacle of music and movement, we might feel the invitation extends to us.

Tommy Albright (Gene Kelly) and Jeff Douglas (Van Johnson) stumble across this captivating community whilst on a hunting trip from New York. The film deadens the mood as it cross-fades to the pair studying a map of the Highlands: subdued browns, greys, greens and blues replacing the effervescent colours of the previous scene. Having swung and dived around the market square, Minnelli pares down his visual style, reducing the camera's movement and creating an innate stillness and inactivity. This toning down is also inherent in the flatness in Tommy and Jeff's voices, their lack of emphatic expression jarring with the energetic vitality of the previous scene. Their flat tones communicate Jeff's cynicism towards and Tommy's disenchantment with life. These qualities are encapsulated in Johnson and Kelly's low-key style of performance, but also in character traits that are revealed to us: Jeff's excessive drinking and disregard for things he does not understand; Tommy's inexplicable unhappiness and sometimes-held belief that he's 'not capable of loving'. The scene's reduced aesthetic registers as a kind of dramatic halt, achieved through the suppression of vivid colour, movement and sound (a harsh silence exists around the characters in the absence of any underscore). This rhymes with Jeff and Tommy having reached an emotional halt in their lives, their respective dissatisfactions rendering them immobile, unsure of which path to take next. In this sense, their being lost in the Highlands takes on symbolic weight, evoking the extent to which they have become lost in life, ill at ease with their own identities. As they try to place their location on the map, Jeff's wry comment that they are in 'nothing' seems to encapsulate their indistinct position within the world generally, an insecurity which Jeff suppresses with dry wit but which causes Tommy's frustration.

Having witnessed the vibrancy of the marketplace in contrast to this undramatic scene, we might feel or expect that something needs to happen (an expectation guided to an extent by a knowledge and experience of the musical genre, which is not usually defined by moments of quiet contemplation). Likewise, having observed Jeff and Tommy's disillusionment and despondency in contrast to the villagers' jubilation, we might feel or expect that something needs to happen to them. Such expectations perhaps correspond with a wider function of the musical experienced as entertainment, defined in terms laid out by Richard Dyer. In a key debate, Dyer illustrates the tendency of such forms of entertainment to present utopian worlds within their narratives. He explains that:

> Two of the taken-for-granted descriptions of entertainment, as 'escape' and as 'wish-fulfilment' point to its central thrust, namely, utopianism. Entertainment offers the image of 'something better' to escape into, or something we want deeply that our day-to-day lives don't provide. Alternatives, hopes, wishes – these are the stuff of utopia, the sense that things could be better, that something other than what is can be imagined and maybe realized.[14]

This account interrogates the viewer's relationship to the utopian alternatives that entertainments such as musicals offer. In this sense, Dyer attends to the broader disparities between the world of the audience and the world on the screen, whereby our real lives are contrasted momentarily with the utopian existences depicted in the films themselves. Quite explicitly, *Brigadoon*'s narrative contains a meta-version of this relationship between the real world and a utopian alternative as it constructs a divide between the drabness of Tommy and Jeff's real world – encapsulated by stillness, quietness, and subdued hues – and the alternative world of Brigadoon – defined by its colour, movement and music. Consequently, Tommy and Jeff's placement in their world throughout this scene comes to resemble our position as viewers, with their need for 'something better' replicating a need for 'escape' that Dyer identifies in our own relationship to the film musical.

Thus, when Tommy forgets his hat, turns around to retrieve it and sees that a village has magically appeared from the early morning haze, it would seem that our desires and the needs of the characters have been simultaneously fulfilled. We cut to a shot of the village in the distance that represents Tommy's point-of-view and the three note theme 'Brigadoon' breaks out on the soundtrack. Although apparently unheard by Tommy and Jeff in their diegetic world, the music seems to symbolize their enthrallment as they both stare out at the view. The soft enchanting theme contrasts with the charmless patter of their previous conversation which occurred in empty silence. Brigadoon has already become synonymous with music and that characteristic infuses the scene now, extending out beyond the boundaries of the community and filling the previously staid environment. The music continues, underscoring their words, as their respective moods soften and warm. Tommy speaks in hushed wonderment; Jeff is almost buoyed with new enthusiasm. The music seems to symbolize a magic that washes over them, at once altering their outlook. Significantly, as we will discover later, this magic endures for one character but not the other.

Tommy and Jeff's speech on the hill placed them as twentieth century characters. As well as Jeff's ironic tone, Tommy's introspection and their shared low-key, free-flow patterns of speech along with terms like 'potentialities', 'depressing' and 'inferiority complex' mark them out as belonging to the modern age. Their speech defines them in the same way as they enter Brigadoon: when they first encounter a native boy (the same boy whom earlier awoke with his dog, also featured here), he runs away and hides behind a rock, so Jeff responds with a wisecrack of post-Freudian logic: 'that kid's gonna have problems when he grows up'. In fact, all of the villagers they approach recoil at the sight of them until a young woman, Fiona Campbell (Cyd Charisse), approaches *them*. As she tells the two men they are in Brigadoon, the three-note musical theme rises in the soundtrack once again before the underscore finally ends. The inclusion of the theme here seems initially to merely repeat Fiona's mention of Brigadoon. Yet this theme has already become synonymous with enchantment and in this moment a second enchantment is occurring between Tommy and Fiona – the music rising as he turns to look at her. It is at this moment, perhaps, that Jeff and Tommy's experiences of Brigadoon begin to diverge as Tommy's love for Fiona takes root. Although Fiona's period dress is discordant with the two men's shirt collars and suits, emphasizing her difference to them, her gaze is magnetized towards Tommy at the expense of Jeff, whom she only glances at from time to time. Likewise, as she is drawn to Tommy, she turns away from Jeff, forming a bond of unity with one man whilst constructing an inadvertent barrier against the other. The theme of Jeff's marginalization from events is thus introduced, to be revisited later. The use of the Brigadoon theme in this moment also binds Tommy and Fiona's burgeoning love to the location, prefacing the later revelation that their love can only survive in this place or not at all. This is crucial to Tommy's final choice as, in choosing Fiona, he chooses Brigadoon itself and a new existence. (The coming together of Kelly and Charisse in this way also conforms to our reasonable expectations of the film as a vehicle for its stars.)

We might propose that the village of Brigadoon has been conjured up to satisfy a lack in Tommy's life, but it might also be said that Tommy has been conjured up to satisfy a lack in Fiona's. In a preceding scene, she expressed her desire to find a match beyond the confines of her world through song (in the number *Waitin' for My Dearie*), much to the puzzlement of her female peers. In that scene, Fiona was set apart from her community and it was appropriate that she ended her song by gazing out of the window beyond the boundaries of Brigadoon, the camera having closed in sufficiently to cut out the other girls around her and so fixing her in a moment of quiet solitude. As Fiona and Tommy first meet, they complete something for each other that previously was absent from their lives. The divide between them, accentuated in their

Brigadoon

costuming and styles of speech (his Brooklyn twang against her Highland burr) evaporates as they mesmerize one another, repeating 'good day' to delay their parting and gazing after one another when finally they are separated (Jeff having impatiently repeated a firm and final 'good day'). After Tommy and Jeff depart, the score resurrects a section from *Waitin' for My Dearie*, restating Tommy's arrival as an answer to Fiona's earlier longing.

When the two men enter the market square, they enter as strangers. The villagers react at first with hostility before the soon-to-be-wed Charlie Dalrymple welcomes them as his guests, and the crowd relent. Both reactions, however, retain Tommy and Jeff's status as strangers, arousing uneasy suspicion and then friendly curiosity within the village. Their strangeness to the village is highlighted through their involvement in the song *I'll Go Home With Bonnie Jean*. Ostensibly, the scene is about integration, as the two New Yorkers are encouraged to join in the group's singing and dancing. They get caught up in the lines of the villager's highland jig, obligingly following the leaps and skips of those around them. Eventually, Tommy and Jeff begin a soft-

Brigadoon

shoe tap routine, much to the delight of the crowd who actually incorporate one particular move – in which they stride, legs half-bent, one arm held out at chest level, palms facing upwards – into the finale of their song. As much as this scene features the coming together of two worlds, it also serves to highlight the distance between them, making clear the incongruity of Tommy and Jeff, suited and shirted, performing the villager's 18th century dance and the villagers in kilts, waistcoats and feathered caps, copying the 20th century moves of their new visitors. The joy lies in two different groups demonstrating their ways and customs to one another, emphasizing the gulf that exists between them. And so, when Tommy and Jeff incorporate a piper motif into their routine, the villagers laugh, acknowledging the mimicry of their distinct 18th century style in the distinct, and foreign, 20th century style. Thus in this film, as with many musicals, movement and musicality are represented as powerful catalysts for the unification of groups and individuals, the utopia of dance here creating an understanding between the men that replaces the need for words and discussion. The distinctions between the New Yorkers and the Brigadoon villagers were inherent in their costuming: the subdued greys and modern style of Tommy and Jeff's hats and jackets contrasting particularly with the patchwork vibrancy of the villager's dress. Tommy and Jeff's clothing was symbolic of their era. It becomes significant, therefore, when Tommy, leaving to pursue Fiona after the dance, gives his hat and coat to Jeff, revealing more fully a deep green shirt and striking orange vest that he wears. We can read this shedding of jacket and hat as Tommy discarding the symbolic traits of his world but also, in uncovering the undergarments that coincidentally resemble the palette of the Brigadoon costumes, unconsciously beginning to attune to this newly discovered world.[15]

Eloquent Steps

When Tommy catches up with Fiona, she mentions that she must gather heather for the wedding decorations and he asks if he could come along. Her answer is a turn back and smile as she walks away from him. He understands her coy invitation and follows. As they walk up the hillside, Tommy replicates Fiona's coyness by telling her how relieved he was to find out it was her sister's wedding day and not hers. Like Fiona's earlier glances back and smiles, there is an emotional undercurrent to Tommy's words; both of their gestures, physical and vocal, reveal the underlying passion that grows between them, which they each understand well enough without speaking of it directly to each other. We also recognize innocence in their relationship as they go collecting heather together, a quality which contrasts with Tommy's earlier world-weariness. As the two continue their journey across the hills, words break into song and song, finally, into dance. This progression marks a move towards Kelly's ultimate performance strength – dancing – and there is a sense that his speech and song occurs in anticipation of the dance, as though he were temporarily curbing his natural instinct to move. Evidently, this impacts upon our understanding of character, evoking the sense that Tommy comes alive when he dances, finding a language that expresses his emotions without words. We notice that his gestures are more eloquent than his speech, as the meandering sentiment and stilted action of his song is replaced by his richer, more fluent articulation of desire through movement. Likewise, there is the suggestion that his movement in dance is instinctive and authentic, whereas the song seemed self-conscious and care-laden, as though notions of propriety and decorum restricted Tommy as he politely related his emotions to the natural scene. In dance, that barrier is apparently and palpably removed and he surrenders to sensuality.

The music marks this change in emotional force, rising in volume and pace as the pair run across the hills to begin their dance. We might notice that Fiona leads this move away from the site of the song to a new location for dance, and might reflect that dance is a natural language for her also. During the song, she merely followed Tommy around as he sang to her, but now she too has come alive, leading him into this new state. They unite through dance. Her leading becomes a matter of teasing as she repeatedly evokes the motif of running away only to be caught again. The motif of his grasping her only to lose her again recalls the potential transience of Fiona and Tommy's wider relationship, unknown to him as yet, whereby they can share one day only to be lost to one another for eternity. The game of his holding and then losing her plays upon this underlying theme. Less forebodingly, the game of catch and letting go also represents a courting ritual between the two, the pattern of capture and loss facilitating brief moments of furtive holding and embracing.

We might also notice the attention paid to the landscape in this scene, a concentration not seen since the film's first opening shots. This is apparent as Fiona and Tommy shape their movements around the contoured surfaces of boulders and trees, replicating the natural lines within their dance, and using the gathering of heather to direct their actions. The attention is also inherent in the movement of Minnelli's camera as it sweeps across the landscape, celebrating the panoramic depth and breadth of the scene. The characters' entwinement with their surroundings and the camera's reverence for the landscape recalls the importance of location in the film and, especially in this scene, stresses the significance of Brigadoon to Tommy and Fiona. Their love can only survive in this place and it follows, therefore, that their evocation of love through dance should involve aspects of the environment to which they are inextricably bound. And yet, crucially, their environment does not confine them. They move freely across the landscape – the camera following their progress in a series of soars and dives – as though there were no borders in the world for them. They dictate the boundaries of their dance, which is a direct reversal of the later situation in which their lives will become dictated by the boundary separating Brigadoon from the world. Tommy and Fiona find a freedom in the landscape that will later be denied to them, and find a space for intimacy which all too soon will cease to exist.

Ultimately, the theme of time is made paramount in Tommy and Fiona's movements. Their dance is balletic, involving a fluid tempo that contrasts rapid gesture with sustained, drawn out motion. This loose temporal pattern resonates with the fluid meter of the accompanying music as it expands the rising, falling melody of *Heather on the Hill*. As the couple curl, stretch, curve and twist in unison they accelerate and decelerate, as though an unseen slow-motion/fast-forward device was manipulating them. And yet, they dictate this pace themselves, creating a unique time-pattern that determines the form of their dance. The effect is most spectacular when it occurs in the various leaps, lunges and supports, where force and motion seem to suddenly dissipate and their actions decelerate as though time had drained from the world. Gene Kelly's choreography in this sequence is accomplished in form alone, but achieves greater resonance as it pertains to the themes of time and temporality inherent in the narrative and particular to Fiona and Tommy's relationship. The great divide between them is time itself: she will outlive him by hundreds of thousands of years whilst he stays confined to his ordinary human lifespan.

Brigadoon

(It is shrewd plotting which dictates that Brigadoon should emerge every hundred years and so anyone who discovers it will almost certainly never see it again.) As the couple dance together against the normal laws of time, it as though they have suspended the rules of temporality, existing outside of its constraints. For a fleeting moment, they create a place in time and space in which they can exist together, resisting the realities that they will later confront. Of course, Tommy is unaware of the temporal gulf between them, yet Fiona must be conscious that their union will be pulled apart after the day ends. Her earlier leading of Tommy to the site of their dance therefore achieves significance as it symbolizes her instigation of their ballet, her desire to suspend time for this moment with him. He is happy to join her and live this moment with her outside of time and regardless of space.

In the sequence described, Tommy and Fiona enact a resistance to time's constraints, creating a hermetic private space in which their devotion to one another can flourish unthreatened. The truth of eternal separation cannot be suppressed, however, and eventually they are left to face the implications of their parting. The moment occurs after the marriage of Fiona's sister Jean (Virginia Bolser) to Charlie (Jimmy Thompson). Harry Beaton (Hugh Laing) has attempted to leave Brigadoon, a chase has been mounted, and Jeff has accidentally shot him. After the women of the village are told the lie that Harry survived, Fiona sets off on a search of her own to find Tommy. They meet in the ruins of the chapel in which Jean and Charlie were married. Previously, this scene was alive with light and warmth as the villagers gathered in celebration of the young couple's union. But the place is changed now. Moonlight filters through the decrepit brickwork and tangled branches, throwing repressive shadows across the gloomy scene.

As it touches the faces of Tommy and Fiona it colours their skin luminous white, so that they appear pale like the statues that punctuate the scene. Like statues, or like ghosts. Looking at each other among these gothic arches, Tommy and Fiona perhaps realize that too soon they will become as ghosts to one another: effectively dead when each return to their own worlds.

Brigadoon

Harry's attempted escape has brought to their minds the notion of this world collapsing, being lost forever, and so their thoughts have at last turned to the prospect of being lost to one another forever. The moonlight, its cold blue glow tinting their features deathly white, evokes the extent to which, as the minutes pass, they draw closer to the moment at which they will become dead to one another. The end of the day brings the end of their love, and this thought seems to propel them towards each other as they embrace instinctively and out of longing for each other, as though pre-empting the loss they will feel when they are parted.

Their moving together instigates dance as the underscore suddenly builds to reprise *The Heather on the Hill*. Yet, the joy and freedom of its earlier performance is lost now, and the dance is enacted almost in mourning for those former sentiments consigned already to the past. Kelly reprises aspects of the earlier choreography, but the moves now possess a sorrowful nostalgia as they are performed in the cold moonlight, surrounded by shadows and ruin, Tommy and Fiona's whole world now facing collapse. Kelly also makes some significant choreographic amendments to the earlier performance. After their first embrace, Tommy and Fiona clasp each other again, but she now allows herself to hang limp in his arms as he leads her into a patch of moonlight and turns in the space. Then, having moved to a new space, he supports her and gently cradles her to the ground until she almost lies flat, before raising her back up again. After this, she again drapes herself across his frame, facing out this time, and allows him to drag her backwards as she again lies motionless, arms outstretched, supported by his body. Finally, having passed through the arch of the wrecked chapel, Tommy lowers her to the ground once more, letting her arms slide slowly through his, until she lies still amongst a patch of growing ferns. Even their final embrace repeats this motif as she sinks to the ground in his arms while they kiss.

I draw attention to the motifs of Fiona lying limp in Tommy's arms and him lowering her slowly to the ground as they seem to perform the event of her being rendered lifeless. As he draws her up each time with a lift or support he seems to revive her, bringing her back to life and embracing her over again. Watching the two perform this dance, it strikes me that they enact death, or a series of deaths, only to relieve the moment as he brings her back to life again. Their play on this theme evokes the death they will experience when they are parted, being dead to each other in their respective worlds. That death will be final, without the guarantee of revival. In evoking the act of death and revival in their dance, Tommy and Fiona seem to embrace the reality of their predicament, realizing they cannot be parted in the way they have just played out to each other. In practising the event of their separation, they acquaint each other with its pain. And so, cradling Fiona for the last time, Tommy makes clear that he cannot be parted from her and leaves to inform Jeff.

Peripheral Concerns

On finding Jeff, however, Tommy's thoughts become confused. His friend is sitting in the village square, hunched over a mug of ale, his posture introverted, closed off from the world. He is lost in thought. Tommy shares his joy at finding love with Fiona but Jeff stops him in his tracks, giving him the story of his evening out hunting while everyone else was out chasing Harry Beaton:

> ...Well after a while Jeff thought he saw a bird perched low in a tree, and he shot at it. Something fell to the ground. He rushed over to it. And what do you think it was? It was hothead Harry, yessir, the boy dervish himself, lying there looking all dead.

Johnson is still as he delivers the first part of this speech, staring out into space, his expression fixed and grim, conveying the bleak trauma that Jeff experiences but keeps hidden from Tommy. On the words 'hothead Harry' Jeff becomes more animated, rolling his eyes and head performatively as he senses Tommy's gaze on the back of his neck (Tommy having turned to face his friend now), constructing a defence again. But the act does not endure. As he delivers the word 'dead' he hangs his head, defeated, as though he himself had been drained of life. The small gesture expresses in undramatic terms Jeff's private anguish, his pain at having killed another man. Only Tommy's interruption revives him, and he instinctively puts on the act once more. Finally, Tommy's sympathy enrages Jeff and he turns on his friend, a dark anger guiding his words. Although his back is turned to us for much of this speech, we appreciate the force of his onslaught and, perhaps for the first time, appreciate how much bigger than Tommy Jeff is; how he towers over his friend and leaves him awkward and lost for words like a child. Tommy remains unsure of whether to stay or leave Brigadoon and Jeff registers this, rounding on him, the words 'you're confused aren't you boy?' delivered in a deep rasp that makes Jeff sound older, bitter and more worn out by life than we have seen him before. After this tirade, Fiona comes running and Tommy must choose between the worlds. With unbearable regret, to the sound of Fiona repeating and repeating 'I love you,' he returns to New York, the world of Brigadoon fading into the mists that gather behind him.

The first part of the town square sequence is striking as it privileges the audience with an insight into Jeff's emotions which no character in his world shares. Minnelli's simple positioning of Johnson towards the camera but away from Kelly achieves this simultaneous act of intimacy and concealment. It is an uneasy moment, more striking perhaps than the actual death of Harry Beaton, which occurred as a strange climax to the musical chase sequence, happening quickly and suddenly overshadowed by its impact on Brigadoon's community. But the pain that Jeff feels, a consequence of Harry's death, is lingered upon, creating an uneasy moment in the film that is apparently unresolvable: Jeff will always live with his guilt. Jeff's actions and attitudes force the shock of reality into the world, dragging Tommy's thoughts back to the real existence outside of Brigadoon and shattering his dream of a life in Brigadoon. The focus on Jeff is not necessarily startling, as the film pays consistent attention to him throughout, recording his acts of often-humorous cynicism. For example, when Mr Lundie reveals the miracle of Brigadoon to him and Tommy, with Fiona in attendance, Jeff sits almost motionless, slumped against a tree, his gaze directed away from the old man in a show of casual disinterest. His only interaction is throw out the occasional dry one-liner. As the scene progresses, a pattern of shots occur that group Tommy, Fiona and Mr Lundie together but exclude Jeff, enclosing him in an isolated shot of his own, highlighting his self-elected marginalization from the group. This sequence is representative of Jeff's distanced attitude throughout the film as he maintains his 20th century sarcasm in the face of inexplicable events. However, when he kills Harry accidentally, this scepticism becomes darker, and he finds that he is not so much unable to live in the world of Brigadoon, as unable to live with himself in that world.

Yet, on returning to New York, Jeff fares little better. Minnelli marks our return to modernity with a shock of noise and activity, the emergence of a cityscape coinciding with a brash burst of cacophonous orchestration, its boisterous intrusion a million miles away from the easy tranquillity of Brigadoon. The theme continues as we enter a bar heavy with the racket of countless fast-paced voices and packed with the frenetic activity of the patrons as they gesture extravagantly to one another and flit across the foreground of the scene. Jeff is at first hidden, seated behind two chattering ladies at the next table from his, but as the camera closes in he leans around and stares at them as they talk. Eyes wide with incredulity, he seems bewildered by the pair's relentless babble, as though he were watching some foreign species of wildlife. He turns his head to register the activity on the next table, where a seated gentleman is aggressively and hilariously asserting his moral integrity to his companions: 'I'll lie, cheat, steal for this company, but I will not give up my integrity!' Jeff turns his head slowly away, the protraction of his gesture contrasting with the unremitting pace of those around him, and looks down in disbelief, breaking contact with the surrounding world. He rises and leaves.

The opening moments of this scene succinctly describe Jeff's sense of entrapment within this world as he sits enclosed by the two groups of boisterous neighbours, but also his distance from it: his expressions depicting the ways in which he struggles to comprehend its nature, his stillness highlighting his incompatibility with the world's unyielding rate. We might have supposed that Jeff, having earlier expressed his desire to leave Brigadoon, would belong in the modern world. Yet, this environment now seems anything but his natural home, as though his experience of Brigadoon had crystallized some of this world's unattractive features for him. Jeff appears removed from his environment and seeks to remove himself from it, leaving the scene to visit the bar where he places two glasses of water and two cigarettes on ashtrays either side of him in an effort to avoid close contact with anyone else. We have already spoken of Jeff's self-elected marginalization from the world of Brigadoon, his cynicism forming a barrier between him and the whimsical community he encountered. But he now performs the same self-distancing in relation to the New York world, his experience of Brigadoon making him wise to the superficiality of his surroundings and its inhabitants. Jeff, incongruous with the worlds of both Brigadoon and New York, is left without a natural home. Lost in the world, he retreats from it, ordering two brandies in rapid succession to further dull the abject reality of his existence. Through the alcohol, Jeff reinvents his world as a hallucination, which is precisely what Brigadoon might seem like to him now.

Of course, Tommy also finds himself to be incompatible with the modern world. Yet, his predicament is profoundly different to Jeff's. As he sits listening to his somewhat monstrous fiancée, Jane (Elaine Stewart), thoughts of Brigadoon and Fiona penetrate his consciousness. It is tempting to suggest that these intrusions, all in the form of songs, are memories of his time spent in that world. Yet, at one point Jane's words 'you certainly wouldn't want to keep me waiting' in relation to their wedding day triggers in his mind Fiona's song Waiting for My Dearie.[16] The difficulties in describing this as a memory lie in Tommy having never witnessed her perform the song, and so the moment is curious. Furthermore, the camera remains in wide shot rather than zooming in on Tommy's face, so resisting a convention that would focus attention upon his internal thoughts and locate the musical intrusions as flashbacks. We might conclude that something beyond the act of everyday remembrance takes place here, and certainly the fantastic nature of the film has from the outset prepared us for such events. It would appear that the world of Brigadoon bleeds magically into the world of New York, mysteriously summoning Tommy back. This notion is certainly consistent with the boundaries of possibility the film has constructed from the outset, and explains why Tommy hears Fiona perform a song which he had never heard before. Thus the convention of temporarily accessing a character's thoughts, which is common to narrative cinema in voice-overs, flashbacks, dream sequence etc, is evoked only to be altered: to show one world magically speaking to another.

Tommy is drawn back to Brigadoon, as echoes from that world invade not only his thoughts but his very existence. To this degree, there is no doubt in his mind where he belongs. Jeff, on the other hand, enjoys no such emotional bond with that ancient world. He remains untouched by it and, when the pair return to the site of Brigadoon, he reveals that 'I have to work hard to convince myself it happened at all'. (There is a question here of why Jeff has to accompany Tommy back to Brigadoon at all, given that he has no clear motives to return and given that it creates a slight imbalance at the film's conclusion, which I discuss later. It would appear that there is something of a ritual in their returning together, as though Tommy wishes to recreate almost exactly the moment in which they first discovered Brigadoon in an effort to force its reappearance for them now, like turning a key in a certain way to open a difficult lock. Perhaps he perceives that, were he to travel alone, the conditions would somehow not be right and any chance of returning to Brigadoon would be lost.) Tommy, in contrast, is mesmerized by the absence of that community, unable to comprehend losing Fiona forever. He slumps down, hanging his head and Jeff, now sensitive to his friend's incurable pain, suggests they leave.

At this moment, mysterious voices sing out gently the name of Brigadoon and Tommy slowly raises his head, as though roused by their sound. Crucially, Jeff does not appear to hear the sounds now and responds only to Tommy's looking up, following his gaze to see that the village has once again magically appeared. Tommy's hearing the voices represents his attunement to Brigadoon's magical world, just as he was able to hear its song when he sat in the New York bar. Jeff's inability to hear them registers his lack of attachment to that world, the extent to which he never properly integrated there. They rush down to the village and find Mr Lundie waiting to explain that the force of Tommy's love for Fiona has miraculously awoken their world once more. Tommy rushes through the village to find Fiona and, magically, she is also drawn towards him. They meet in the market square, walk slowly towards each other, arms outstretched as though impelled by a force they are helpless to control. They touch hands and the screen fades to black.

This ending emphasizes the coming together of two worlds through Tommy and Fiona's love, yet leaves Jeff suspended on the threshold between Brigadoon and his own world. Indeed, he cannot stay in Brigadoon because the laws, according to Mr Lundie version of events, dictate that he must love someone who resides there. So, we assume that he must return home to New York, alone, to resume his somewhat bleak existence. And yet, there would be nothing to keep him in Brigadoon either. The film does not allow Jeff happiness of that kind; does not reward him with a symmetrical relationship to Tommy's. Instead he becomes an unbalancing element that cannot be accommodated in the film's happy ending. Deborah Thomas has suggested that a symmetry exists in the film that makes Tommy Charlie's equivalent, and pairs Jeff and Harry together.[17] Certainly, Jeff and Harry share a similar disaffection with the world, and become dreadfully joined as Jeff accidentally ends Harry's life. Yet, Harry's frustrations emanate from his perceived entrapment within the world of Brigadoon, and his desire to escape the 'dimensions of my jail'. Jeff faces no such restrictions, yet still struggles to find a place in the world, and remains disenchanted with the worlds of Brigadoon and New York. Furthermore, the film reduces Harry's characterization to a few encapsulating outbursts, whereas Jeff is afforded a lengthier consideration in the ways already detailed. So Thomas' useful pairing of Jeff and Harry requires qualification based upon the characters' consistent representation within the film.

Likewise, Thomas asserts, quite correctly, that 'Brigadoon, if constructed more consistently from Jeff's or Harry's point of view, rather than from Tommy's, would be a much more melodramatic film'.[18] Yet, this overarching statement neglects to mention the ways in which the film does, from time to time, provide access to Jeff's complex point of view, more so than with Harry, and finishes with Jeff held in a melodramatic predicament, whilst Harry is absent through death. In that sense, it is possible for an audience to read Brigadoon melodramatically in the way that Thomas suggests based upon some of the events and attitudes that are disclosed to us. The camera does not linger on Jeff at the end of the film, but this only emphasizes his marginalization and lack of belonging in the world: the extent to which he has no place to call his own. The film contains two distinct and discontinuous worlds within its narrative but, in Jeff, presents a character belonging to neither. Attending to this does not drag the film out of shape to fit our concerns, but rather highlights an extra complexity to the plot that exists in stark contrast to the central pleasure of Tommy and Fiona's reunion as he crosses from one world to the other. In a film ruled by magic, Jeff stands outside of the enchantment, an uneasy counterpart to the story of enduring love. At the end of the film, his future is far from certain, his status far from secure.

Jeff represents a melancholic figure not normally found in Hollywood musicals.[19] A consideration of his position might expand into the broader suggestion that *Brigadoon* is a musical film that bears a hard, uncompromising logic, resisting the opportunity for easy resolution that might be found in other examples of the genre. In Jeff's case, he is left, somewhat tragically, without a place in the world, and the film devotes significant attention to his character to make this a legitimate concern. The only apparent option left to him is a return to the New York represented emphatically in the movie as an unbearable and lonely place: a harsh and critical depiction of modern life. Yet, we might also reflect that the film does not offer Tommy or Fiona a particularly easy choice and that, by opening up the possibility of an existence in another world, it forces upon Tommy the necessity of deciding upon a life in one world or the other as he is explicitly told that Fiona's leaving Brigadoon would mean the end of that world forever. So the selection of one world equates to the absolute rejection of another, the film constructs no compromise solution.

In this way, the two worlds are hermetically sealed from one another, with the possibility of passage between the realms limited to a miniscule window of opportunity that relies upon chance and can only occur in one direction. This rigidity is reminiscent of the films such as *A Matter of Life and Death*, *Flatliners* or *The Others*, discussed in the previous chapter that represented death as another world and showed passage between those worlds as a violation. *Brigadoon* makes its two worlds equally distinct, ruling out the possibility of lasting interactivity between the realms. In this sense, the characters are unyieldingly confined to their own worlds for their entire lives once Brigadoon disappears again for a hundred years. For Tommy, this offers the prospect of an existence within a kind of utopia but for Harry Beaton it was a prison that he escaped only through death, whilst Jeff ultimately finds neither comfort nor fulfilment in either realm and is thus condemned to a bleak future as the film concludes.

Notes

1. At the same time, away from the world of the film, narration of this sort also reasserts the notion of authorship, re-emphasizing the fact that someone (or some people) has designed and shaped a story to be seen and heard by an audience. It makes sense, therefore, that Orson Welles' voice should be heard and recognized at the beginning of *The Magnificent Ambersons*.
2. George Gibson was responsible for producing the backdrops in Brigadoon, just as he had been on Minnelli's earlier film *An American in Paris* (1951). Accounts suggest that Gibson's painting was so realistic that birds were drawn to it, flying in through open stage doors and colliding with it. (Hugh Fordin *M-G-M's Greatest Musicals: The Arthur Freed Unit* Da Capo Press, 1996, p. 426).
3. Colin McArthur *Brigadoon, Braveheart and the Scots: Distortions of Scotland in Hollywood Cinema* London: I.B. Taurus & Co. Ltd., 2003, p. 118.
4. Ibid.. p. 119.
5. Stephen Harvey *Directed by Vincente Minnelli* New York: Harper & Row, 1989, p. 130.
6. Gene Kelly quoted in Vincente Minnelli *I Remember it Well* London: Angus & Robertson, 1974, p. 279.

7. McArthur, pp. 110–111.

8. V.F. Perkins *Film as Film: Understanding and Judging Movies* New York: Da Capo Press, 1993, p. 121. Perkins' book first appeared in 1972 when, naturally, it was impossible to check images derived from 2001. The fact that the images of the film *2001: A Space Odyssey* (Stanley Kubrick, 1968) would not match the world of 2001 as we experienced it would seem to strengthen Perkins' points regarding authenticity and fictional worlds in film.

9. Even the film's opening credits display this same editing pattern, with the names of cast and crew appearing and disappearing in gentle dissolve, referencing the appearing and disappearing village at a remarkably early stage.

10. The magically lifting fog was achieved in reality by shooting the scene in reverse. Minnelli started with the clear view of the village and then flooded it with chemical fog; when the film was reversed, the fog appeared to slowly lift (Fordin, p. 426).

11. Minnelli, p. 280.

12. McArthur, p. 78.

13. My reference to the Vermeer painting here gives only a surface appreciation. Edward Snow provides a full and detailed analysis of *Woman Holding a Balance* that explores in careful terms the thematic and compositional intricacies of the work. Edward Snow *A Study of Vermeer* London: University of California Press, 1994, pp. 158–166.

14. Richard Dyer, 'Entertainment and Utopia' in Dyer *Only Entertainment* second edition London: Routledge, 2002, p. 20.

15. Tommy later wears the hat and jacket to sing *Almost Like Being in Love* after his encounter with Fiona on the hill. The song is distinctly 20th century, climaxing with a burst of showy brass section, and Tommy's style of dance is markedly of the modern age. His return to the modern mode seems strange (Harvey describes it as 'egregious') unless he evokes his world in order to reject it once more. We might regard Tommy's final act in the song – his throwing away his hat and then his jacket – as a more emphatic discarding of these 20th Century symbols. His re-emphasizing would then relate to him, having spent time with Fiona, realizing the implications of discarding his old life and willingly accepting them. Taken this way, Tommy puts the hat and jacket back on in order to replay the act of discarding them, of disowning his former existence.

16. Minnelli performs a clever trick with sound and image here by contrasting the graceful sound of Fiona's voice with Jane's pompous gestures, emphasizing the fact that this precious sound could never emanate from this woman.

17. Deborah Thomas *Beyond Genre: Melodrama, Comedy and Romance in Hollywood Films* London & Moffat: Cameron & Hollis, 2000, p. 137.

18. Ibid. p. 138.

19. But found in another Minnelli musical, *An American in Paris*, with the cuckold Georges (Henri Baurel) who must step aside in order that Jerry (Gene Kelly) and Lise (Leslie Caron) can be united. This earlier film also finds time to linger upon the melancholy of a figure left out of the romantic unions the musical genre demands.

10

REHEARSAL SPACE

Pleasantville (Gary Ross, 1998)

Placing the World

Pleasantville is reaching its first point of dramatic climax.[1] David (Tobey Maguire) and his twin sister Jennifer (Reese Witherspoon) are at home, fighting over the use of a television remote control. David had anticipated watching the 'Pleasantville Marathon', a back-to-back run of episodes from his favourite television show from the 1950s, while Jennifer insists on tuning in to an MTV concert which she intends to watch with her date, who will arrive any minute. Their preference for each television choice represents a succinct encapsulation of their divergent personalities. David is somewhat marginalized from his society, as disclosed in an opening scene where he imagines talking to an attractive female classmate while in fact standing over fifty feet away from her. Just as he remains at the periphery in that moment, so David also retreats into the distanced, nostalgic fantasy that the show 'Pleasantville' provides. Indeed, he seems to assume nostalgia for a period he has never experienced, in place of meaningful memories derived from his own life. Jennifer, on the other hand, is firmly in touch with her immediate society, a fact expounded in an earlier scene in which she boldly approaches and propositions a male classmate against the reservations of her female peers, thus setting up tonight's date. Her choice of television viewing correspondingly emphasizes her close investment in contemporary culture, forming the basis of her engagement with others (as Jennifer makes explicit, a sexually motivated engagement here) whereas David's choice of show marks his withdrawal from everyday society.[2]

This is the second remote control the pair has fought over, supplied during the unexpected visit of a TV repairman (Don Knotts) after they had inadvertently smashed the first control against a wall. As the two begin to tussle we cut first to an exterior tracking shot, where the TV repairman sits in his van outside their house, apparently satisfied with his evening's work, and then to an extreme close-up of the TV screen inside the house, where 'Pleasantville' is currently showing. On the black and white screen, the show's two juvenile children, Bud and Mary-Sue, fight over a transistor radio. We move out to a shot that incorporates David and Jennifer's hands in front of the television screen as they pull at the remote control, and then to a wider shot that

Pleasantville

emphasizes the physical correspondence of their tussle to the one taking place on screen: David matching Bud's positioning and Jennifer matching Mary-Sue's.

Indeed, the choice of shots used to depict Bud and Mary-Sue's battle on screen are replicated in the framing of David and Jennifer's tug-of-war, creating a mirrored association between the living room's reality and the television's fictional world. However, while the struggle on screen is portrayed as light-hearted and playful, with exclamations of 'gee-whiz' accompanying the background noise of canned audience laughter and a jaunty, carefree orchestration, David and Jennifer's battle has a greater intensity: a move to close-up emphasizing the pair's somewhat brutal expressions, the orchestration becoming sharper and militaristic; her shouting 'God, David! Just give it to me!' and him yelling back in her face 'Forget it!' In this way, the film constructs a series of visual resemblances in order to express the difference between a stylized, constructed argument in the television's fictional world and its harsher, more visceral equivalent in the real world.

As the two continue to struggle, Jennifer accidentally presses the 'power' button on the remote control and suddenly their motion seems to become blurred and hazy as they pull one way and the other. The music has grown frenetic now and, as we cut to a reverse medium-long shot of the pair, we see them become more indistinct, a glow emanating mysteriously from the remote until, cutting back to the original shot of them in front of the television, they disappear altogether and reappear miniaturized in the television set, literally taking the places of Bud and Mary-Sue. An overhead shot of the empty room emphasizes the gap where they once stood. From that moment on, David and Jennifer are in the world of Pleasantville.

David and Jennifer's cross over into the television's fictional world defines the film's narrative as a fantasy. Their departure from one realm to the next is not entirely surprising, however, as the film had built to this moment through a series of uncanny occurrences surrounding the remote control: the unexplained appearance of the TV repairman; the dissonant theme that underscores his arrival; the flash of lightning when David mentions 'Pleasantville' to him and again when he takes the control; the tense delay and portentous swelling of music as David and Jennifer first consider using the remote. Indeed, the film anticipates the event of the pair's absorption into the television world to the extent that, when the camera earlier tracked across the repairman's van to capture him smiling slightly as he gazes at the house, there was a firm, if enigmatic, sense that his expression carried further meaning, a notion emphasized by the somewhat ominous music that accompanied the camera's sideways movement in that shot. The film in fact declares its narrative mode at an earlier point even than the delivery of the remote control when, at the beginning of the film (after a brief sequence of apparent channel-hopping followed by a kitsch commercial for the 'Pleasantville Marathon') the simple words 'Once Upon a Time...' fade up in silence and remain on screen for around four seconds before fading away again.

Pleasantville

Following the audio-visual onslaught of the channel-hopping sequence and the 'Pleasantville' commercial, the silent, calm punctuation of the words allow a moment for pause, encouraging an appreciation of what 'Once Upon a Time...' might imply at the start of a film. We could reasonably take the words as a declaration of fantasy, and this expectation is certainly rewarded early on in the film's narrative as David and Jennifer are inexplicably drawn into their TV set.

The early establishment in *Pleasantville* of a storytelling tone rooted in fantasy (evoking memories of childhood fantasy-making in particular with the words 'Once Upon a Time...') defines a set of dramatic boundaries similar to those which I suggested were being laid out in *Brigadoon*. Indeed, a direct link might be taken to exist between the wording of *Pleasantville*'s inserted title and the first words spoken in Minnelli's film: 'Once in the Highlands...' Each film's explicit declaration of their fantastic mode is rewarded by the subsequent narrative events: two characters magically entering a world suspended in time in *Brigadoon*; in *Pleasantville* two characters magically entering a television world. The comparison between the two films endures if we consider that, just as *Brigadoon* attracted criticism on the grounds of historical accuracy in its portrayal of the Scottish Highlands, so the world of 'Pleasantville' might be confused with an attempted depiction of 1950s America, rather than a satirized depiction of 1950s American television. Paul Grainge attends to this misapprehension by comparing the film to an earlier but contemporaneous work, *Forrest Gump* (Robert Zemeckis, 1994), which involves a literal recasting of historical periods. Grainge explains that:

> Unlike the status of 'docu-fable' that *Forrest Gump* claimed for itself, *Pleasantville* does not play with boundaries of fiction and history in the same manner. Instead, *Pleasantville* creates a hyperreal past, entirely defined by, and within, the fictional conventions of television (sitcom) genre. Where *Forrest Gump* is based on the archival and historical referencing of 'real' events and peoples...*Pleasantville* creates a satirical iconography of projected cultural values.[3]

The technological progression of film stocks dictate that events before the widespread use of colour have been seen as black and white, since older film was most usually monochrome, whereas events occurring after the more widespread use of colour are seen as contemporary.[4] This is clearly becoming less true as moments from a shared cultural past appear increasingly in colour, yet the convention of representing the past in black and white and the present or future in colour persists in film and television, to the point of cliché.[5] It is perhaps this recurrent tendency to represent the past as a black and white world and the present or future in colour that might give rise to the confusion surrounding the kinds of worlds that are being contrasted in *Pleasantville*. The shots comparing David and Jennifer's struggle with the remote to Bud and Mary-Sue's tussle with the transistor radio could be misconstrued as contrasting a real past with a real present, the historically specific technologies of the radio and remote perhaps inviting such assumptions. Yet, David and Jennifer do not move back through time when journeying to Pleasantville. That would involve them moving to a realm spatially, chronologically and dimensionally continuous with the real world they already inhabited. Instead, they transfer into a fictional world, discontinuous with the world they have left.

Understanding Pleasantville's customs and attitudes depends upon a knowledge of the past to an extent, but it is not a real past world, only a fictional depiction of that world. Thus, the plot of *Pleasantville* does not share the same fundamental logic of time travel films that transplant a character from the present into the past or transport them into the future. The film asks us to understand the world of Pleasantville as existing even beyond the conventional borders of science-fiction logic and certainly beyond the confines of everyday logic. After all, the show 'Pleasantville', filmed at some point in the 1950s features a cast of real actors that have aged, changed and perhaps even died since, yet David and Jennifer interact with physical versions of them as they were in the fifties filming of the show. Pleasantville is defined, therefore, as a fictional realm.

The consequential danger in recognizing Pleasantville as a fictional place might be that we are led to conclude that nothing that occurs there matters: the place and its people do not exist according to everyday logic and therefore the importance of the town's events can be discounted. Scepticism of that kind would involve reading against the dramatic structure of the film, overlooking the themes and issues that are placed at stake in the narrative. Later in this discussion, I hope to suggest ways in which the film convinces us that matters taking place in Pleasantville have significance and, indeed, lasting relevance. However, the disregarding of Pleasantville's importance as a world might also result from a misinterpretation of the word 'fictional,' misreading it as 'fantasy'. We have seen the lasting significance of fantasized worlds in *The Wizard of Oz* and *Woman in the Window* through the ways in which Dorothy and Wanley's imagined worlds can be seen to reference an emotional poverty they each experience. In each of those films I suggested that, for example, the creation by each character of companions in whom trust and dependence could be placed, served to highlight the lack of such figures in Dorothy and Wanley's waking lives: their rendering of such people in their dreams making clear the lack each experienced in their everyday existence. Pleasantville, however, is not like Oz or the mirror-Gotham that Dorothy and Wanley respectively invent in their dreaming: both an actual and impossible place, it exists independent to the thoughts of either David or Jennifer. Their experiences there are as real as any other experiences and when David returns the world of Pleasantville continues, with Jennifer actually choosing to stay. When it becomes apparent that a disproportionate amount of time has elapsed in the real world compared to the duration of David's stay in Pleasantville's fictional world, it is clear that the film has fused concepts of realness and impossibility whereby the alternative world tangibly exists, but in isolation to the pervading laws of time and space.

Related to these matters, in his appraisal of the film Grainge describes *Pleasantville* as 'Existing somewhere between the historical time-travelling of *Back to the Future* (1985) and the media voyeurism of *The Truman Show* (1998)...'[6] This statement hardly constitutes a main facet of his argument, but it is worth lingering further on the distinction provided, especially in relation to what the film actually presents diegetically and thematically. The comparison with those other two films is perhaps understandable and, coincidentally, the cover notes for the *Pleasantville* DVD release contain a similar statement, attributed to *Total Film* magazine, which reads: '"THE TRUMAN SHOW" MEETS "BACK TO THE FUTURE"'. Surface accounts of the films uncover some of their potential connections to *Pleasantville*: in *The Truman Show* a character unknowingly lives in a television show for real, only finding out this truth at the end; in *Back to the Future* a character, roughly David's age, inadvertently travels back to 1955 and then has to find a way of returning to 1985. However, it is crucial that the literalness of those two films set them apart from the dramatic structure of *Pleasantville*: Truman Burbank (Jim Carrey) is *actually* living in a television studio; Marty McFly (Michael J. Fox) *actually* travels to the past. Where David and Jennifer travel to is less distinct both spatially and temporally, and the film seems to engage with a brand of fantasy that is removed from the storytelling structures of *The Truman Show* and *Back to the Future*.

Indeed, in those two films the characters' situations and journeys are explained and accounted for within the narrative: Doctor Emmett Brown (Christopher Lloyd) goes to some lengths to elucidate the scientific processes of time travel, including the essential need for plutonium; Truman's studio existence is eventually made clear to him when he discovers its borders and, ultimately, he simply leaves that space to move his life elsewhere. Although *Back to the Future*, and to a lesser extent *The Truman Show*, rely upon an acceptance of sets of rules different to those governing our everyday life (no one has yet travelled back in time, no one has yet unknowingly lived in a TV show for their entire life) they are at least based upon certain societal realities: science could conceivably make it possible for time travel to occur, someone could conceivably spend their life in a massive TV studio and think it was real life. In this sense, we might regard the two films as branching from but maintaining a connection with the ordinary. The events of *Pleasantville* cannot be measured against real life in the same way, as nothing related to everyday society could explain the transference of two individuals into a hermetically sealed fictional space, which takes the form of a television show recorded four decades earlier. Taken this way, the differences between *Pleasantville* and the two other films might become more critically useful than the similarities when referring precisely to its narrative structure and storytelling form. Rather than existing somewhere between *Back to the Future* and *The Truman Show*, *Pleasantville* makes a departure into a type of fantasy that those films do not and so, beyond certain surface correlations, it remains fundamentally distinct from them.

Expanding the World

The existence of a fictional world of Pleasantville within the film's narrative leads to a dramatically heightened revisiting of some of the debates surrounding the nature and structure of fictional worlds in film, as raised by a number of critics whose work is surveyed in chapter one of this study. Indeed, we might interpret V.F. Perkins' theoretical interests in 'Where is the World: The Horizon of Events in Movie Fiction,' for example, as an intellectual, near-anthropological, exploration of a series of fictional worlds in films. In the course of his discussion, Perkins seeks to orientate himself within a number of cinematic landscapes according to sets of potentials and possibilities that he finds to be inherent in the nature of their representation on screen. As we may recall, this involves an appreciation of a fictional world's 'worldhood' – the extent to which it is a world, of which we are only ever shown selected aspects. Indeed, as Perkins elucidates in relation to Douglas Sirk's *All I Desire* and its central character Naomi (Barbara Stanwyck):

> Within the larger world, the isolation of any one space or community and its value system (with its internal conflicts and sub-systems) is always far from complete. There are always Elsewheres that may be, for instance and in various mixes, familiar, remote, rumoured, desired, feared, imagined, sought, envied, shunned or demonised. A problem for Naomi, and potentially for her daughter, is whether a move from Riverdale should be welcomed as a liberation or lamented as an exile. Riverdale is not the whole world but it is the world that imposes the immediate context for the characters' actions and prospects. At every moment the film faces stylistic choices over the degree to which it will scale its gestures to the proportions and values of the depicted world.[7]

In this passage, Perkins balances a need to appreciate the extent to which a larger world exists around the society of Riverdale with an acknowledgement that our understanding of the fictional world is always dependent upon those aspects we are provided access to, and the nature of their presentation to us through the stylistic choices the film makes. In this sense, Perkins places emphasis upon the restrictions implicit in our status as viewers outside of a film's fictional world, reminding us that:

> We are offered an assembly of bits and pieces from which to compose a world. Fragmentary representation yields an imagined solidity and extensiveness. The malleability of the image is in a reciprocal relationship with the seamlessness and continuity that the image can evoke in our minds.[8]

Perkins' argument thus acknowledges the ontological borderline between viewer and fictional world, and consequently reinforces the fact that our suppositions are based upon a series of representational choices taken by the film-maker.

We are reminded here of Deborah Thomas' statement that 'The fact that we are given access to the film's geography, architecture and décor from a predetermined set of positions inevitably shapes what we, as spectators, see, and influences what we make of it'.[9] In this way, our 'predetermined' perspective on the fictional world's events impacts upon our understanding of what is possible within that world, dictating our boundaries of reasonable expectation. It may lead us to consider whether, for example, the event of a happy ending is a conceivable possibility in the fictional world we view on screen. We might here return to Thomas' assertions regarding the worlds of *My Darling Clementine* and *Party Girl*, as she maintains that the former provides far greater potential for harmonious resolution in its narrative world than the latter, where the pervasively repressive, misogynistic and self-serving tone (defined by characters' actions and attitudes) makes the likelihood of eventual reconciliation far more precarious.[10]

In their critical investigations, both Thomas and Perkins acknowledge the extent to which our reactions and responses to a fictional world are fundamentally shaped by what is shown to us at any given moment through a film's strategy of representation. However, in its fantasy of a physically accessible fictional world of Pleasantville that can be reached and visited by David and Jennifer, *Pleasantville* provides a level of interaction unachievable in real life. Within this structure, the central characters are able to not only investigate but also test the limits of the fictional world they encounter, literally exploring its geographical features, its residents, and the pervading ideologies found there. By crossing the ontological divide of the television screen, David and Jennifer advance the ordinary viewer's potential for supposition about the fictional world in dramatic fashion, enjoying an interactive relationship unattainable in everyday viewing experiences. Crucially, their actions within the fictional world of Pleasantville impact upon the potentials and possibilities of that society, fundamentally expanding the boundaries of reasonable expectation within that world.

Taking into account Thomas' account regarding the impossibility of harmonious resolution in the narrative world of *Party Girl*, it could be said that that David and Jennifer reshape the prevailing spectrum of possibility in Pleasantville and actually progress that society from a status quo of convenient, unquestioned and inflexible resolution to a much more unstable, enlightened and empowered democracy where the possibility of safe, rigid, homogenous rule is left untenable. Where fictional worlds, as experienced by the ordinary viewer, are already shaped and predetermined by a film's stylistic and representational choices, David and Jennifer actively reconstruct the borders of Pleasantville's fictional world, creating new narrative potentials by (sometimes inadvertently) overhauling a set of prevailing attitudes and ideologies. This fact is encapsulated in two features that are introduced to and made significant in the world of Pleasantville, and made significant in relation to each other: fire and literature.

Literature and fire are joined dramatically in the film as certain residents of Pleasantville's community enact a mass book burning in the town square. Scenes of burning books in *Pleasantville* perhaps invite allegorical readings in reference to the oppressive regime of the Nazi party in the thirties and forties. In many respects, this type of critical response serves to emphasize the potency of a set of iconic images from a period of the twentieth century, to the extent that monochrome images of massed burning books causes us almost involuntarily to recall Nazi officers burning Jewish texts, just as images of massed piles of assorted spectacles immediately form the word 'Holocaust' in our minds. It is no doubt part of the film's strategy to play upon the immediate powerful impact of such images, but a purely allegorical reading of the burning of books in Pleasantville is by no means the only interpretation of the event made available in the film. As residents of a fictional reality divorced from certain guiding contexts of 'exterior' reality, a group of the town's citizens register the threat of subversive knowledge through literature to their sense of normality and propriety.

Crucially, it is David and Jennifer's influence that has brought literature into the lives of Pleasantville's residents. Before their arrival, the pages of books are blank in that world, appropriately like props on a television set, and so the townspeople are never required to explore beyond a certain scheme of ideas and principles that guide their daily lives. However, when Jennifer and then, more expansively, David relate the plot of *Huckleberry Finn* to a group of schoolmates in the diner, the pages fill up with words and illustrations, an action which then has magical repercussions as hundreds of other books in the town library likewise become full. A scene occurring after David and Jennifer's revelations in the diner depicts groups of young people queuing outside the library and others emerging with armfuls of books. The cut between the two scenes is indicative of a short gap in time, with a cross-fade being employed that keeps both scenes on the screen rather than a fade which might have suggested an extended passage of time. This serves to illustrate the instantaneous way in which the town's books become full following David and Jennifer's interventions. We might reasonably suggest that this alludes to the particular brand of fantasy at work in the film, whereby events do not possess a clearly defined logic according to ordinary expectation. Neither David nor Jennifer can know the topics contained in all of Pleasantville's books, and so a force beyond their personal control seems to carry on their actions for them, with the two merely starting a chain reaction of events that extends the potential for knowledge and understanding in the fictional world.

The town's discovery of fire is similarly magical. In an earlier scene, Jennifer has told her Pleasantville mother, Betty Parker, (Joan Allen) the facts about sex. Sex is something that the Pleasantville citizens apparently have no knowledge of and, as we have seen in previous scenes, Jennifer seems to have appointed herself as something of an ambassadorial representative on the subject. When Betty reveals that her husband, George Parker (William H. Macy) 'would never do anything like that' Jennifer responds enigmatically: 'Well, y'know mom...there are other ways to enjoy yourself...without Dad'. A pause follows this lingering innuendo as the two females exchange looks, framed in reverse shots, and Jennifer tilts her head slowly and reassuringly at the older woman. We cut to later that night as Betty runs herself a bath while her husband prepares for bed. Shots of George drinking his bedtime milk, vigorously plumping his pillows and attempting to sleep in his single bed are intercut with those depicting Betty bathing, clearly following her daughter's advice. As she approaches climax, items of décor are suddenly turned to colour and, at the point of climax, a tree in the Parker's front garden bursts spectacularly into bright orange-white flame.

Here, Betty's private act of sexual pleasure is made public in the world of Pleasantville, albeit in an ambiguous and indirect fashion. This contradicts the general representation of sex in films as an illicit, intimate, private or secret act, making the introduction of sex into the world of Pleasantville such a crucial act that it requires announcing in such visually dramatic terms (echoing the way in which the town's teenagers have been turning to colour after sex). The symbolic use of fire in the scene naturally equates to notions of passion, but the theme of destructiveness is also evoked in the burning tree, as if to illustrate that moments of sexual awakening inherently threaten the fabric of this world, constituting a major breach of Pleasantville's routine equilibrium. As an active, vigorous force, fire is an appropriate means of representing this, and it is similarly significant that the fire is colour, burning in a black and white world, anticipating the way in which forces such as sexual desire will eventually turn Pleasantville to colour. A crucial change to the society's order – the introduction of sex and, particularly, masturbation – is thus announced in the visually dramatic form of a blazing tree, incorporating themes of liberation and release alongside those of threat and volatility.

Pleasantville

It falls to David to run to the town's fire station and alert the crew (the fire department have only ever rescued cats in Pleasantville so, amusingly, they do not understand David's cries of 'fire': eventually he has to shout 'cat' in order to get their attention). At the scene of the fire, the crew still fail to comprehend events, and so it is David's duty to teach them how to use their equipment and put out the blaze. His actions result in him receiving a commendation for bravery, an event that represents the people of Pleasantville's eventual understanding of fire as a destructive force and therefore recognizing David's act as heroic. The precise reason for the fire is, apparently, never discovered nor debated.

As a consequence of their actions, Jennifer and David inadvertently introduce two new elements to Pleasantville: literature and fire. There is a poetic sense later on, therefore, in one new force being utilized by some sections of the community to destroy another: fire to burn books. Although clearly resonating with some of the imagery associated with the Nazi's destroying of forbidden literature, the book burning sequence in the film brings together two developments in Pleasantville's society and has a logical function within that world's parameters of possibility. There had never been a need to burn books before because in the first part the books didn't contain words and in the second part fire ostensibly didn't exist. Thus, the burning of books marks the response to a changing world from a faction of Pleasantville's society, explainable within the coherent framework of that world. Importantly, it is David and Jennifer who have introduced these elements, thus expanding the possibilities and potentials of the fictional world they inhabit. The burning of books represents a futile attempt to halt progress in straightforward fashion, removing the potentially subversive and foreign elements (represented here in literature) in the hope that it will effect a reversal of time, returning the society to the moment before the boundaries of their world began to expand dramatically.

It is testament to the power of those images from 1930s Germany that black and white footage of groups burning books should evoke associations with the spectre of Nazism. Yet, a reading based solely upon allegorical reference risks missing the power and significance of such moments within the film's world, precisely that the introduction of fire and literature into the society of Pleasantville comes to symbolize the extent to which Jennifer and David have reshaped the contours of their world, appropriately bringing forth powerful scenes of positive revolution as well as reactionary fear and suppression of new ideas.

Rather than attempting direct correlations with pre-existent social contexts – by revisiting the specific historical fact of Nazism in Europe, for example – the film succeeds in integrating such potent images and themes within Pleasantville's particular (fictional) society, providing clear causal relationships between actions and outcomes as I have suggested with the fire/literature pattern of discovery and use. One interesting statement the film seems to make here is that, even in a community once removed (as a fictional creation) from our wider social and historical context, the same kinds of prejudices and frustrations emerge. Indeed, the expression of some of these prejudices and frustrations happen to take the same form as acts of violence and oppression we recognize from our own history. That notion is far more general than any attempt to address a specific historical injustice (a dubious project given the film's dramatic tone and structure) but more successful as it addresses an inclination across human society as well as remaining coherent within the film's fictional world of Pleasantville. The burning of books in Pleasantville represents the last desperate attempts of factions of its citizens to regain control of their world, having seen it expand beyond their comprehension, by destroying an element that they identify as bringing about this ideological shift: knowledge gained from books. Thus, even as allegorical resonances emerge within *Pleasantville*, the film does not stretch the internal logic or credibility of its fictional world in the attempt to make such connections.

Identity Found Elsewhere

One of the curious aspects of *Pleasantville*'s narrative is its general avoidance of common themes that might well have been exploited: namely notions of entrapment and escape. Given the film's dramatic structure, an obvious emphasis could have been placed upon David and Jennifer's pursuit of a return to their normative existence. This is certainly one of Marty McFly's objectives in *Back to the Future* (to refer back to the earlier comparison with *Pleasantville* made by Grainge). Kristin Thompson suggest that Marty has two interrelated goals, explaining that:

> Marty must induce his parents to fall in love at a high school dance in 1955, thus ensuring his and his siblings' existence in 1985. He must also, with Doc's help, arrange to take advantage of the bolt of lightning to return to 1985 in the time machine...The failure of either goal would be fatal for Marty's future existence.[11]

Accounts of this kind perhaps risk reducing *Back to the Future*'s story to a straight line of causal motivation based upon set goals, providing a very limited spectrum of narrative possibility. In this sense, they represent a limited response to the film's achievements and, indeed, if Marty were to fail either goal, it might simply result in a different kind of film. It may be more precise to suggest that *Back to the Future* places strong emphasis upon Marty's successful return to 1985, and 'success' here also involves his pairing of his mother and father before that act takes place. The film skilfully makes this issue of escape crucial by imposing a time limit upon his actions: he has to be at the clock tower at a certain hour in order to harness the power of the lightning and thus escape 1955. Failure to achieve his goals will result cataclysmically in his ceasing to exist or being forced to remain in the past, and the film inventively draws explicit correlations between the past Marty finds himself in and the present he wishes to return to. Marty and Doc's race against time becomes one of the climactic pleasures in Zemeckis's film.

Pleasantville, however, does not create such a vital relationship between the world the characters leave and the alternative world they find themselves in. The duration of time spent in Pleasantville is not made a crucial factor in the narrative and, indeed, the film entertains this issue of escape only to a limited extent, and only firmly in relation to Jennifer who is initially horrified at the prospect of an extended stay in Pleasantville. Yet her objections lessen as she first finds a ready means to continue her sexual exploits and then experiences an intellectual awakening. (Although still surprising, the film succeeds in making this transformation in the character's interests less jarring by amusingly having the first author Jennifer takes an interest in D. H. Lawrence, whom she considers to be 'kinda sexy', thus fusing her past and future investments in one moment. These sorts of joke references are indicative of the film's wider comedic strategy that is crucial to Pleasantville not becoming a nightmare world.) Indeed, it is Jennifer who finally opts to stay in that world, choosing to adopt the persona of Mary-Sue indefinitely, whereas at first this very notion represented a breach or suppression of her identity.

The film marks Jennifer's transition in a sequence where she sits reading alone at a desk in her bedroom. Her hair is tied back for the first time in the film to avoid it spilling over her book. A close-up of the open window by the side of her shows a breeze that flutters the light net curtains. Cutting back to a wider shot of Jennifer at her desk, we see her rub her bare arms and shiver slightly in the wake of the draught. Looking around, she spots the staid-looking cardigan hanging over the back of her chair and, out of practicality, puts it on. Witherspoon's particular talent for sharp, instinctive movement conveys the no-nonsense processes of Jennifer's thoughts and actions here, making the putting on of the cardigan seem like a simple and arbitrary act, rather than one marking a gradual transition in identity. This is also true in a subsequent close-up that captures Jennifer frowning slightly at her page of writing and then looking across at another object on the desk. A cut reveals a pair of glasses which she picks up and slowly puts on. Witherspoon upturns her mouth into a small, inconsequential expression that merely denotes a half-hearted curiosity on Jennifer's part, rather than a weighted discovery. The slowness with which she puts on the glasses might suggest an extension of the moment for dramatic purpose, but her nonplussed attitude ensures that it is not laboured. Complementarily, Randy Newman's score resists building to an emphatic crescendo, instead providing variations on an already established musical motif. Once the glasses are on, Jennifer looks for a while and then tilts her head back and down slightly, as though moderately surprised by the improvement offered through the magnifying lenses.

It is when we cut to a panning shot from behind her head that the meaning of the sequence is made emphatic. As it moves from right to left, the camera captures first the edge of a typewriter, a portrait of a ballerina, two framed commendation certificates and the book that Jennifer reads. As the camera moves to the other side of Jennifer's head we see a cheerleading statuette, a stack of three more books before resting upon a framed photograph of Jennifer 'as' Mary-Sue and a china lamp in the shape of a woman wearing a low-cut ball gown, in a pose reaching up with both arms to smooth her tightly curled hair.

The framed photograph acts as a mirror replicating the image of Jennifer as she sits at her desk: the same black-rimmed glasses, the same patterned cardigan, the same tied-back hair. The relationship of the image to Jennifer is complicated as, although it is her features in the frame, it is definitely a picture taken of Mary-Sue before Jennifer adopted that role and name in Pleasantville. In this way, the picture expresses the extent to which Jennifer has inadvertently moulded herself into the likeness of Mary-Sue, consequently taking on aspects of a character that she originally found to be repellent and actually rejecting some of her own traits that are

Pleasantville

encapsulated visually in the alluring design of the lamp. Indeed, the lamp and the statuette have immediate and explicit attractions – the raised arms of each female depiction denoting a performance or show, the surfaces of both either shiny or glowing. In contrast, the books and photograph require further scrutiny to uncover their meaning and value; both appear less attractive in visual terms than the statuette and lamp do on first glance.

The contrast between surface appearance and meaningful depth in the objects displayed on Mary-Sue's desk indexes the shift in attitude Jennifer makes in terms of her own self-perception. Whereas previously she felt secure of and revelled in the power her appearance held over others, she now discovers resources and qualities that set her on a different course, one which involves a rejection of surface effect and requires others to investigate the facets of her personality to discover her value. Shortly after this scene, Jennifer will lean out of her window, annoyed to have been disturbed from her study, and reject a sexual advance from Skip (Paul Walker), whom she had earlier introduced to sex. When she awakes in the morning, she has turned to colour.

This shift in Jennifer's self-perception results in her opting to stay in the alternative world she and David found themselves in, to go to college. The college is in Springfield, now signposted as twelve miles from Pleasantville.[12] Pleasantville therefore ceases to be a world contained within its own parameters, but a town that forms part of a larger alternative world whose borders have magically expanded as the people's vision has extended though David and Jennifer's actions. In a final montage sequence, we see Jennifer sitting on the steps of her new college reading from a book to a male peer of hers. As the camera pans across them, she looks up from her reading and catches his eye; he makes a comment – unheard to us as the overlaid musical soundtrack (Fiona Apple's version of 'Across the Universe') is the only audio element – and she smiles back at him, laughing as she returns her gaze to the book she holds. This shared moment of closeness and humour between the two characters is important in establishing the fact that Jennifer has not simply made a choice between the two binary oppositions of being attractive to males or being intelligent. In the brief glimpse we catch of her in the film's final stages, we are led to understand that she has remained intelligent *and* attractive, or attractive through her intelligence; capable of forming an engagement both with words and with those around her. Without this short sequence, it might seem as though Jennifer had merely rejected all of her former traits and thus suppressed a guiding (and in many respects liberated) aspect of her personality. Instead, the film has avoided such a simplistic portrayal by fusing together her past and present characteristics, meaning that she doesn't give up being Jennifer to become Mary-Sue.

It is also made certain that returning to the 1990s is no longer an attractive option for Jennifer: her sense of identity depends upon staying in the alternative world. However, the film does not make a dramatic issue of her decision to stay by making it a final choice. Instead, she tells David as she waits for the bus: 'I gotta do this for a little while'. The implication is that the door to the present-day is left ajar, and return is an option should she choose it. Indeed, David even says that he will come back and check on her soon, suggesting that the portal operates in both directions indefinitely. Again, we might link this to the ways in which the film resists those themes of entrapment and escape that are made available within the dramatic setup. As we saw in the previous chapter, *Brigadoon* does not allow for the same kind of movement between worlds that apparently allows David and Jennifer to revisit and return from Pleasantville. In this sense, Pleasantville has traits in common with the land of Narnia that a group of children visit in *The Chronicles of Narnia: The Lion, the Witch and the Wardrobe* (Andrew Adamson, 2005). In that film, Narnia can be visited, returned from, and revisited, in the way that it is suggested Pleasantville can be here.

Saving Face

David is actually offered the opportunity to leave Pleasantville on two occasions, a fact he apparently doesn't share with Jennifer. The magical TV repairman who originally sent the pair into Pleasantville visits him twice to voice his growing dissatisfaction with events taking place in the town, especially those surrounding David's relationship with Margaret (Marley Shelton), who according to pre-existent 'Pleasantville' plotlines is betrothed to a character called Whitey (David Tom). David opts to stay on both occasions; in the first instance due to an impending date he has with Margaret that evening and in the second because he refuses to allow the TV repairman return Pleasantville back to its original monochrome repression. David's liberation of the town is given melodramatic weight in a final court scene in which he manages to turn first his 'father', George, then the despotic town leader Big Bob (J. T. Walsh), and then the entire world to colour. David's actions effectively reverse his nostalgic attachment to the values and procedures inherent in his favourite television show, as he opts to bring forward change and progression within his adopted society.

Likewise, his relationship with Margaret corrects his timidity and detachment at the beginning of the film when he acted out the beginnings of asking a girl on a date whilst actually standing a long distance from her. Indeed, when propositioning Margaret he begins to repeat verbatim the same long-winded speech he enacted at the beginning of the film, starting with 'look...you probably don't think I should be asking you this...' before pausing and looking away from her for a moment, as though recognizing that this is the wrong approach and, in recognizing this, realizing the extent to which he has changed since he entered Pleasantville. David's sense of personal worth has escalated not only through his adopting the pre-existent persona of Bud but through his acts since then at the centre of his community, such as putting out the fire and introducing his peers to literature. These actions stray from the narrower possibilities offered in Bud's life before David inhabited the character: the climax of his achievements apparently consisting of winning first-prize in the science contest. Thus, David's success is due to his distinctly un-Budlike behaviour that, concurrently, marks a change in his own attitudes and actions.

In the instant that David looks away from Margaret he seems to acknowledge the shift that has occurred in himself, and when he looks up he is more direct and certain, asking simply 'Will you go out with me tonight?' Margaret smiles and nods in agreement. Before David became Bud, it is made clear that Margaret would not have chosen Bud and, likewise, before David became Bud it is also made clear that he held little attraction for girls in his world. Thus, by becoming someone else, but crucially not merely adopting their characteristics, David realizes a sense of worth never before experienced, expanding the spectrum of possibility both for himself and for the character of Bud.

It is suggested that David's liberation of the town and his successful relationship with Margaret will have a tangible effect on his life once he leaves Pleasantville and returns home, such are the magnitude of his accomplishments and the dramatic contrast this constitutes in relation to his former demeanour and status. However, these effects are only implied and the film stops short of providing the viewer with precise assurances. It is, however, more emphatic when detailing the change in David's relationship with his real mother (Jane Kaczamarek) once he has returned from Pleasantville's alternative world. Their estrangement from one another was a marked feature at the beginning of the film as he sat in the front room mouthing lines of a 'Pleasantville' re-run and she paced the kitchen impatiently arranging custody times with David's father. As the characters in the television show exchange pleasantries, the mother's aggravated voice continually interrupts, disrupting David's viewing and, when she declares down the phone-line 'Barry, if I want to have a *mud bath* with my new boyfriend that's really none of your business,' he turns the television volume up two notches in an effort to drown her out.[13] Immediately following this action, there is a shot from the direction of David's viewpoint which captures the image of the television screen in the foreground and his mother on the phone in the background.

The shot emphasizes the disparity between the sterile perfection of the nuclear family in 'Pleasantville', with mother and father Parker framed symmetrically on the screen, and the condition of David's domestic life where his mother stands alone, distanced from him, arguing with her ex-husband. Significantly, there is no communication between mother and son – they are both involved in conversations on the telephone and with the television respectively – and there is no eye contact between them, whereas on screen the television family engage in a shared celebration of Bud's top science grade, a final shot emphasizing their equal positioning within the frame and their attention to one another. When we next see David's family home, on the night of the magical TV repairman's visit, his mother has already left, and at no point do we see the two have any kind of interaction with one another.

The estrangement that is shown to exist between David and his real mother contrasts with his later relationship to Betty Parker, his 'adopted' mother in Pleasantville. However, when David experiences his first significant engagement with Betty, it does not follow the lines of impossible perfection expounded in the Pleasantville episode he viewed earlier. Instead, he finds her at a moment of acute insecurity and hopeless anxiety. George Parker and Big Bob, the town leader, sit in the Parker's living room, Big Bob having just made George a member of the Pleasantville Chamber of Commerce so that he can help combat some of the 'changes' that are occurring in the town. Once this deal is made, Big Bob requests one of Betty's 'swell pineapple kebabs' but when she doesn't respond to George's call, David intervenes and offers to find her. (There

Pleasantville

is not space in this chapter to properly detail the complexities of William H. Macy's exquisite comic timing, as exhibited in this scene where he pauses for just the right amount of time to perfectly depict George's waiting for a routine response and then subtly captures the character's mixture of despondence and utter confusion when the reply does not arrive. Macy's intricate sense of the rhythms of human interaction is crucial to this portrait of a man coming farther and farther adrift in his world.)

David discovers Betty in the kitchen, leaning over the sink, hands squared on the surface to support her frame. She has her back to him and, while the sounds of her distressed, uneven breaths are audible, the cause of her anguish is still unclear. He approaches her and, in a closer shot, gently lays a hand on her turned shoulders. His reaching out to her in this sensitive, supportive gesture represents his first moment of real human contact with anyone in Pleasantville (his relationship with Margaret having been marked up to this point only with her gift of some cookies). Indeed, as he touches her back he provides an emotional support that rhymes with the physical support she seeks to gain from the kitchen surface as she leant against it. David's tender gesture discloses his awareness of Betty's emotions and conveys the extent to which his time in Pleasantville has begun to change him, bringing him closer to others where once he was distant and reclusive. As Betty turns to face him he sees for the first time that her face has now turned to colour, her transparent tears distinct against the blush of her cheeks. A reverse shot captures David's uncertain reaction, and we are perhaps also surprised by her appearance as she is dressed in monochrome colours, her hair black, so that when turned away there was no sign that she had changed.

Her transformation fits with a chain of causal events, however, stemming from her lingering exchange of mesmerized gazes with David's boss at the soda store, Bill Johnson (Jeff Daniels), with whom she will later form a passionate romantic relationship. From that moment of seeing Bill differently for the first time, colour affects Betty. In a neighbourhood bridge game, her suit of hearts turns to red (appropriately symbolising her growing but suppressed desire) then, as has already been described, her pursuit of Jennifer's sexual advice has the effect of turning her bathroom to colour and causes a tree in the front yard to burst into bright orange flame.[14]

The redness of Betty's deck of cards is mirrored in the redness of her lips when she turns to face David in the kitchen now. Again, the deep crimson hue of her lips seems to fulfil the function of conveying the desire that is building uncontrollably within her and which, were it to be revealed in Pleasantville society, would elicit a response not dissimilar to Hester Prynne's scarlet letter 'A'. As David looks at Betty, his open-mouthed awe and wide eyes seem to communicate his passing over these consequences in his mind as he realizes the implications of her appearance and fears for her. Moreover, as he gazes upon her, he seems to see her as a different person now – as a person at all in fact, capable of a depth of feeling, desire and emotion he had

Pleasantville

never thought possible in her. Up to this point Betty had performed the archetypal domestic duties that corresponded with her one-dimensional depiction in the television show he knew so well. Now, however, he sees in her simultaneous fervour and fragility, qualities that define her 'realness' as opposed to surface details that he observed previously. David is aware by this point in the story that colour is potentially equated to sexuality, thanks to Jennifer's busy exploits, and so must recognize the significance of Betty's appearance. In this moment, he ceases to regard her as the single-dimensional mother figure shown in the reruns of 'Pleasantville' and engages with her as a complex, emotional person.

His engagement takes the form of reassurance. Straining against her emotions, Betty asks: 'What am I going to do? I can't go out there this way. How can I go out there this way?' She is overwhelmed once more as she finishes 'Look at me...' speaking the words through welling tears. David responds by saying: 'It's okay...it's alright...' and then 'Have you got any makeup?'[15] She tells him there's some in her handbag and they sit down together, David opening a compact of face powder. In the sequence that follows, he applies the powder to her face, covering over the colour of her skin with the makeup that remains grey. Following this, he applies lipstick to her, again covering over her colour with its dark tone. During this process, a series of close-ups on David's face reveal his rapt concentration as he applies Betty's camouflage.

Indeed, the dedication and care required to complete this task are immense, involving a careful responsiveness and appreciation of the subject themselves. If the sight of Betty's coloured face brought to David's mind her inner depth, this tactile activity convinces him of her tangible realness as he gently passes the powder-puff over her face and hands. If his laying a supportive hand on her shoulders represented an engagement with another human, then this process repeats that engagement again and again, deepening the connection with each stroke of his hand. And, of course, David is no make-up artist: the procedure of making over that he undertakes requires a particular determination and care as he has no prior aptitude for the task. The possibility exists for David to simply tell Betty the solution to her dilemma and leave her to apply the makeup, drawing upon years of experience and skill. Yet, he elects to perform the task himself, providing comfort and intimacy as well as a solution to her problem.

By applying the makeup to Betty, David creates a bond between them as they both share in the secret of her colour and he becomes complicit in the process of camouflaging her for the outside world. The act exposes his special awareness that surfaces can conceal truths, and that the nature of an appearance is not necessarily a reliable measure of its substance. This characteristic perception endures throughout the film, as David systematically allows others to engage with and express their interiority, in turn allowing them to appreciate for themselves that things are not always as they seem. In this scene, particularly, David must understand what he conceals in order to conceal: to know what the truth beneath the surface is in order to successfully mask it.

The specialness of this union between the characters reverses the previous mother-son relationship they had in Pleasantville, where she would regularly be seen providing hearty breakfasts and snacks. Now, he provides for her, offering safety and protection and forging a bond with her against the world. Once the process is completed, David's gaze lingers on her, as though he were appreciating the new closeness that exists between them, but also recognizing for the first time that this woman is beautiful – that she has a potency he never before recognized in her. In this sense, David sees Betty properly for the first time. When she has smoothed down her dress and left the room to attend to her husband, he sits in motionless silence, partly exhausted by the effort he has had to expend and partly overwhelmed by the strength of the engagement he has made with Betty. With his gaze tilted down, away from the world, it reads as a moment of contemplation on David's part, as though this act of closeness with his adopted mother had profoundly defined him. It makes sense later in the film, therefore, that David should turn to colour having defended Betty from a group of thuggishly aggressive youths. In that later scene, Betty shows him his reflection in her compact mirror, as if connecting his moment of ultimate self-realization with those moments they spent together in the kitchen.

The connection persists when, in the film's conclusion to the climactic trial sequence, Betty tosses down the compact from the public gallery of the courthouse so that David can reveal to Big Bob that he has now also turned to colour, just like the other residents of Pleasantville. (Bob's turning to colour occurs as a result of his rage at David's fluent courtroom performance in which he suggests that any number of unpredictable changes could occur at any moment in Pleasantville.) The arcing, spinning compact is captured in slow-motion, the film lingering on the object's movement to heighten its motion and perhaps also to propose its significance. The inclusion of this object at this stage carries thematic weight as David's ultimate triumph in turning the whole town to colour - Big Bob included - is related back to the quieter kitchen sequence involving himself and his adopted mother, Betty, through the reintroduction of a key souvenir from that earlier scene: the compact. In this way, David's final achievement takes its place in a sequence of self-discoveries, connecting back with his defence of Betty in the street and his care of her in the kitchen. Betty's tossing of the compact so that David can make plain his triumph places her back within the sequence of his accomplishments, referencing the extent to which she has been involved in each of his previous self-awakenings. Significantly, then, David's emphatic, widespread achievements in Pleasantville originate from a moment shared with Betty in the kitchen, which can be seen to have acquainted him with the fragile complexities of another human's emotions, causing him to look beyond surface appearance to discover the person, rethinking notions of what a mother might be to him.

The nature of this mother-son relationship is thus made crucial to David's time in Pleasantville. The final affinity between mother and 'adopted' son is emphasized as David prepares to leave the town. At the Parker house, Betty has unexpectedly prepared for him a packed lunch of meatloaf sandwich, a hard-boiled egg, marshmallow squares and some fried chicken for his trip. David had thought she wasn't coming, but she replies plainly that she had to and, as he approaches her, she drapes his high school sweater around his shoulders, to wear on the trip 'in case you get cold'. These simple gestures – the preparation of lunch and the offering of the sweater – illustrate a thoughtfulness that is distinct from the automated, mindless household routine that had been Betty's previous existence before David's arrival. As she smooths David's lapel, she lingers slightly and emotion rises within her, tears welling in her eyes (the moment is shot from behind David so that Betty's reactions register most clearly). She draws him close to her in an embrace, murmuring 'Oh Bud', and as they stand, continues 'I am just so proud of you'.[16] Their embrace continues as we reverse to a shot from behind Betty to frame David's reaction as he closes his eyes, half-burying his face in the curve of her neck. Eventually he sighs 'I love you too' in response and they slowly break their hold, stepping back from each other as Betty lightly touches David's chin. The pride that Betty feels for David and his stated love for her reinforces the bond between the characters that has evolved and matured during David's stay in the fictional town. The film therefore provides a point of resolution for their relationship, allowing them a moment in which to express their love for one another (David's expression 'I love you *too*' references his understanding of Betty's pride to be a statement of her love for him). At this point David can withdraw from Pleasantville, his emotional maturation complete and Betty left in a position that, although unresolved, includes a series of options previously unavailable to her and an independent strength she never before possessed. For these respective changes, David and Betty have each other to thank.

The newly available options that emerge for Betty naturally relate to Jennifer and David's expanding the boundaries for potential within the fictional world of Pleasantville. It is significant that we can easily recognize Betty's former entrapment within an oppressive social order alongside other depictions of 1950s life in film. Specifically, we might recall melodramas such as Max Ophüls' *The Reckless Moment* or Douglas Sirk's *All I Desire* (films briefly mentioned already in this study) which interrogate traditional notions of maternal and domestic duty through their portrayal of a mother's extra-marital love. The extraordinary – and extraordinarily moving – relationships that develop in these films occur against the background of a socially repressive order, so that mothers are, at different stages, made to choose between duty and desire.

Pleasantville revisits such themes of maternal repression in order to move beyond them, concluding with the crucial images, once David has returned to his world, of Betty sitting alongside her husband and then her lover, Bill, involving herself in a relationship of mutual dependence and cooperation with both. Implicit here is the extent to which the actions of David, and Jennifer, have led not only to a change in the fictional world's potentials, but crucially to a change in what is permissible in that world, advancing the society of Pleasantville beyond the ideological orders inherent in films like *The Reckless Moment* and *All I Desire*, where the impermissibility of extra-marital relations became a central narrative constraint for the characters.

Returning to his real world via the magic remote control, David does not discover a similar state of harmony. He finds himself back in his real front room, standing in front of the television screen, from which a voice announces the first hour of the 'Pleasantville' marathon has concluded. David immediately switches the television off, as though ending his association with a programme that had previously dominated his life; his understanding of that fictional world has, after all, altered significantly. Looking around the room, he notices his Pleasantville High School sweater folded over a chair (this item from the alternative world effectively removing the possibility that David's time in Pleasantville was merely a fantasy). As he walks over to pick it up, his movement is underscored by a rich, slow variation of the 'Pleasantville' theme, the tonal warmth of which references David's nostalgia as he touches an object brought back from that other realm.

His moment of reflection is cut short, however, as female sobbing is audible in the background. Following the sound, he pushes open the kitchen door to find his mother sitting at the table, the camera tracking forward and tilting upwards to take in the packed luggage at her feet, suggesting that she didn't go away for the weekend after all. As she catches sight of David at the door she covers her face with her left hand, saying 'Hi' in a faltering tone that undermines her attempt at casualness. Her gesture of hiding her face closely resembles Betty's action earlier in the film when David found her standing at the sink: as he entered the kitchen in that house she angled herself away from him so that he was unable to see her face. Although Betty had other reasons for hiding her face, the visual resemblance between the mothers' actions in both scenes establishes a correspondence that will endure as this scene progresses.

Interestingly, both mothers' hiding can be understood as a way of protecting themselves from a discovery that would leave them vulnerable, but also as a means of instinctively shielding their child from the trauma of sharing in their distress. David says 'I thought you went out of town,' to which she simply replies 'Came back,' the brevity of her response acting as a barrier in a similar way to the hand that she uses to shield her face from his view. At this reply, David pauses, assessing the situation, the camera framing his expression in a reverse medium-close up, and then he seems to reach a decision as a slight smile forms across his mouth. This small change represents his new confidence in his ability to handle this situation, and this situation particularly as he had a parallel encounter in the alternative world of Pleasantville. His real mother, like Betty in Pleasantville, has become the victim of her world, unable to find a clear route in which to manoeuvre herself out of her hopelessness. Here, as in Pleasantville, David is capable of guidance. As he moves to sit down we cut to a new shot of the table that frames his mother's features from the front, making plain the extent of her distress as black patches of runny mascara have formed underneath her teary eyes. On David's asking what is wrong, she begins her sentence 'Everything's just so fucked up,' emphasizing the disparity between this nineties reality and the fifties fictionality of Pleasantville. David, however, remains unfazed and, as his mother explains that she turned around instead of meeting her young boyfriend because 'it doesn't make me feel younger, it just makes me feel older,' her son simply listens and, as she pauses, a reassuring smile spreads again across his face, disclosing his ease at this display of raw emotional reflection.

In fact, as he smiles, David seems to also experience his own moment of reflection, his gaze dropping away from his mother temporarily as though his mind were half-elsewhere in the silence. Perhaps his mind is back in Pleasantville for those seconds, as he realizes his ability to cope with this new crisis due to the nature and frequency of human crises he encountered and overcame there. Particularly, he might now feel equipped to support the fragile emotions of his

Pleasantville

mother, just as he did Betty's in that other realm. David's security in this situation allows him to meet his mother's anxieties with calm reassurance and a tenderness that is beyond his years.[17] Indeed, he refers back to experiences in Pleasantville when he advises her 'there is no right house, there is no right car...' in response to her longing for the predictable future she once saw mapped out for herself. David's legacy in Pleasantville, of course, was founded upon the rejection of such notions of rightness, and his lasting achievement was his ability to encourage the town to embrace the unpredictable. Such sentiments find a place here again as he seeks to guide his mother away from her overwhelming sense of despair. His tenderness towards her continues as he reaches for a box of tissues and begins to slowly wipe away the patches of mascara beneath her eyes.

The framing of this moment mimics almost exactly its counterpart in Pleasantville, with the camera placed behind David to frame his mother and him reaching across from the right, with his right hand, to touch her face.

Although clearly replicating his behaviour towards Betty in Pleasantville, this sequence possesses none of the heightened melodrama of that earlier sequence: no equivalent tension of a husband waiting in the other room; no poignant underscore to complement the scene's affection; no lingering close-ups of the two individuals; no equivalent visual satisfaction of the grey make-up applied to the coloured skin. Instead, the editing maintains the steady pattern of shot-reverse-shot and the camera remains at the same distance from the characters, resisting the move closer that might heighten the significance of David's repeated gesture. Indeed, as he puts the tissue to his mother's eye, she continues to talk: 'I'm forty-two, it's not supposed to be like this,' to which he replies calmly 'It's not supposed to be like anything. Hold still'. The equivalent sequence in Pleasantville occurred with the characters remaining silent, as though privileging the moment's weight and import. Here, however, the rhythms of ordinary speech continue to flow over the action, placing it more firmly in the realm of everyday life. Consequently, we might consider that the style of this sequence results in a portrait of the everyday, far removed from the pervasive melodrama of Pleasantville. Style fuses with story here, marking David's return to the real world from the fictional realm by depicting the same type of action in more recognizably authentic terms.

The pared-down simplicity of everyday language is continued and completed when David's mother asks finally 'How come you got so smart all of a sudden?' and he replies straightforwardly 'I had a good day'. Our knowledge of David's days spent in Pleasantville clearly allows us to appreciate the irony of his statement, but his mother cannot share our insight. Nevertheless, his simple answer is sufficient for her and she smiles back at him for the first time in the sequence (her first smile of the film, in fact). David's closing statement also suggests that he will not choose to reveal the nature of his departure; that he might never be compelled to. Indeed, as the scene cross-fades into a montage of Pleasantville images, we might reflect that David has left that world behind and instead engages with his own world in a way he never felt able to before. His reaching out to his real mother in the gesture of wiping away her tears represents his re-embracing the real, reclaiming it as his home. It might be tempting to suggest that David simply applies the lessons learnt in Pleasantville to good effect in the real world. This is partly the case, but it is also true that David must reapply those lessons in the real world, understand its disparity to the fictional realm of Pleasantville, in order to succeed there. Crucially, he must appreciate that his mother is different to his Pleasantville mother, a realization that ironically rests upon his viewing her as a sensitive, complex individual – a lesson that he learnt from Betty, a fictional character in that other world. His ability to raise a smile from his mother suggests his achievement in this, and reaffirms his new belonging to the world he once left behind.

David's return to his real world exposes a narrative trait that *Pleasantville* shares with each of the alternative world films discussed in detail in this study. Each film dedicates itself to representing ends as beginnings. In each case, as the film concludes, the characters themselves rejoin a world (a real world or, in the case of *Brigadoon*, an alternative) and in doing so start again there. The period away has without exception opened up revelations and insights about their world that they can either dramatically act upon in the pursuit of change (in the cases of *It's a Wonderful Life* and *Groundhog Day*), temporarily or permanently suppress (in the cases of *The Wizard of Oz* and *The Woman in the Window*), inadvertently forget and then struggle to comprehend (*Eternal Sunshine of the Spotless Mind*) or find so revolutionary to their thinking that they elect to adopt an existence in another world entirely (*Brigadoon*). In each case, the flights from the real world result in characters having to face reality again, equipped with new knowledge and experience, and find a way of living there from that day on. To this degree, alternative world films include departures in order to facilitate returns, and present endings that are truly beginnings.

Notes

1. The word 'Pleasantville' has different meanings which I hope to clarify in the following ways: *Pleasantville* is the title of the film, 'Pleasantville' is the title of a television show, and Pleasantville is the place that the film's central characters travel to.

2. It is also interesting to consider the role of social groups as depicted in David and Jennifer's television choices. The MTV concert features a return to visual depictions of a mass audience sharing in the thrill of a cultural experience whereas the presence of an audience of 'Pleasantville', although possibly present in the studio during filming, are a non-diegetic element of the show, not part of the character's world. We might relate these screen representations to Jennifer and David's proximity to their societies: her actively engaged, him significantly removed.

3. Paul Grainge 'Colouring the past: Pleasantville and the textuality of media memory' in Paul Grainge (ed.) *Memory and popular film* Manchester: Manchester University Press, 2003, p. 208.

4. Colour was of course a feature of cinema almost from its beginning, with the early films of George Méliès perhaps providing the most dramatic early example of colour film.

5. This is certainly a pervasive convention, but one that has not always been adhered to in the history of cinema. *With Bonjour Tristesse* (1958) Otto Preminger creatively inverts the associations of past as black and white and colour as present, thus using colour, or its lack, as an expression of a central

character's emotional state, to depict Cecile's (Jean Seberg) nostalgia for the past and her sense of loss in her present.

6. Grainge, p. 204.

7. V.F. Perkins 'Where is the World? The Horizon of Events in Movie Fiction' in John Gibbs & Douglas Pye (eds.) *Style and Meaning: Studies in the detailed analysis of film* Manchester: Manchester University Press, 2005, p. 33.

8. Ibid. p. 26.

9. Deborah Thomas *Reading Hollywood: Spaces and Meanings in American Film* London: Wallflower Press, 2001, p. 9.

10. Ibid. p. 31.

11. Kristin Thompson *Storytelling in the New Hollywood: Understanding Classical Narrative Technique* London: Harvard University Press, 1999, p. 15.

12. Like Pleasantville, Springfield is a ubiquitous town name in America, but also functions self-consciously is this film as it is also the fictional setting for a US television show of the fifties, *Father Knows Best*, which would almost seem to suggest that television communities of the past are starting to link up at the end of the film. For a contemporary audience, however, Springfield is also where *The Simpsons* live.

13. This sequence represents a fairly scathing critique of the conditions of modern life, similar to Minnelli's depiction of a boisterous, shallow New York in *Brigadoon*.

14. The bathroom may signify a small inconsistency in the film's plot. If we are to take it that the room actually changes to colour, as other objects in Pleasantville do, rather than Betty being suddenly able to see in colour, then it seems implausible that her husband George would not discover this and ask questions.

15. From the other room we hear George continue to shout 'Betty', hilariously attempting to follow the pattern of expectation that has been built up over years and not quite appreciating that its change might indicate something more.

16. Betty addressing David as 'Bud' reminds us that he only inhabits this persona. We never know whether, when David returns to his world, the character of Bud still remains, reverting back to his old incarnation before David's arrival. The finality of David's farewell perhaps suggests that this is not the case, but it would certainly produce a complicated scenario in that alternative world once he had departed.

17. Indeed, David is literally beyond his years when he rejoins the real world as his lengthy experience in Pleasantville has only amounted to an hour when he returns.

Conclusion

I suggested in chapter ten that events in Pleasantville might be discounted by the sceptical viewer due to their occurrence within a fictional place, divorced from the regiments of everyday existence and so, somehow, less important for that. This position could conceivably be expanded to fit all of the places that the characters visit in the films that I have discussed. From there, it would be no great leap to propose that none of the films dealing with such places matter; that the events they disclose to us can confidently be dismissed as only works of fantasy: stories without basis in authentic human experience. Fantasy, then, becomes a negative critical judgement.

In partial response to this hypothetical position, my analyses of the films contained within this study implicitly propose those films' value as works of fantasy which are pertinent to the human condition in ways both complex and profound. Specifically, these films all have something to say about the shared experience of existing in the world. In each case an imagined, potential or other world is introduced as a contrast to the character's everyday world: a new existence provided or invented as an alternative to theirs. Thus, a relationship between the worlds is established that brings the character's reality into sharp focus, demanding a vital re-engagement with ordinary life. The films use the fantasy of an alternative world to debate a series of universal conditions associated with human experience: insecurity, ambition, loneliness, apprehension, bravery, vanity, inarticulateness, anxiety, ambiguity, introversion, love, and so on. This kind of exploration, I would suggest, is a feature of many variations of fantasy cinema, of which alternative world films constitute a discrete group, that include an audacious or inventive narrative development in order to re-examine the human condition, forming a sincere and serious connection with everyday life. Once this key characteristic is recognized and starts to be evaluated, dismissing such films on the grounds suggested above becomes a less secure enterprise.

The seven films I have selected for extended consideration invest in these existential questions with a degree of complexity and perceptiveness that justifies close analysis in order to adequately describe their achievements. In this sense, a summarising approach would not be appropriate to the task. That is not to say all films containing alternative worlds merit such detailed scrutiny, however, and I am receptive to the notion that a counter body of films could be found, with a little searching, that deal with the narrative convention in ways that are facile, incoherent or inconsequential. An inquiry of that kind, however, lies beyond my critical interests here.

A central contention in this study is that it *matters* that a disillusioned small town hero doesn't imagine the world of Pottersville, for example, or that a land called Oz does not exist outside of a young girl's mind. Knowing whether a world a character experiences is Imagined, Potential or Other is crucial if we are to appreciate fully the statements each film wishes to make about the experiences, emotions and actions of its protagonists. Without these important distinctions, we are liable to misinterpret alternative worlds in films, falsely reading George Bailey's encounters as only products of his imagination, for instance, or missing the tragic significance of Dorothy Gale's inventing a world in which she takes a central, active role that could never be replicated in her waking life. It is crucial that our understandings of such narratives are exact and properly formulated; while the nature of the alternative world remains ambiguous to us, the nature of the film's particular quality and achievement remains potentially underdeveloped. Our judgement might become clouded as worlds like Brigadoon seem imbued with aspects of dreamlike wish-fulfilment, whereas the world of Oz seems just as coherent and tangible as the worlds of Pottersville and Pleasantville. These are some of the challenges faced in an attempt to accurately describe alternative worlds; challenges that are actively embraced and negotiated in my analyses. As I have strived to demonstrate throughout this work and through the close scrutiny of particular films, engaging in precise terms with the alternative world a film proposes is integral to an exact evaluation of the resonances created between the realms it presents.

The themes of credibility and coherence in film narratives have constituted a central focus throughout the study, based upon critical contributions such as V.F. Perkins' founding assertion, cited in chapter one, that 'As an illusion-spinning medium, film is not bound by the familiar, or the probable, but only by the conceivable. All that matters is to preserve the illusion'.[1] To this end, an enduring interest throughout my work has been the extent to which the films discussed have successfully accounted for the event of an alternative world within the internal logic of a broader fictional world. A fundamental challenge for the films, it seems, is to balance an audacious narrative device with a need to retain the credibility of the fictional world, making it coherent and rational for an audience. It has therefore been a notable achievement of the films discussed that they handle a complex departure from the rudiments of everyday existence without fracturing the coherent relationships essential to our making sense of the events we witness as viewers. Indeed, it is testament to the coherence of the films that they develop a series of crucial relationships and resonances between the worlds they create, ensuring that their real and alternative worlds matter in relation to each other.

Such conclusions are pertinent to the broader study of fictional worlds. Although in many respects the study of alternative worlds in film constitutes a specialized intellectual enterprise, I have suggested that it brings forth concerns surrounding the coherence, credibility and internal logic of those worlds: questions which are in turn pivotal to an evaluation of fictional worlds in film. In my analyses, I have strived to articulate the various ways in which alterative realms are made credible within the films' broader fictional worlds, ensuring balance and cohesion whilst avoiding rupture and fragmentation. These types of assertions might be profitably expanded to allow for a better-developed sense of fictional worlds on screen, beyond the theoretical concerns of this study. The attention paid to the somewhat extreme dramatic occurrence of an alternative world in a film's narrative might then serve to crystallize a series of issues surrounding the nature and composition of broad fictional worlds within films: the extent to which they are imbued with sets of rules and characteristics that we either accept or query and, in doing so, accept or query them as worlds at all. With this in mind, a study of alternative worlds that attends to issues of coherence, credibility and internal logic continues and complements the work of critics, detailed in the opening chapter of this book, who sustain an intricate engagement with fictional worlds *as* worlds. This study emphatically refocuses attention upon worlds as they are created in films, suggesting a methodology and critical approach that extends beyond an analysis of *alternative* worlds in film.

Furthermore, this study of alternative worlds has consistently evaluated the extent to which significant relationships are established and maintained between elements within the films. Thus, details such as the colour of a jacket, the positioning of a photo frame, the wiping of a tear, the throwing of a hat, light cast onto a face or the fractional pause between two words have been shown to possess particular weight and meaning within a narrative. But not only within a narrative: they have particular weight and meaning within a world. This becomes particularly pronounced within the films that I engage with, as a contrast is struck in these narratives between the arrangement of elements in one world and in its alternative. So the significance of a set of characters' warm embraces in Oz is enhanced as they contrast with the relative coldness exhibited by another set of characters in Kansas. Likewise, a wife's utter lack of emotional recognition in Pottersville can forcefully remind us of the intimate support she provided her husband in Bedford Falls.

Contrasts of this kind are representative of achievement in the films I discuss, but they are only a version of the kinds of complex correspondences and distinctions that are made between compositional elements in fiction films. For the critic sensitive to matters of style and meaning, the extent to which a film handles such relationships and develops them into significant arrangements becomes a measure of its accomplishment. Crucially, such elements belong to a fictional world, defining that world and in turn being defined by it. Films containing alternative worlds concentrate our attention upon the orders and arrangements of the worlds they propose and contrast, but we might profitably expand that awareness to an appreciation of fictional worlds in films more generally. In this way, we are concerned not only with what events are possible and potential within a fictional world according to the societal regimes established there, but also how elements of that world are shown to meaningfully interact, so that events are made significant within the world on screen. Again, a study of alternative worlds brings such issues to the forefront, as it centres upon the contrasting of elements from one world to the next, but that kind of focus should make us alert to the types of comparisons that films continually make between elements contained within their fictional worlds, leading us to evaluate in detail the achievement in making those relationships meaningful. In this way, the work complements and continues the interests expressed by critics such as Deborah Thomas and V.F. Perkins, particularly, whose recent work has been defined by an engagement with matters of film style in relation to the structure and tone of fictional worlds on screen.[2] It is appropriate, therefore, that their theoretical contributions have formed a substantial part of the critical context for this study of alternative worlds, and that their assertions have been revisited consistently throughout the work.

Although taking into account examples outside American cinema, this study has predominantly focused upon films made within Hollywood. The inclusion of titles from both classical and contemporary Hollywood has performed the function of demonstrating the endurance of alternative world narratives across periods and styles of film-making in American cinema. In addition, as I have hoped to demonstrate, Hollywood has proved a particularly rich source for the types of films I wish to discuss. However, this selecting of films from both eras of American cinema also responds to certain assumptions regarding 'old' and 'new' Hollywood, namely that the former represents tight causality and narrative transparency whereas the latter possesses a greater propensity for narrative fragmentation and complexity.

This is a claim that Kristin Thompson contends with directly in *Storytelling and the New Hollywood*, a work to which I have made periodic reference throughout this study.[3] Thompson attempts to complicate notions of a rupture between classical and post-classical Hollywood film-making, questioning whether shifts in production and regulation (such as the fallout of the antitrust proceedings against Paramount or the dismantling of the Production Code) have significantly impacted upon narrative structure and storytelling.[4] However, in asserting that there are a number of key correlations that can be found between old and new Hollywood storytelling, Thompson makes a case for a type of narrative straightforwardness she takes to be inherent in classical and contemporary Hollywood films. One of the central arguments in this formulation relies upon the notion of cause and effect chains in Hollywood narratives, a concept inherited from Thompson's earlier work with Bordwell and Staiger on *The Classical Hollywood Cinema*.[5] It is Thompson's contention that:

> The most basic principle of Hollywood cinema is that a narrative should consist of a chain of causes and effects that is easy for the spectator to follow. This clarity of comprehension is basic to all our other responses to films, particularly emotional ones... Hollywood favours unified narratives, which means most fundamentally that a cause should lead to an effect and that effect in turn should become a cause for another effect, in an unbroken chain across the film.[6]

A difficulty arises when thinking about narratives in terms of linear chains, in that we might risk misreading an event as being motivated by another action in the story, as a straightforward effect in response to a cause. In *Brigadoon*, for example, the world of Brigadoon emerges directly after Tommy has expressed his disillusionment with his own world, but its appearance in no way occurs in response to his needs as a character within the story. The reasons for its emergence are in fact entirely unrelated to Tommy within the fictional world, and require explanation according to a set of circumstances proposed by the film itself according to its internal logic. Importantly, in relation to my study, Brigadoon is not a linear response to Tommy's disillusionment but a world in its own right, replete with a spectrum of hermetically sealed customs and orders. Engaging with that fact, I maintain, produces a more appropriate and accurate appraisal of the film's narrative rather than an account limited only to chains of cause and effect. Brigadoon is not an effect, it is a world. This is certainly the basis for the chapter on the film contained in this study.

Furthermore, these points regarding Tommy in Brigadoon connect with another suggestion of Thompson's, that:

> In virtually all cases, the main character in a classical Hollywood film desires something, and that desire provides the forward impetus for the narrative. Hollywood protagonists tend to be active, to seek out goals and pursue them rather than having goals simply thrust upon them.[7]

Returning again to Minnelli's film, it is hard to square this account with events in Brigadoon as, in Tommy's case, at the film's opening he has no clear objectives inasmuch as he is unaware of what he might desire, beyond the fact that he is unenthusiastic about his life at that moment. His journey into the Highlands of Scotland is one of recreation, a break from life without any firm purpose or intention and, indeed, when we first encounter him he has come to a standstill, inactive and inert. The challenge of being reunited with Fiona at the film's conclusion is certainly thrust upon him by the dictates of Brigadoon's magical disappearance, but he journeys back to the site of that lost world without any firm knowledge that his actions will be successful, as no one has ever mentioned that Brigadoon can appear between its hundred years enchantment. In this sense, it is unclear what his goal might be in returning. Yet, it is not essential to completely understand Tommy's motivation, to have it spelt out to us, in order to appreciate his actions. Indeed, the lack of clear explanation might actually lend his character depth and definition through the allusion to an interiority beyond surface appearance.

We might also relate this kind of ambiguity to films from the contemporary period, such as Groundhog Day, where Phil Connors appears utterly unaware of his need for change and inadvertently ends up in the cycle of repeating potential worlds. Even at the film's conclusion, it is relatively unclear whether it was Phil's goal to escape the cycle of Groundhog Days, since he had no means of knowing how that might be achieved, or rather to create that day as perfectly as he could, altruistically repeating the ideal day for certain residents of Punxsutawney forever more. As with Tommy's ambiguous motivation in Brigadoon, it is not vital that we understand this precisely one way or the other, as this lack of clarity might lead to our appreciating Phil as a real person in his fictional world, with a private psychology that even he might not understand. Importantly, such ambiguities regarding the causality of events in Brigadoon and Groundhog Day do not compromise the extent to which these films present a coherently structured world in which events make sense to us. It is not necessary to reduce these narratives to lines of cause and effect dictated by character motivation in order to make a case for their achievement in terms of coherence and credibility.

The films contained in this study balance the ambition of their storytelling structures with an ability to preserve the internal logic of the worlds they present, meaning that their audacious narratives make sense to us. This does not equate to simplicity, however, and my intention through a series of close analyses of films in this study is to exemplify the kinds of complexities the films create and handle. This level of complexity joins films from old and new, classical and post-classical Hollywood cinema, emphasizing the extent to which Hollywood has always been capable of intricately structured, carefully constructed narratives replete with relationships and metaphors that warrant further interpretation and evaluation. Indeed, I would contend that an appreciation of the coherent relationships that the films create between elements within their narrative worlds – from features such as costumes, possessions and structures to others such as movements, gestures and words – is fundamental to our making sense of the themes and issues the films wish to raise and engage with. This runs against Thompson's assertion (actually made in defence of Hollywood against accusations of slightness and thinness in comparison to European counterparts) that:

> the best Hollywood films of any era, whether a classic of studio era like Ford's *How Green Was My Valley* (1940) or a recent film like *Silence of the Lambs*, are as complex in their own terms as their art-house equivalents. They do tend, though, to be much easier to understand, lacking the ambiguities and symbolisms that can make many art films fascinating or pretentious, depending on one's tastes.[8]

This statement, although setting out ostensibly to champion Hollywood cinema, makes a series of assumptions that I find to be inconsistent with my experience of the Hollywood films contained in this study. Unlike Thompson, I do not recognize an incongruity between a film being 'easier to understand' and also proposing a series of 'ambiguities and symbolisms'. I have hoped to demonstrate in this study that Hollywood has a history of producing stories where ambiguity, symbolism and complexity feature as traits that attract us as audience members, drawing us back to the films in an attempt to better appreciate the themes and issues represented in their narratives. In this sense, there is no perceivable rupture between classical and post-classical Hollywood, but the continuity is based upon a propensity for complexity, coherence and profundity in narratives rather than simplicity, linearity and redundancy. Ultimately, to re-emphasize a central contention made throughout this study, the films I discuss not only present alternative worlds within their narratives and make those worlds credible to us, they also create *resonance* between those realms, meaning that such worlds matter *in relation to each other*.

Notes

1. V.F. Perkins *Film as Film: Understanding and Judging Movies* New York: Da Capo Press, 1993, p. 121.
2. V.F. Perkins 'Where is the World? The Horizon of Events in Movie Fiction' in John Gibbs & Douglas Pye (eds.) *Style and Meaning: Studies in the detailed analysis of film* Manchester: Manchester University Press, 2005, pp. 16–42; Deborah Thomas, *Reading Hollywood: Spaces and Meanings in American Film* London: Wallflower Press, 2001.

3. Kristin Thompson *Storytelling and the New Hollywood: Understanding Classical Narrative Technique* London: Harvard University Press, 1999.
4. Ibid. pp. 2–4.
5. David Bordwell, Janet Staiger and Kristin Thompson *The Classical Hollywood Cinema: Film Style & Modes of Production to 1960* London: Routledge, 1985. The concept of causality occurs most prominently in a section of the work attributed to Bordwell, 'The classical Hollywood style, 1917–60,' in a chapter entitled 'Story causality and motivation,' pp. 12–23.
6. Thompson pp. 10 & 12.
7. Ibid. p. 14.
8. Ibid. p. 11.

FILMOGRAPHY

8½
Federico Fellini, Cineriz/Francinex, Italy, 1963

Afterlife (Wandâfuru raifu)
Hirokazu Kore-eda, TV Man Union/Engine Film, Japan, 1998

Amelie (Le Fabuleux destin d'Amélie Poulain)
Jean-Pierre Jeunet, Victoires Productions, France/Germany, 2001

American Psycho
Mary Harron, Am Psycho Productions Inc/Muse Productions/Lions Gate Films/P.P.S. Films, USA/Canada, 2000

An American in Paris
Vincente Minnelli, Metro-Goldwyn-Mayer/Loew's Incorporated, USA, 1951

Arrivée d'un train en gare à La Ciotat
Auguste Lumière/Louis Lumière, France, 1895

Back to the Future
Robert Zemeckis, Amblin Entertainment/Universal Pictures, USA, 1985

Back to the Future Part II
Robert Zemeckis, Amblin Entertainment/Universal Pictures, USA, 1989

Back to the Future Part III
Robert Zemeckis, Universal City Studios, Inc./Amblin Entertainment USA, 1990

Being John Malkovich
Spike Jonze, PolyGram Holding, Inc./Gramercy Pictures/Propaganda Films/Single Cell Pictures, USA, 1999

A Beautiful Mind
Ron Howard, DreamWorks SKG/Universal Pictures/Imagine Entertainment, USA, 2001

Bigger than Life
Nicholas Ray, Twentieth Century Fox Film Corporation, 1956

Blind Chance (Przypadek)
Krzysztof Kieslowski, Zespol Filmowy 'Tor,' Poland, 1987

Brigadoon
Vincente Minnelli, Metro-Goldwyn-Mayer, USA, 1954

The Chronicles of Narnia: The Lion, the Witch and the Wardrobe
Andrew Adamson, Walt Disney Pictures, USA, 2005

The Company of Wolves
Neil Jordan, Palace Productions/ITC Entertainment, UK, 1984

The Countryman's First Sight of the Animated Pictures
R.W. Paul, UK, 1901

The Devil's Advocate
Taylor Hackford, Warner Bros./Regency Enterprises, USA, 1997

Donnie Darko
Richard Kelly, Pandora Inc./Flower Films, USA, 2001

The Dream of a Rarebit Fiend
Edwin S Porter, Edison Manufacturing Company, USA, 1906

Eternal Sunshine of the Spotless Mind
Michel Gondry, Focus Features, USA, 2004

eXistenZ
David Cronenberg, Alliance Atlantis, Canada/Great Britain, 1999

The Family Man
Brett Ratner, Beacon Pictures/Saturn Films, USA, 2000

Fight Club
David Fincher, Twentieth Century Fox Film Corporation, USA/Germany, 1999

Finding Neverland
Marc Forster, Mirimax Film Corporation, USA, 2004

The Fisher King
Terry Gilliam, TriStar Pictures, USA, 1991

Flatliners
Joel Schumacher, Columbia Pictures Corporation, USA, 1990

The Fountainhead
King Vidor, Warner Bros., USA, 1948

Groundhog Day
Harold Ramis, Columbia Pictures Corporation, USA, 1993

Hook
Steven Spielberg, Amblin Entertainment/TriStar Pictures, USA, 1991

It's a Wonderful Life
Frank Capra, Liberty Films, USA, 1947

Labyrinth
Jim Henson, Labyrinth Enterprises/Jim Henson Organisation/Lucasfilm, UK, 1986

The Last Temptation of Christ
Martin Scorsese, Universal Pictures, USA/Canada, 1988

Let Me Dream Again
G.A. Smith, UK, 1901

Letter from an Unknown Woman
Max Ophüls, Rampart Productions/Universal-International, USA, 1948

Liliom
Fritz Lang, Fox Film Europa, France, 1934

The Locket
John Brahms, RKO Radio Pictures, USA, 1946

Lone Star
John Sayles, Castle Rock Entertainment, USA, 1996

The Magnificent Ambersons
Orson Welles, Mercury Productions/RKO Radio Pictures, USA, 1942

The Matrix
Andy Wachowski/Larry Wachowski, Warner Bros., USA/Australia, 1999

A Matter of Life and Death
Michael Powell/Emerich Pressburger, Archers Film Productions/Independent Producers/J. Arthur Rank Film Productions, UK, 1946

The Never Ending Story (Die Unendliche Geschichte)
Wolfgang Petersen, Constantin Film AG, Germany, 1984

Open Your Eyes (Abre los ojos)
Alejandro Amenábar, Sociedad General de Cine S.A., Spain/France/Italy, 1997

Orphée
Jean Cocteau, Films du Palais Royal, France, 1950

The Others (Los otros)
Alejandro Amenábar, Sociedad General de Cine S.A./Mirimax Films, Spain/USA, 2001

Peter Pan
P.J. Hogan, Columbia Pictures Industries Inc./Universal Pictures, USA/UK/Australia, 2003

Pleasantville
Gary Ross, New Line Cinema, USA, 1998

The Purple Rose of Cairo
Woody Allen, Orion Pictures Corporation, USA, 1985

The Reckless Moment
Max Ophüls, Columbia Pictures Corporation, USA, 1949

Return to Oz
Walter Murch, Walt Disney Productions, USA, 1985

Rosemary's Baby
Roman Polanski, Paramount Pictures Corporation/William Castle Enterprises, USA, 1968

Run Lola Run (Lola rennt)
Tom Tykwer, X Filme Creative Pool, Germany, 1998

Sherlock Jr.
Buster Keaton/Roscoe Arbuckle, Joseph M. Schenck/Buster Keaton Productions/Metro Pictures Corporation, USA, 1924

Sliding Doors
Peter Howitt, Mirage Enterprises/InterMedia Film Equities/British Screen, USA/UK, 1998

Spellbound
Alfred Hitchcock, Vanguard Films/Selznick International Pictures, USA, 1945

The Thirteenth Floor
Joseph Rusnack, Columbia Pictures Industries Inc., USA/Germany, 1999

The Usual Suspects
Bryan Singer, Rosco Film/Bad Hat Harry Productions/PolyGram Filmed Entertainment/Spelling Films International/Blue Parrot, USA/Germany, 1995

Vanilla Sky
Cameron Crowe, Paramount Pictures Corporation, USA, 2001

Vertigo
Alfred Hitchcock, Alfred J. Hitchcock Productions/Paramount Pictures Corporation, USA, 1958

Waking Life
Richard Linklater, Twentieth Century Fox Film Corporation, USA, 2001

What Dreams May Come
Vincent Ward, Polygram Filmed Entertainment Inc./Interscope Communications/Metafilmics, USA/ New Zealand, 1998

Who Framed Roger Rabbit?
Robert Zemeckis, Touchstone Pictures/Amblin Entertainment, USA, 1988

The Wizard of Oz
Victor Fleming, Loew's Incorporated, USA, 1939

The Woman in the Window
Fritz Lang, Christie Corporation/International Pictures, USA, 1944

BIBLIOGRAPHY

Allen, Richard & Murray Smith (eds.). *Film Theory and Philosophy* (Oxford: Oxford University Press, 1997).

Baldick, Chris. *Oxford Concise Dictionary of Literary Terms* (New York: Oxford University Press, 2001).

Barr, Charles. *Vertigo* (London: BFI Publishing, 2002).

Barrie, J.M. *Mary Rose: A Play in Three Acts* (London: Hodder & Stoughton, 1929, first published 1920).

——. *Peter Pan: A Play in Five Acts* (London: French, 1977, first published 1904).

Baum, L. Frank. *The Wizard of Oz* (London: Penguin Books, 1994).

Bjorkman, Stig. *Woody Allen on Woody Allen* (London: Faber & Faber, 1993).

Bordwell, David. *Making Meaning: Inference and Rhetoric in the Interpretation of Cinema* (London: Harvard University Press, 1989).

——. 'Film Futures,' *SubStance* vol. 31, no. 1, 2002

——, Janet Staiger and Kristin Thompson. *The Classical Hollywood Cinema: Film Style and Mode of Production to 1960* (London: Routledge, 1985).

Branigan, Edward. *Narrative Comprehension and Film* (London: Routledge, 1992).

——. 'Nearly True: Forking Plots, Forking Interpretations: A Response to David Bordwell's "Film Futures,"' *SubStance* vol. 31, no. 1, 2002

Braudy, Leo & Marshall Cohen (eds.). *Film Theory and Criticism: Introductory Readings 5th Edition* (New York: Oxford University Press, 1999).

Britton, Andrew. 'Hitchcock's *Spellbound*: Text and Counter-Text,' *CineAction!*, no. 3/4, Winter 1986

——. 'The Philosophy of the Pigeonhole: Wisconsin Formalism and the 'Classical Style,'' *CineAction!*, no. 15, Winter 1988–89

Bronfen, Elisabeth. *Home in Hollywood: The Imaginary Geography of Cinema* (New York: Columbia University Press, 2004).

Cameron, Ian (ed.). *The Movie Book of Film Noir* (London: Studio Vista, 1992).

Carroll, Noel. *Philosophical Problems of Classical Film Theory* (Princeton, New Jersey: Princeton University Press, 1988).

Cavell, Stanley. *The World Viewed: Reflections on the Ontology of Film* enlarged edition (London: Harvard University Press, 1979).

——. *Pursuits of Happiness: The Hollywood Comedy of Remarriage* (Cambridge MA: Harvard University Press, 1981, reprinted 1997).

——. *Contesting Tears: The Hollywood Melodrama of the Unknown Woman* (London: The University of Chicago Press, 1996).

——. *Cities of Words: Pedagogical Letters on a Register of the Moral Life* (Cambridge, Massachusetts; London, England: The Belknap Press of Harvard University Press, 2004).

Christie, Ian. *The Last Machine: Early Cinema and the Birth of the Modern World* (London: BFI Publishing, 1994).

—— & David Thompson (eds.). *Scorsese on Scorsese* (London: Faber & Faber, 2003).

Clarke, Gerald. *Get Happy: The Life of Judy Garland* (London: Time Warner, 2002).

Cohan, Steven & Ina Rae Hark (eds.). *The Road Movie Book* (London: Routledge, 1997)

Coniam, Matthew. 'Rodents to Freedom,' *Philosophy Now*, June/July 2001, Vol. 32

Connelly, Mark (ed.). *Christmas at the Movies: Images of Christmas in America, Britain and European Cinema* (London; New York: I.B. Taurus, 2000)

Culbertson, Andrew. 'Revisiting *Groundhog Day*,' *Film Journal* 2003: 1(5) http://www.thefilmjournal.com/issue5/groundhogday.html (accessed 5/6/2007)

Currie, Gregory. *Image and mind: Film, philosophy and cognitive science* (Cambridge: Cambridge University Press, 1995).

Daughton, Suzanne M. 'The Spiritual Power of Redemptive Form: Steps Towards Transcendence in *Groundhog Day*,' *Critical Studies in Mass Communication* No. 13, 1996

Davies, Jude. 'Gender ethnicity and cultural crisis in *Falling Down* and *Groundhog Day*,' *Screen* 36:3 Autumn 1995

Dickens, Charles. *The Christmas Books* (London: Penguin Books Ltd., 1994, first published 1876).

Dyer, Richard. *Only Entertainment* second edition (London: Routledge, 2002).

Elsaesser, Thomas (ed.). *Early Cinema: Space Frame Narrative* (London: BFI Publishing, 1990).

Feuer, Jane. *The Hollywood Musical* (London: BFI Publishing, 1982).

Fordin, Hugh. *M-G-M's Greatest Musicals: The Arthur Freed Unit* (New York: Da Capo Press, 1996).

Fowkes, Katherine A. *Giving Up the Ghost: Spirits, Ghosts and Angels in Mainstream Comedy* (Detroit, Michigan: Wayne State University Press, 1998).

Framework editorial. 'The Reckless Moment,' *Framework* 4, Autumn 1976.

Frank, Gerald. *Judy* (London: W.H. Allen & Co. Ltd., 1975).

Freud, Sigmund *The Interpretation of Dreams* Joyce Crick, trans., (New York: Oxford University Press, 1999).

Gibbs, John. *Mise-en-scène: Film Style and Interpretation* (London: Wallflower Press, 2002).

—— & Douglas Pye (eds.). *Style and Meaning: Studies in the detailed analysis of film* (Manchester: Manchester University Press, 2005).

Girgus, Sam B. *The Films of Woody Allen* second edition (Cambridge: Cambridge University Press, 2002).

Goodrich, Frances & Albert Hackett. *It's a Wonderful Life* (California: O.S.P Publishing Inc., reprinted 1994).

Gordon, Andrew. 'You'll Never Get Out of Bedford Falls: The Inescapable Family in American Science-Fiction and Fantasy Films,' *Journal of Popular Film and Television* vol. 20, no. 2, 1992

Gunning, Tom. *The Films of Fritz Lang: Allegories of Vision and Modernity* (London: British Film Institute, 2000).

Grainge, Paul (ed.). *Memory and Popular Film* (Manchester: Manchester University Press, 2003).

Graves, Robert. *The Greek Myths* complete edition (London: Penguin Books, 1992).

Halpern, Leslie. *Dreams on Film: The Cinematic Struggle Between Art and Science* (Jefferson, North Carolina: McFarland & Company, 2003).

Harvey, Stephen. *Directed by Vincente Minnelli* (New York: Harper & Row, 1989).

Hoberman, J. 'Under the Rainbow,' *Sight and Sound* vol. 9, no.1, January 1999

Horton, Andrew (ed.). *Buster Keaton's Sherlock Jr.* (Cambridge: Cambridge University Press, 1997).

Humphries, Reynold. *Fritz Lang: Genre and Representation in his American Films* (London: Johns Hopkins University Press Ltd., 1982).

Jackson, Kevin (ed.). *Schrader on Schrader & Other Writings* (London: Faber & Faber, 1992)

James, Nick. 'I forgot to remember to forget,' *Sight and Sound* vol. 14, no. 5, 2004

Jensen, Paul M. *The Cinema of Fritz Lang* (London: Zwemmer, 1969).

Kawin, Bruce F. *Mindscreen: Bergman, Godard, and First-Person Film* (Princeton, New Jersey: Princeton University Press, 1978).

——. *How Movies Work* (London: University of California Press, 1992)

Kelly, Richard. *The Donnie Darko Book* (London: Faber & Faber, 2003)

Klevan, Andrew. *Disclosure of the Everyday: Undramatic Achievement in Narrative Film* (Trowbridge: Flicks Books, 2000).

——. 'The Purpose of Plot and the Place of Joan Bennett in Fritz Lang's *The Woman in the Window*,' *Cineaction!* No. 62, 2003

Langley, Noel, Florence Ryerson & Edgar Allan Woolf. *The Wizard of Oz* (London: Faber & Faber, 1991).

Lindroth, James. 'Down the Yellow Brick Road: Two Dorothys and the Journey of Initiation in Dream and Nightmare,' *Literature Film Quarterly* vol. 18, no. 3, 1990

Mamet, David. 'Crisis in happyland,' *Sight and Sound* vol. 12, no. 1, January 2003

Martin-Jones, David. 'Two Stories, One Right, One Wrong: Narrative, National Identity and Globalization in *Sliding Doors*,' *CineAction* 64, 2004

Matthews, Peter. 'Spinoza's Stone: The Logic of *Donnie Darko*,' *Post Script* vol. 25, no. 1, Fall 2005

McArthur, Colin. *Brigadoon, Braveheart and the Scots: Distortions of Scotland in Hollywood Cinema* (London: I.B. Taurus & Co. Ltd., 2003).

McDaniel, Robb. '*Pleasantville* (Ross, 1998),' *Film and History* vol. 31, no. 2, June 2002

Minnelli, Vincente. *I Remember it Well* (London: Angus & Robertson, 1974).

Naremore, James. *The Films of Vincente Minnelli* (New York: Cambridge University Press, 1993).

Nayman, Ira. 'Film, Dreams and Stolen Pocketwatches,' *CineAction!* No. 67, October 2005

O'Hehir, Andrew. '*Pleasantville*,' *Sight and Sound* vol. 9, no. 3, March 1999

Perez, Gilberto. *The Material Ghost: Films and their Medium* (London: The Johns Hopkins University Press, 1998).

Perkins, V.F. *Film as Film: Understanding and Judging Movies* (New York: Da Capo Press, 1993)

——. 'Must We Say What They Mean?: Film Criticism and Interpretation,' *Movie* 34/35 (Winter 1990)

——. *The Magnificent Ambersons* (London: BFI Publishing, 1999).

Poague, Leland A. *Another Frank Capra* (Cambridge: Cambridge University Press, 1995).

Popple, Simon & Joe Kember. *Early Cinema: From Factory Gate to Dream Factory* London: Wallflower, 2004

Powdermaker, Hortense. *Hollywood: The Dream Factory* (Boston: Little Brown, 1950).

Pullman, Philip. *His Dark Materials* (London: Scholastic Press, 2001).

Ray, Robert B. *A Certain Tendency of the Hollywood Cinema 1930–1980* (Princeton, N.J.: Princeton University Press, 1985).

Rohrer Paige, Linda. 'Wearing the Red Shoes: Dorothy and the Power of the Female Imagination in *The Wizard of Oz*,' *Journal of Popular Film and Television* vol. 23, Winter 1996

Rose, Brian G. *An Examination of Narrative Structure in Four Films of Frank Capra* (New York: Arno Press, 1980).

Rothman, William. 'Hollywood and the Rise of Suburbia,' *East West Film Journal* vol. 3, no. 2, 1989

——. *The Eye of the Camera: Essays in Film Criticism, History, and Aesthetics* second edition (Cambridge: Cambridge University Press, 2004).

—— (ed.). *Cavell on Film* (New York: State University of New York Press, 2005).

Rubin, Danny. Telephone Interview with James Walters (21 November 2003).

Rushdie, Salman. *The Wizard of Oz* (London: British Film Institute, 1992).

Schrader, Paul. *Transcendental Style in Film: Ozu, Bresson, Dreyer* (Berkeley: University of California Press, 1972).

Silverman, Kaja. *Male Subjectivity at the Margins* (London: Routledge, 1992).

Singer, Irving. *Reality Transformed: Film as Meaning and Technique* (London: MIT Press, 1998).

Snow, Edward. *A Study of Vermeer* (London: University of California Press, 1994).

Thomas, Deborah. *Beyond Genre: Melodrama, Comedy and Romance in Hollywood Films* (London & Moffat: Cameron & Hollis, 2000).

——. *Reading Hollywood: Spaces and Meanings in American Film* (London: Wallflower Press, 2001).

Thomson, David. *The New Biographical Dictionary of Film* (London: Little Brown, 2002).

Thompson, Kristin. *Storytelling in the New Hollywood: Understanding Classical Narrative Technique* (London: Harvard University Press, 1999).

Todorov, Tzvetan. *The Fantastic: A Structural Approach to a Literary Genre* (Ithaca, New York: Cornell University Press, 1975).

Valenti, Peter. 'The Theological Rhetoric of "It's a Wonderful Life,"' *Film Criticism* Vol. 5, No. 2, 1981

Von Gunden, Kenneth. *Postmodern Auteurs: Coppola, Lucas, De Palma, Spielberg and Scorsese* (Jefferson, North Carolina, and London: McFarland & Company Inc., 1991)

Walton, Kendall L. *Mimesis as Make-Believe: On the Foundations of the Representational Arts* (London: Harvard University Press, 1990).

Willis, Donald C. *The Films of Frank Capra* (Metuchen, N.J: Scarecrow Press, 1974).

Wilson, George M. *Narration in Light: Studies in Cinematic Point of View* (Baltimore; London: The Johns Hopkins University Press, 1986).

Wood, Robin. *Hitchcock's Films Revisited* (London: Faber & Faber Ltd., 1989).

——. 'Ideology, Genre, Auteur,' *Film Comment* Vol. 13, No. 1, 1977, reprinted in Braudy, L. & Cohen, M. *Film Theory and Criticism: Introductory Readings* (Oxford: Oxford University Press, 1999) pp. 668–678.

——. *Hollywood from Vietnam to Reagan...and Beyond* (New York: Columbia University Press, 2003).

Young, Kay. '"That Fabric of Times" A Response to David Bordwell's "Film Futures,"' *SubStance* vol. 31, no. 1, 2002.

INDEX